TAKE
AWAY
ONE

TAKE AWAY ONE

Thomas Froncek

St. Martin's / Marek
New York

Design by Doris Borowsky

Library of Congress Cataloging in Publication Data

Froncek, Thomas.
    Take away one.

    1. Kidnapping, Parental—United States—Case studies.
2. Custody of children—United States—Case studies.
I. Title.
HV6598.F76 1985   364.1'54   85-8402
ISBN 0-312-78342-6

First Edition
10 9 8 7 6 5 4 3 2 1

*For my
mother and father*

AUTHOR'S NOTE AND
ACKNOWLEDGMENTS

This is a true story. The characters, scenes, and dialogue are based on conversations with the chief participants, especially the members of the family whose story this is.

For reasons that will become apparent, the names and identities of the main characters have been changed and many of the settings have been altered in order to protect the privacy of those involved.

A number of individuals have been instrumental in the evolution of this book and to them I extend my gratitude: Richard Mazolla, who first brought the story to my attention; Joseph Hotchkiss, who encouraged me to pursue it; William Reiss, whose advice and support helped it along; Norman and Zane Kotker, in whose home it found a house, and Richard Marek, at whose house it found a home. Thanks also to Barbara Morgan for her suggestions; to Tracy Brigden, whose irrepressible enthusiasm buoyed my spirits, and to Stan Lieberfreund, who kept it all in perspective.

Finally, special thanks to my wife Ellen and to my son Jesse, for their support and encouragement and for their (mostly) patient acceptance of the fact that while this book was being written a whole lot of other things would just never get done.

And the king said: "Fetch me a sword."
And they brought a sword before the
king. And the king said: "Divide the
living child in two, and give half to
the one and half to the other."

—First Kings, III, 24–25

CHECKPOINT
Saturday, April 23, 1977, 12:30 A.M.

Sarah did not realize the car was slowing down until it swerved and hit the gravel at the edge of the road. Suddenly she was wide awake.

"We there, Mum?" she heard the boy ask his mother for what must have been the hundredth time. "We in Spine?"

"I don't know, luv," the woman said.

"Then why are we stopping?"

"Shh. I told you, I don't know."

The car rolled to a stop.

Outside in the dark Sarah could see nothing. No lights, no houses, only a mass of black mountain silhouetted against the night sky. She glanced at the green dial on the dashboard. Twenty minutes past midnight. Against her shoulder the window felt cold.

The driver put the car into neutral and dimmed the lights. His name was Peter Wilkes. They had been instructed to do exactly as he said.

"Where are we?" Sarah's father asked from the front seat. He sounded groggy, as if he had been asleep too.

Wilkes ignored him. "Still up then, lad?" he asked over his shoulder.

"It's all the excitement," said the boy's mother apologetically. "The airplane ride and all."

"And no bloody chance for 'im to get comf'table, neither," said the boy's father.

"I'm well aware of the inconvenience, Mr. Hardy," said Wilkes.

They had been traveling that way for hours: five adults and a sharp-elbowed six-year-old crammed ridiculously into a space intended for four. In front were Wilkes and Sarah's father, whose name was Edward Novack. In the back Sarah sat shoulder to shoulder with the English couple, David Hardy and his wife Sheila, who had sniffles and kept pulling up her nose. Their boy, Adam, was slouched on his father's lap. He had his legs stretched across his mother's thighs. His stocking feet were jammed against Sarah's rib cage. There was luggage piled on the back window ledge and an airline bag shoved under Sarah's legs. It was impossible to move.

"I know you could all do with a stretch," Wilkes said. "So could I. But not here. Not yet. We're tired and we should look tired. When we cross the border I want the guards to see a car full of sleepy tourists."

Cold and hard and wary. That had been Sarah's impression when she met Wilkes for the first time that afternoon. And so far nothing had happened to change that impression. Good-looking, yes. But wintry cold. And suspicious of everyone.

"How far is it now?" her father asked.

"We're almost to the pass. From here it's three miles to the checkpoint."

"We in Spine, then?"

"Not yet, lad."

2

"I won't forget," the boy said, squeezing his eyes tight.

"Good," Wilkes said. He turned his attention to Sarah. "You know your part," he told her. "You're Adam's mother now and Adam is your Joey. He's asleep and you don't want him wakened. If the guard wants you to get out, stay where you are. Be stubborn. Remember, you're a tired mother and you're not going to let anyone disturb your child."

She nodded. Suddenly she was beginning to be afraid. Why Wilkes should be so nervous about getting into Yugoslavia she did not understand. She knew it would be dangerous getting out again. But getting *in*? She held the boy closer.

"Now, let me have your passports please," Wilkes was saying. "Sarah?"

"My father has ours."

"All right. Mr. Novack? . . . Thank you. . . . Hardy?"

When he had them all, he sorted them as carefully as a bridge player arranging his suits. He put his own passport on top, Ted's under it, Sarah's and Joey's next. The Hardys' passports he put on the bottom. Then he tucked them all into the side pocket of his tweed jacket and put the car in gear.

"Okay," he said. "Here we go."

The main road from Klagenfurt, in southern Austria, to Ljubljana in northwestern Yugoslavia, crosses over the craggy Karavanke mountains at Loibl Pass—or Ljubelj Pass, as it is called on the Yugoslav side of the frontier. There, a tunnel—dug by Nazi slave labor during the Second World War—cuts beneath the top of the pass, shortening the distance and making the frontier passable even in winter. The Yugoslav checkpoint lies a little over a mile beyond the southern end of the tunnel.

At the checkpoint a pair of gatehouses stand on either side of the roadway. They are built of stone, the windows are high

5

and wide, and each is lit inside by a single ceiling fixture. Between the two buildings, a hand-winched barrier, painted in red and white candy-cane stripes, falls across the roadway.

The gatehouses reminded Sarah of the toll booths on the Garden State Parkway back home in New Jersey. But the area was not nearly as well lit as the toll plazas. That surprised her, and so did the flimsy-looking crossing gates. She had expected something more formidable of an Iron Curtain border post. Floodlights. Barbed wire. Machine guns. If there were such things around, none of it was in sight. At least not on a dark night like tonight.

There was one car ahead of them as they approached the gate house, none on the opposite side of the road. Holding the boy close, Sarah wondered if it wouldn't have been wiser to cross in daylight, when heavier traffic might have made their crowded little car seem less conspicuous. But Wilkes had insisted. At this time of night, he said, the guards were likely to be tired and bored and more careless than usual. Besides, in the dark they were less likely to notice the differences between the boy asleep on her lap and the boy in the passport photo. And that was the crucial point: getting little Adam into the country on Joey's passport.

There seemed to be only two guards on duty, one at each gate house. They wore baggy gray uniforms and each had a pistol at his belt. Sarah wondered where the third man was, then noticed another small building off to the left: some sort of administration building perhaps. There was a light on inside. Maybe that's where the third man was.

The car ahead was waved through. Now it was their turn. Wilkes rolled down his window. *"Guten abend,"* he said.

The guard said something in German. Wilkes handed over the passports. No one said anything. Sarah stopped breathing.

Suddenly the guard's face was at the window, his flashlight

probing the darkness inside the car. The light flashed on Wilkes' face, on Novack's, on the Hardys'. One by one he checked them against the passport photos. Then the light was in Sarah's eyes. It made her wince. She didn't know whether to shield her eyes or to stare brazenly into the glare. She clutched Adam tighter, felt him burrow his face deeper into her shoulder. And still the light did not go away. What was the guard looking at? Had he noticed something? She felt her heart pounding, her stomach tightening.

And then it was gone. The light was gone. She breathed again. It was over. Now they could drive on. They had made it through.

But no. The guard was waving Wilkes over to the side of the road.

"My God, what does he want?" her father whispered.

"He says to wait here."

"Wait? Why? What for?"

"I don't know. He just said to wait."

"What's going to happen to us?" asked Sheila Hardy.

"I don't know. Maybe it's nothing. I don't know."

The guard had turned away. Walking across to the administration building, he opened the door, stepped into the light, and disappeared inside, taking the passports with him. It was 12:45 A.M.

Five minutes passed. Then ten. With the engine turned off the car began to get cold inside.

"What the hell is keeping that guy?" her father muttered to himself.

Wilkes said nothing. Sitting perfectly still, he was staring straight ahead into the darkness.

Sniffling, Sheila Hardy dug in her purse for a tissue and blew her nose loudly.

"Damn it," said Ted. "At least they should tell us why they're holding us here."

7

"Should?" Wilkes said without turning his head. "You'd better understand one thing, Mr. Novack. We are in Yugoslavia now. They do things differently over here."

For a long time Wilkes' words hung like frost in the cold air.

A big sedan came out of the darkness behind them, following the bright path made by its headlights. It rolled to a stop at the gatehouse. The guard from the other side came over, checked the driver's papers, then passed him through and returned to his own post. The road was empty again. The darkness beyond the gatehouse lights seemed darker than before. Sarah felt her legs tingling. The boy's weight on her thighs was cutting off her circulation. Her back hurt. Down low, around her kidneys. She shifted slightly and realized that the boy had fallen asleep.

"Do you think the guard noticed something?" she said quietly, so as not to wake him. "About Adam, I mean."

Wilkes said, "I couldn't tell."

"Otherwise wouldn't he just stamp the visas and let us go?"

"Usually."

The man was infuriating. Of course the guard had noticed. How could he *not* notice, when even here in the half-light of the gatehouse lamp the difference between the two boys seemed so obvious to her. Dutifully, she had been trying to imagine that the small stranger on her lap was her own son —wishing even that it were true. But there was nothing the same about Adam and Joey. Height and age, but that was all. Adam's hair, his eyes, his voice, the smell of the cheap soap his mother used to wash him—all of it was different and strange. Part of her resented Adam because of it. Resented his parents too, because they had their son and she did not have hers.

Were they happy together, she wondered, the Hardys' and their mousy little boy? Was any family really happy together?

She could not imagine it. Not after all that had happened in the last few years. How had she put up with it for so long? *Why* had she put up with it? It made no sense at all.

Or did it? Knowing what she knew now, it was easy to upbraid herself for having got trapped the way she did: trapped by love, by such awful need. But when she thought about it she doubted she could have done anything very different at the time.

Not that it mattered now. Not that anything had mattered to her for months except getting back her son.

Only now, sitting there cramped and cold, she was beginning to wonder if she ever would.

Part One

Coming Apart

Labor Day Weekend, 1976

one

It had been Jovan's turn to have Joey for the weekend. Visiting rights. There had been nothing she could do.

Sarah had prepared as usual for Joey's visit with his father. On Friday, after lunch, she packed his suitcase with a couple of clean T-shirts, underwear and socks, an extra pair of shorts, a bathing suit and towel, a comb, a lined jacket in case it got chilly. She put in crayons and a pad of paper so he'd have something to do on the train.

When it was time, she called him in to wash up and change. She combed his hair and gave him an apple to tide him over until supper. Then she drove him to the station to meet Jovan's train.

Not that she had to, of course. Her father was right about that. Jovan could just as well get a taxi out to the house and pick Joey up by himself. "You're always bending over backwards to make it easy for him," her father kept reminding her. "If he wants to see Joey, let *him* make the effort." But Sarah had had enough of rancor and recriminations. Why make the separation more difficult than it already was? If she could save Jovan time and taxi fare, she was willing. Besides, it meant she could have the boy with her right up until the last minute. Just in case.

From her parents' house on the west side of Sommerton, New Jersey, it was a twenty-minute drive downtown to the station. Jovan's train from New York was due at three. But Sarah liked to allow extra time. She didn't want Jovan getting there first and having to wait for her. She didn't want to give him any excuse for flying into one of his rages.

Turning up the music on the car radio, she headed north on Mercer Street for three blocks, then east on Hamilton Avenue, past Sommerton West High School, past the apartment houses, past St. Cecilia's, past Eberhardt's Tool and Die plant, with its great crenellated clock tower. It was twenty minutes to three. She'd be in good time.

"Mom," Joey said, "why d-d-do I have to g-go with Daddy again? Why can't I s-s-stay with you?"

She glanced over at him. He was slumped morosely in the seat beside her. Usually he liked to kneel so that he could see out the window. But today he seemed to have no interest in the scenery. And his stutter was back.

"It's only for the weekend," she told him. She felt like a traitor.

He was five-and-a-half. He had Jovan's almond eyes and broad Slavic cheekbones; he had her tawny curls. She loved his curls. She had let his hair grow long and the curls covered his ears and the back of his neck almost to his collar. Sometimes, when the sun was behind him, his hair shone like amber: a rich mellow brown at the center, a golden halo around the edges. In shops and at bus stops other people's grandmothers were forever running their fingers through his hair and telling her sweetly what a pity it was to see such beautiful curls wasted on a boy.

"I'll tell you what, though," Sarah said to him now. "On Monday, when you're back, we'll do something special."

14

"Like what?"

"What would you like to do?"

"G-go to the z-zoo?"

"Okay. Let's do that. And afterward we can stop over and see Grandma Helen."

They were downtown now, driving past the urban-renewal project, the Sommerton County Court House. Swinging the loop under the expressway, she pulled into the station parking lot. It was ten to three. Getting out, she lifted Joey's suitcase out of the back seat and locked up. Joey was already waiting at the meter. She handed him a quarter and waited while he pushed it into the slot. It was one of their little rituals.

He turned the dial. "Bzzzt," he said, mimicking the sound it made.

She took his hand and led him into the air-conditioned building. They went past the coffee shop and the newsstand and out onto the platform.

They waited in the usual place, on a bench halfway along, just where the fourth car would be when the train came to a stop. The bench was in the shade of the platform roof, but just barely. The toes of Sarah's sandals stuck out into the hot sun that glared on the concrete. The tracks shimmered. Joey sat very still, his hands jammed into the pockets of his shorts. He hardly ever sat still.

"You'll have fun," she said. "You'll see."

Joey shrugged, said nothing.

"I'm sure Daddy's got some nice things planned for you to do."

He shrugged again and looked away. She wasn't being very convincing.

"Didn't you have fun the last time you saw Daddy?"

Joey shook his head.

She gave up. Obviously her talk was only making him more

unhappy. She watched the line of sunlight inch away from the toes of her sandals.

"D-Daddy just wants to w-work all the t-t-time," Joey said. "He n-n-never wants to d-do anything that I want to d-d-do."

"That's not true. He took you to the beach last time, didn't he?"

"He took a b-b-book, too."

"Well, his work is very important to him," she said, then immediately wished she hadn't. She of all people should know how little comfort there was in hearing over and over again how important Jovan's work was. She'd heard it from him herself too many times.

Not that she'd ever begrudged Jovan his dream, his vision. It was one of the things that had attracted her to him in the first place. Science. To him there was nothing more challenging in its complexity, more beautiful in its well-ordered simplicity.

He was especially fascinated by chemistry, by the miracles that could be performed in a test tube. One day, he vowed, he would make important discoveries. He would find a way to dissolve and eliminate cholesterol in the bloodstream. Maybe even find a cure for cancer. He would be asked to lecture at universities. He would be welcomed in his homeland as a hero. He would win the Nobel Prize!

Granted, Sarah had not always understood the work he was doing. The formulas and equations that he scribbled endlessly on his notepads made as much sense to her as Urdu. But from the beginning she had admired his dedication, had reveled in his fervor. Eventually, though, his dream had become an obsession, had taken over his life completely. Hurrying down to the lab early in the morning, he would not return until seven or eight at night, then spend the rest of the evening at his desk, poring over his papers. If she finally managed to persuade him to spend a Sunday afternoon in the park with her and Joey, he would be forever glancing at his watch, worrying about the time he was wasting. It was almost as if he were under siege, fighting off everything and everyone that might sap his energies or intrude on his concentration. And the harder Sarah and Joey tried to reach him the harder he fought them off. What he could not seem to understand was that as much as Sarah loved his dream, she loved him more, needed him more—to see her, to hear her, to love *her*.

Not until last December, when she'd finally taken Joey and gone home to her parents for good, did it even seem to occur to him that he, too, might need something separate from his work.

It was then that he had first threatened to take Joey away from her.

She reached over and took Joey's hand. "You're important to Daddy, too," she told him. She knew that in some sense it must be true, even if Jovan himself had no idea how to show it. "He loves you and wants to be with you. You love him too, don't you?"

"Mom?"

"Don't you, Joey?"

"Yes. But Mom?"

"What is it?"

"How long is a w-w-weekend?"

"Tonight and tomorrow and part of the day after that. Daddy will bring you back on Sunday afternoon, just like he always does." She wished she felt as confident as she was trying to sound.

It was five past three when the train's headlight came dancing through the distant haze. The light grew. Behind it, the train took form, swelled in size and sound, and then was rushing alongside the platform. As it slowed to a stop, the front of the fourth car came level with where Sarah and Joey were sitting.

The door opened, a few people got out.

Then there was Jovan, book in hand as usual. He was wearing dark slacks, banged-up loafers, and a short-sleeved dress shirt with the top two buttons open. A hank of wavy dark hair fell rakishly over his forehead and his face was lit with that incredibly charming smile of his. Once upon a time Sarah had found that smile absolutely irresistible. Now it only made her wary.

"Hello, Sarah," he said.

"Hello."

She let him kiss her on the cheek, then pulled away. His smile flickered out.

"Hot out here," he said. "Why didn't you wait inside where it's cool? You didn't think of that?"

The nasty edge on his voice made her suddenly tense. Would he never change? Must he always make me feel small? "Please," she said. "Don't start."

He scowled and turned from her. He bent to kiss his son. "Hello, Joey. How are you?"

Joey looked at his feet. "Okay," he said, so quietly they almost didn't hear.

"What's wrong with him?" Jovan asked.

"Nothing," said Sarah. "He'll be all right."

They had a half hour to wait for the train that would take Jovan and Joey back to New York. They went inside to the coffee shop, took a booth, ordered Cokes, a Tab for her. Joey sat next to his father. Subdued, he busied himself with the Bicentennial sugar packets from the dispenser, arranging them in neat geometric patterns on the table in front of him.

"Who's th-this one?" he asked his mother.

"George Washington," Sarah said.

"Who's th-th-this one?"

"That's . . . let me see it. That's John Adams."

With a straw Jovan stirred the ice in his glass. He looked

18

tired, on edge, older somehow than when Sarah had last seen him two weeks before. But then, part of her still thought of him as the young man she had first fallen in love with ten years ago: the suave continental with the dark hair, the charming manners, the strange yellow-brown eyes. Tiger eyes.

He was thirty-nine now. His hair was thinning. He was getting thick around the middle. In his eyes she rarely saw the warmth anymore, only the hardness. But she was used to that. What puzzled her now was why he seemed so tense, so edgy. One hand kept darting to his shirt pocket for a cigarette, though he hadn't smoked for months and the pocket was empty. It must be his work, she decided. Had he finished his dissertation yet? Was he preparing for his orals? Was he still planning to finish up in October? She sipped her Tab. She wouldn't ask.

"Sarah," he said, without looking up from his glass, "come back with us, will you? We could have a nice weekend together. Go to Jones Beach. Whatever you want."

Joey looked at her hopefully. "Oh, Mom, will you?"

"Joey, stay out of it."

"Will you, Sarah?"

"No. I can't."

"Why?"

"I have plans."

"A date?"

"I have plans, that's all." She said it firmly, but then held her breath, waiting for the reaction she knew would come. What would it be this time? she wondered: icy silence? a fist slammed down on the table? the Coke glass smashed on the floor? She was surprised when all he did was shrug indifferently and go back to fidgeting with the ice in his glass. Once he would have kept after her, pleading and raging and cajoling, wearing her down until she'd finally agreed to give him

19

"just one more chance." Was it possible that he had finally resigned himself to the fact that it was all over between them? She hoped so. It would make everything so much easier.

They finished their drinks and went down to the platform. When the train came in they waited together as the conductor stepped out and made way for the people getting off.

Scooping Joey up in her arms, Sarah hugged him to her and kissed him on both cheeks. "Good-bye," she said. "Have fun."

Joey threw his arms around her neck. "P-please, Mama, d-d-don't m-make me g-go," he cried into her shoulder.

"It'll be okay. You'll see." She gave him one last hug, then put him down. Or tried to. Joey did not want to let go, but held her bent over.

"All aboard, miss," said the conductor.

"P-please, Mama. Please."

She gave him another kiss, then gently pried loose his arms. "See you on Sunday," she said.

Straightening up, she found herself looking into Jovan's eyes—those strange eyes. It seemed to her that she was seeing him from a great distance, and it struck her that he looked very sad just then. Or maybe just tired. His eyes held hers and for a moment she thought he was going to kiss her. Or was waiting for her to kiss him. Part of her wanted to, just as part of her wished they could be a normal family, loving each other, doing things together, enjoying each other's company. But she'd realized long ago that it could never be that way with Jovan. She stood her ground. "Bye," she said.

He seemed about to say something, but changed his mind. He nodded, accepting. "Good-bye," he said. Then, reaching down, he picked up Joey's suitcase, shepherded the boy onto the train, and followed him in.

She looked for them in the windows but the glass was too heavily tinted to see inside. She waved anyway, then caught

20

a glimpse of a small hand waving back as the train pulled away.

From the start, Sarah's parents, Ted and Emma Novack, had been against letting Jovan have visiting rights. Her mother had been especially adamant.

"Hasn't he threatened?" she warned. "Hasn't he said he would take Joey the first chance he got?"

Sarah knew her mother was right, but to battle Jovan in court? to prevent him from ever seeing Joey again? It seemed so hard-hearted, so spiteful. She'd never intended it to be that way. She had left Jovan to save *herself*, not to punish *him*. If he could see Joey whenever he wanted, maybe he'd be satisfied. Maybe their separation could be amicable after all.

Besides, her parents knew as well as she did that Jovan was not about to go anywhere, with or without Joey, until New York University handed him the piece of paper that would allow him to call himself *Doctor* Jovan Stefanovic. He had worked too long and hard. He was not about to turn his back on the prize now that it was almost within his grasp. Nor was he about to assume the day-to-day responsibility of looking after Joey—not while he was trying to finish his thesis and prepare for his orals. If for no other reason than that, he was likely to keep bringing Joey back to her. At least for a while. At least until October.

It was Bob Koenig, the Novacks' lawyer, who had clinched the argument. "Look," he'd told them, "you can't deny the man the right to see his own son. Even if the court did go along with you—which I doubt it would do—what guarantee do you have that he won't just come and grab the boy off the street? You can't watch the kid every minute. Not a five-year-old."

"But if something happens," Emma had persisted, "if he does what he says, there'll be nothing we can do."

"Maybe, maybe not. It depends. Anyway, it's like Sarah says: he's not likely to do anything before October. Let's see how it goes this summer. Then we'll talk again after Labor Day."

Koenig had been right, of course. In the end, the County Court of Sommerton County, New Jersey, had granted Sarah custody. According to the court decree, Jovan was permitted to have the boy with him

> every other weekend in Yonkers, New York, from
> Friday night to Sunday night, and to pick up the
> child in Sommerton, New Jersey, and transport
> him to Yonkers, New York, and transport the child
> back to Sommerton at the end of his visitation.

That was in the middle of June. Since then, Jovan had taken Joey with him for five weekends.

For Sarah, the first few times had been nerve-racking. From the minute she left them at the station on those Fridays until the time Jovan brought Joey back on Sunday afternoon, she was unable to think or do anything without being distracted by fear and worry, without wondering if he would do what he had threatened to do: take Joey and never bring him back.

But the first weekend came and went, and the second, and the third. And each time, the two of them had been there at the station on Sunday afternoon, Joey with his hair a mess and needing a bath, but home at least, his sticky hand in hers. Gradually the leavings had ceased to be quite so difficult, until now, as she watched Jovan and Joey's train disappear down the tracks toward New York, she found she could almost ignore the small, nagging, irrational fear that lay curled in the pit of her stomach.

Friday evening went by quickly: dinner and a movie with friends, drinks afterward at a bar downtown. She did not get home until two in the morning. She fell into bed exhilarated. Saturday night she would be going out again. She was enjoying herself immensely. She and Jovan had rarely gone out anywhere together, especially after he'd started working on his doctorate. She had a lot of catching up to do.

Saturday she did errands: laundry, groceries, shopping at the mall for a blouse to wear that evening. Then it was time to get ready. She had just gotten out of the shower and was drying her hair when she heard the extension phone ringing in her parents' bedroom down the hall. A moment later her mother was calling up the stairs to tell her it was Jovan.

Won't he ever let me alone? Sarah wondered. He often called on Saturdays. He pretended it was to let her know that everything was all right with Joey. But what he really wanted was to keep her from forgetting he was there.

"I'll take it up here," Sarah called back. She wrapped the towel around herself, tucked it under her arm, then took another one off the rack and wrapped her hair in it. She went down the hall.

The phone was on the night table on her father's side of the bed. She picked up the receiver. "Hello."

"Just wanted to say hello," said Jovan.

"Yes," she said. "How's everything going? How's Joey?"

They were having a good time, he told her. They had been shopping, had had lunch at Burger King. "Oh, and I took him to a barber for a haircut."

"Oh, no, Jovan. You didn't."

"Now, come on, don't get excited. It was only a little trim, just to neaten it a little. He needed a haircut. He looks much better."

She did not believe him. She had an awful picture of all those beautiful curls strewn on the tiles of the barber-shop floor.

But then Joey was on the line, telling her about his new clothes, and the Tonka truck Daddy had bought for him. What new clothes? she was about to ask, but before she had a chance he was telling a joke that the barber had told him: "A cabbage, a faucet and a t-t-tomato are having a r-r-race. Who's the w-w-winner?"

"I don't know. Who?"

"The c-c-cabbage is ahead, the faucet is r-r-running, and the tomato has to c-c-catch up."

It was more than the joke that made her laugh. It was her own relief at hearing him sounding so happy and excited.

"That's a wonderful story, Joey. That's very funny."

When he said good-bye it was in his father's native Serbian: *"Do vidjenja, Mami."*

"Do vidjenja, Joey."

She was pleased. Not about the haircut. That was awful; she dreaded to see what Joey was going to look like. But at least Jovan hadn't pressed her too hard and Joey sounded like he was enjoying himself. Maybe the separation would work out well after all. Maybe it just took getting used to.

At any rate, the call helped put her mind at ease. That evening, over drinks and dinner at the Towne House, she found herself thinking about Jovan and Joey only once. Her date, an architect who acted in amateur theatricals, kept her talking and laughing from the moment he picked her up. It was when she was almost through with her coffee that she happened to glance at her watch and wondered fleetingly if Jovan had gotten Joey to bed at a reasonable hour.

But that was all. Blessedly, that was all.

Not until Sunday afternoon did she begin to think that something might be wrong.

Usually Jovan called her early on Sunday to let her know which train he and Joey would be taking back to Sommerton. That way, she could pick Joey up at the station and Jovan could catch the next train back to New York.

But noon came and went and still he did not call.

Would he phone from the station? she wondered. He did that sometimes: waited until the last minute before letting her know. Most of the time it didn't matter since she never did much on Sundays anyway except sleep late and dawdle over breakfast and browse through the magazine sections of the Sunday newspapers. Today, though, she had already decided to drive over to the swim club with her parents and she did not want to give that up. This was the last weekend before the pool closed for the season. Besides, it was just too beautiful a day to sit around the house waiting for a phone call that might not come until two or three in the afternoon.

She finished lunch and went up to her room to change into her bathing suit. There was still a chance that Jovan would call before her parents were set to go, and in the meantime, she thought, she might as well get ready.

The suit she pulled out of her beach bag was a two-piece in electric blue, which highlighted her tan and always attracted appreciative glances. Which was why Jovan had never liked it. "It shows too much," he'd growled the first time she wore it to the beach. Instead of being proud of the way she looked, he had acted as if every man who glanced at her was trying to take her away from him, and as if she were egging them on. Well, maybe she had been. Maybe she had needed some reassurance just then: a man's admiring eyes to tell her that in spite of being thirty and a little overweight from her pregnancy, she was still an attractive woman.

Not that she could have explained any of that to Jovan. She hadn't even tried. Why bother? It would only have led to another argument. Better to just put the suit away and forget about it, as she had put away so much else of what she was and what she could be.

She had found the suit again a few months ago, at the bottom of a drawer. And tried it on, and looked at herself in the mirror, and discovered to her delight that it fit even better than when she'd first bought it.

Now she wore the suit whenever she went to the pool or the beach. She loved the way it made her feel: younger and trimmer and more womanly than she had felt in years—and just a little bit pleased with herself.

She slipped a white terry jacket on over the suit, then brushed her long hair and tied it back with a scarf. She collected her sandals and sun screen and towel, and then had to hunt for her sunglasses. By the time she found them—in the kitchen, on top of the refrigerator—Jovan had still not called and her parents were almost ready to go.

She could not wait any longer. If Jovan was not going to call her, she would have to call him.

She was just starting to dial, using the wall phone in the kitchen, when her father came clopping into the room in his sandals. He was bare-legged and wore a red-and-white striped polo shirt over his swimsuit. He was carrying a vinyl beach bag and had the Sunday *New York Times* tucked under his arm. He was obviously looking forward to spending a long, leisurely afternoon in the sun.

"Hey, you coming or not?" he asked impatiently. "I thought you were ready to go."

"I'm just trying to reach Jovan." The phone was ringing now on the other end.

"You had to wait until now to do that?"

"I'll only be a minute," she said, and turned away to listen.

The phone kept ringing. How many times? Six? Eight? Had she missed them? Were they already on their way to the station? Had they gone out for lunch somewhere? Feeling vaguely uneasy, she traced the outline of the phone box with one finger and wondered if she should wait at home for him to call. Or was he just playing games with her again? Keeping her off balance?

He would tie her in knots if he could.

If she let him.

She wouldn't let him. She was going to have her swim.

She hung up. Turning around, she found her father still there, hovering, expectant.

"No answer," she said, in reply to his unspoken question.

He frowned. "Did he say anything about his plans when he called yesterday?"

"No. Nothing. Just that he had taken Joey shopping and they were having a good time."

"Well, a nice day like this, they probably went to the beach or something."

"I don't know. He would have said something."

"Anyway, you can always try calling from the pool. Come on, let's go."

"Isn't mother coming?"

"She decided she needs a nap more than a swim. Her back's been bothering her again."

Sarah picked up her beach bag and glasses off the table. "Good. Then she'll be here if he calls."

"Right. So you can stop worrying. Anyway, I'm sure everything's all right."

———

But two hours later she wasn't so sure. Standing at the pay phone near the entrance to the bathhouse, she dialed the apartment for the fourth time and for the fourth time listened as the phone rang and rang without being answered.

Annoyed, she hung up. Jovan was spoiling her day after all.

How could she enjoy the afternoon when she had to keep worrying?

Then she picked up the phone again. Maybe he'd called the house. Anyway, her mother would be done with her nap by now.

But oddly, there was no answer at home either. Why not? What if Jovan *was* trying to call? There was no way he could reach her. Suddenly apprehensive, Sarah hurried back toward the cluster of lawn chairs where she and her father had parked themselves.

Thanks to the holiday weekend, the pool was more noisy and crowded than usual. Whooping teenagers were cannonballing off the diving board one after another. Children were splashing in the shallows. On the pavement around the pool and on the grass beyond, sunbathers slick with oil and cream lay sprawled on towels or sat propped up in aluminum chairs, their glistening faces turned to the sun. As Sarah picked her way among them, a woman in sunglasses and straw hat waved to her and called her name. But Sarah did not stop. She was too preoccupied to sit and gossip.

Her father was stretched out in a chaise, with the Business and Finance section open in front of him and one of his long dark cigars clamped between his teeth. He was big-shouldered and barrel-chested, with chestnut hair about half gray —a man of fifty-eight who prided himself on keeping fit. This afternoon he had already done a fast two dozen laps in the pool.

She stood beside his chaise. "Dad?"

He looked up at her over the top of his sunglasses. "Well?"

"I want to go home," she said, as calmly as she could.

"So soon?"

"There's still no answer at the apartment and mother's not answering at home either."

he's not there. If we drive up there now, chances are we're just going to miss him on the highway or somewhere."

"Please, Dad." It was maddening. Was she crazy? Wasn't anyone concerned but her?

"Now, just sit tight, hon. He's probably on his way down here right this minute. Tell you what, though. If it'll make you feel better, we can drive down to the station after supper. It could be there's some problem with the trains. Holiday tie-ups or something."

"You go. I want to stay near the phone."

He was gone about an hour and a half. When he got back he looked tired and drawn. Large sweat stains blotted his shirt. "Everything's on schedule," he reported. "No delays, no track work, no accidents." He forced a laugh. "Funny, after all the times I cursed those trains for being late, there I was tonight cursing them for being on time." Wearily, he sank into a chair at the kitchen table. "You know, while I was standing there I got to wondering if maybe Jovan didn't make a mistake because of the three-day weekend. I'll bet he's planning on bringing Joey back tomorrow."

Sarah shook her head. "He knew it was supposed to be today. He told me Sunday."

"He must have meant Monday."

"Dad, for God's sake, can't you hear me? Why won't you listen? He said today! He *knows* it's today."

"She's right, Ted," her mother said quietly. "You're just hoping against hope. You're just trying to find excuses."

He looked at her for a long moment, then let his gaze drop. "I know," he said. "I know."

They decided then: if Jovan did not call that evening, Ted and Sarah would drive up to the apartment first thing in the morning. Emma would stay home and listen for the phone.

———————

It was just after nine-thirty the next morning when Sarah and her father stepped off the elevator on the third floor of the apartment building. The corridor smelled of cigarettes and cat boxes and other people's cooking. Sarah had almost forgotten that smell.

She wanted to run away, wanted to turn right around and go back. She didn't want to be here. *Not again. Not ever.*

"Go ahead," her father said behind her.

Mechanically, trying not to think, trying not to feel anything, she walked down the corridor.

She stopped at 3-B. The hand-lettered nameplate over the buzzer said "Stefanovic."

She was uncertain what to do. Press the buzzer? Use the key and go right in? Her hands were shaking. She hadn't been back here since that morning in December when she'd called her father to come and take her and Joey away from this place.

Ted pressed the buzzer. "Just in case," he said.

They waited, heard nothing: no shuffling footsteps from inside, no one calling out.

"Let's go in," he said. "Got the key?"

"I'll do it." She fit the key into the lock, turned it, pushed the door, and stepped inside.

"Hello?" she said.

Something was different. She knew it immediately. But what?

"God, it's stifling in here," her father said, coming in behind her.

Puzzled, she scanned the living room. The pictures on the walls were the same: the garish abstracts that Jovan had promised to sell for a Belgrade artist friend. On the sofa was a dust jacket from one of his albums of Serbian folk music. Joey's blocks and toy cars were strewn on the floor as if he'd just gotten up from playing. But that, too, was usual enough.

Stepping over Joey's blocks, her father threw open the windows to the terrace. "There," he said, "that's better."

Suddenly she realized what it was: the drapes were gone. Why would Jovan take the drapes down?

In the kitchen, dishes were piled in the sink. The countertop was littered with breadcrumbs, coffee mugs, an open jar of peanut butter. Except for one dessicated philodendron, the plants that Sarah had nurtured on the windowsill were all gone; the spider plant, the geraniums.

Home.

Had this place ever really been home? she wondered. Is it possible that I lived here for six years?

Her father picked up a pitcher of milk from the dining room table, sniffed it, made a face. "It must be a while since anybody's been here," he said.

Sarah turned the corner to the bedroom. The door was partly open. With the tips of her fingers she pushed it back.

The first thing she saw were the clothes scattered on the floor: the Mets T-shirt and the pair of shorts she had dressed Joey in on Friday, the extra clothes she had packed in his suitcase. Why? she wondered. It didn't make sense.

She bent and picked up the clothes. Then she noticed the bed, the bare mattress. Stripped of sheets and blankets, it looked cold and barren. Their bed once—hers and Jovan's. Once.

The bed was littered with bits of paper: cellophane wrappers, stick pins, little paper tabs. Odd. She went closer, picked up one of the tabs. It was a Macy's price tag. The labels and wrappers were from new clothes. Shirts, pants, socks.

Boys.

Size four.

Suddenly her legs felt weak. She sat down on the edge of the bed, her body trembling uncontrollably. "No," she whispered. "Please, God, no."

Her father was in the doorway. For some reason he was holding a wire clothes hanger. "I checked the closets," he was saying. "They're empty, Sarah. Both of them. Everything's gone."

And then she heard a voice screaming, her voice, screaming over and over and over, "No, no, no, no, no . . ."

CHECKPOINT
Saturday, April 23, 1:05 A.M.

Sheila Hardy shifted in her seat and tried to arrange her stockinged legs. First she tried propping up both feet on the hump that ran down the middle of the car. Then, she placed a leg on either side of the hump. Next, she tried both legs on her husband's side.

"Cripes," he muttered. "Do you have to keep fidgitin'?"

"I'm just tryin' to get comfortable," she said, wiping her nose with a tissue.

"Yeah, well, while you're at it I'll thank you to take your elbow out of me ribs."

"Move yours, why don't you."

"'Cause I got no room, that's why."

"Well, neither do I."

"All right, knock it off, you two," Wilkes snarled from the front seat. "The last thing we need now is to listen to your bickering."

Sarah grimaced. She had been taking advantage of the woman's squirming to shift her own position in the backseat, but now her right arm was being pinched between the window frame and the shoulder of the boy asleep on her lap.

Gingerly, trying to avoid waking the child, she worked the arm free.

It was now twenty minutes since the guard had walked away with the passports and disappeared into the administration building. Since then, Wilkes had turned the engine and the heater back on. Now, instead of being too cold, the car was hot and stuffy. And little Adam had become a dead weight in Sarah's lap. If she had to sit like this for even five more minutes she didn't know what she'd do. What was that guard up to? Was he suspicious? What if he had found something wrong with the passports? Would they all be arrested?

In the front seat her father stirred impatiently. "How long do we wait before doing something?"

Wilkes shrugged. "It's their show. We wait as long as they want us to." But Sarah heard the edge on his cultured English voice. He was not as calm as he was pretending to be.

"Maybe we should just turn around and go back," she offered.

"Forget it," said Wilkes. "The minute we tried anything they'd pull us in for questioning. And they've got fast cars. We'd never make it."

"So what do we do?" her father asked. "Just sit here and wait?"

"That's right."

"Jesus," said Ted.

Sarah shifted in her seat. "We can at least ask them what's going on, can't we?"

"No," Wilkes snapped. "We sit tight."

"That's ridiculous," said Ted. "It can't hurt just to ask."

"I'll decide what can hurt and what can't," said Wilkes through clenched teeth. "You may be paying the bills on this trip, Mr. Novack, but I'm still giving the orders and don't you forget it."

"Well then, do something, goddamn it!" said Ted. "Hell,

we look more suspicious just sitting here than we would if we got out and talked to these bastards."

Wilkes glared at Ted but said nothing. He looked over at the administration building and at the gatehouse, where the lone guard sat. The man was reading a magazine and seemed to be paying them no attention whatever.

"Maybe you're right," said Wilkes.

"It's a damn sight better than just sitting here," said Ted.

"Amen," murmured David Hardy.

"All right," Wilkes pushed open his door. A welcome draft of cold air blew in. Sheila Hardy sneezed.

"You stay here," said Wilkes. "I'll see what I can find out."

Stepping out of the car, he shut the door behind him. At the sound, the guard looked up from his magazine. Wilkes made a show of looking nonchalant. He stretched his arms and legs, did three deep knee-bends, and jogged in place a few times. Then, while Sarah and the others watched, he strolled across the tarmac. Reaching the administration building, he opened the door and went in. For an instant he was silhouetted against the light in the doorway. Then he was gone.

Inside the car they waited and watched. Minutes passed.

"Dad, could you turn the heat down?" Sarah asked. "It's roasting back here."

"Not too much, please," said Sheila Hardy.

"Look," said David Hardy, "'e's comin' back."

Wilkes was alone, striding toward them purposefully. A good sign? Sarah couldn't tell.

With one graceful motion Wilkes swung open the car door and slid behind the wheel.

"What did they say?" her father asked. "What are we waiting for?"

Instead of answering, the Englishman held up a hand. In it were three passports. Two of them he tipped back toward Hardy, who took them. The other he kept for himself.

"But that's only three," Sarah tried to quell the alarm in her voice. "What about ours?"

"There's been a hitch," Wilkes said grimly. "It could be nothing. I don't know. The guard inside told me that the man with the visa stamp is down in the town. Taking his break."

"What?"

Hardy groaned. "Bloody 'ell."

"God, I don't believe it." Sarah slumped in her seat. She felt as if she had just taken her first breath of air in twenty minutes. She almost laughed in relief. But something in Wilkes' manner stopped her. "You don't believe it either, do you, Mr. Wilkes?"

He did not turn around. "I don't know. The man could be telling the truth. Or he could be trying to put us off our guard."

No one said anything. Sarah shuddered. What would happen now? Getting Joey's passport stamped was the key to the whole operation. Without it, there was no hope of getting Joey out of the country. Without it, they may as well turn right around and go home.

two

"We're going to get him back," her father said. Fierce with rage, he was driving fast down the parkway toward the towering arches of the George Washington Bridge. "We're going to get him back if it's the last thing we do."

Sarah wasn't listening. Numb, dazed, she sat stroking the small pile of clothes on her lap, trying to press out the wrinkles with the palm of her hand. Stroking and stroking. "He has nothing of his own now," she murmured. "Nothing from home. Why would Jovan do that to him?"

Swinging the wheel hard, Ted headed for the ramp that led to the lower deck of the bridge. He took the turn so fast that Sarah was thrown against the door. "He was probably afraid we'd give the police a description before he could get away."

Sarah righted herself. Police? Would Jovan really have thought of that? Or was it that he did not want Joey to have any reminders of home, of her?

With one finger she traced the outline of the N.Y. Mets logo on Joey's T-shirt. Tears kept blurring her vision.

"I'll send him a package," she said. "Just a small one. It

won't cost much. I'll send him Mr. Monkey to keep him company."

Mr. Monkey was Joey's favorite "pillow friend": a cuddly stuffed version of Curious George, the character from the children's book. At home, Joey went to sleep every night with his arms around Mr. Monkey. The doll's grinning red felt mouth had come unglued long ago and one of the button eyes had fallen out, but she could repair it all easily enough before she sent it to him. He'd be so happy to see Mr. Monkey. He needed a friend.

"He must be so lonely over there," she murmured.

Over there.

In Belgrade.

They had gotten the news over the telephone, when her father called home to report what they had found at the apartment: the empty closets, the price tags on the bare mattress. Sarah, sitting on the edge of the bed, stunned and exhausted from weeping, had heard his voice in the next room—had heard the quiet murmur turn abruptly to explosive rage. "Goddammit," he'd said, slamming down the receiver. "Goddammit to hell."

"What, Dad?" she'd said. "What is it?" But she knew. With absolute certainty she already knew.

Her father loomed in the doorway, fists clenched. "Jovan just called the house. From Belgrade."

"Yes." She felt very cold, as if it were winter and she were out in the snow.

"He says to tell you that Joey's safe with him."

"Yes."

"He says to tell you—" He cleared his throat, passed a hand through his hair, started again. "He says to tell you that if you

40

want to be Joey's mother again, you'll . . . have to go and live with him over there."

Sarah nodded. Belgrade. Of course. It was what she had known all along, what she had feared and turned away from: Belgrade.

You are my wife. You cannot leave me.

It's over, Jovan. I can't take anymore. I won't.

We belong together. You belong to me.

You're wrong, Jovan. I don't belong to anyone. I belong to myself.

Come back, Sarah.

No. Not again. Not ever.

I'll make you sorry. I'll take Joey. I'll make you hurt. I'll take him home with me, where he belongs.

His words. *His.* He had been telling her all along. But how could she live with being afraid every minute that he would actually *do* such a thing—tear Joey away from her, tear her very life away, rip open her insides and maul the heart out of her. It was impossible. It was more than she had been able to bear, more than she'd ever dared to think about.

P-please, Mama. D-don't make me g-go.

It'll be okay.

P-please, Mama. Please.

And then remembering, she had wept and wept, burying her face in the small pile of clothes and shaking with grief. Joey. Oh, Joey.

———————

"We'll call Bob Koenig," her father said now as they sped south down the New Jersey Turnpike. Eyes straight ahead, both hands fixed on the wheel, he kept to the passing lane, overtaking one car and truck after another. "We'll call him as soon as we get home. Koenig will know what to do."

Around and around the Mets logo Sarah ran her finger.

Around and around and down and over to where it stopped and then back again. Hopeless, hopeless.

Outside her window the bleak landscape rushed by: the railroad yard; the car dumps; the Meadowlands, with their reeking plateaus of garbage a hundred feet high, where clouds of sea gulls wheeled and dipped above fresh truckloads of filth.

Could she do it? she wondered. Live with Jovan again? *No. Not again. Not ever.* But she would have to now, wouldn't she?

"Jovan will never give him back." She said it coldly, matter-of-factly. It was nothing but the truth.

"I never said he'd give him back. I said we'd *get* him back."

She shook her head. "It's too late."

"No, dammit. It's not too late. You can't give up before we've even tried."

"Tried what, Dad? Tried what? Can you tell me that?" She was shouting now. "You can't, can you? Because there *is* nothing we can do."

"The hell there isn't. Jovan has broken the law. He's violated a court order."

"Oh, right. I forgot. So I guess all we do now is call him up and ask him to please come back to the States so we can have him arrested."

"Dammit, of course not. But it gives us some legal recourse, that's the point. It gives us some place to start."

Sarah turned away. She didn't believe any of it. Not a word. Because she knew that Jovan had won. Jovan always won. And now it was all up to her. Her choice. No way out: go back and live with Jovan. Or never see Joey again.

―――――――

Her father was on the telephone almost from the minute they got home. Using the wall phone in the kitchen, he began calling friends, relatives, business associates—everyone he could think of who might have some idea how to get Joey back.

Upstairs her mother listened on the extension phone and made calls of her own.

Useless, Sarah kept thinking as she wandered absently from room to room, or stood at the window looking out— yard empty, swing set empty. Useless.

The clock on the mantel struck the half hour, a single plangent note. Eight-thirty. Joey's bedtime. She would have just finished reading him his bedtime story and would be tucking him in, kissing him his last goodnight, her nose pressed against his sweet, soft child's hair—

Joey. Joey.

Later, wandering into the kitchen, she found her father still on the phone. She sat down across from him.

"Call me as soon as you get back," he was saying into the receiver. "Thank you."

Hanging up, he made a note on a yellow legal pad. "Still no word from Koenig," he told her as he wrote. "I left another message on his answering machine. We'll just have to wait."

Sarah shrugged. It didn't matter. None of it mattered. Because none of it would do any good.

"What about Jovan's friend?" he asked her. "You know, what's-his-name, the doctor?"

"Marko?"

"Yeah, Marko. Maybe he knows something. Got his number?"

"I don't know. I'll see."

Listlessly she began looking for her phone book among the litter that covered the table: the Sommerton and Manhattan telephone directories; the directories for Trenton, New Brunswick, and Newark; the family phone book; the family birthday, Christmas card, and anniversary book; her father's at-home directory of his current business contacts. There were also assorted pens and pencils, a half-empty coffee mug; an ashtray overflowing with cigar ashes. And scattered everywhere, like unraked leaves, were pages torn from the yellow legal pad, each page scrawled with lists and notes and names and doodles. She smiled to herself. Her father was in his element. On home ground.

This was the way he'd spent most evenings and weekends for as long as she could remember: telephone in one hand, cigar in the other; talking, hustling, only really *alive* when he had a telephone in his hand. He was a salesman. It was what he did. It was what he was good at.

Unearthing her own phone book from the mess, Sarah flipped through the pages, found Marko's number, and showed her father the place.

"Thanks, kitten." He picked up the phone and dialed again. "Hello, is this Marko Markovic? My name is Ted Novack. I'm Jovan's father-in-law and I'm calling because—"

She didn't stay to hear the rest. What was the point? It was over. There was nothing to be done. It was only a matter of her making a decision now. One way or the other.

"I am sorry," Marko Markovic was saying in the thick Slavic accent Ted had come to know so well over the last ten years. "It is unhappy situation. I am very sorry to hear of it. But I cannot help you. As I have said, Jovan tells me nothing about his plans before he goes or even that he is leaving the country."

"Yes, you did say that. I just thought . . . Well, thanks anyway."

"Please."

"Yes?"

"Please tell Sarah how sorry I am that this thing has happened."

"Perfect weather the whole time," he told Ted. "It couldn't have been better."

Normally Ted would have let him run on. Koenig was not only Sarah's lawyer, he was also a friend—one of Ted's regular partners on the squash court. But tonight, Ted had no patience for small talk. "Look, Bob, it's about Joey. . . ."

When Ted told him what had happened, Koenig's mood changed abruptly. "Oh, hell," he said. "I was afraid this might happen."

"*You* were afraid?" Emma said over the extension. "Since when were *you* afraid? I was the one who kept saying we should stop him. But you didn't want to do anything. We'll talk again after Labor Day, you said. Well, it's Labor Day, Mr. Koenig, and Joey's gone."

"Emma, I realize how upsetting this must be but let me assure you—"

"We don't want assurances, we want Joey back."

"Emma, please," Ted said. "Let me handle this."

"Let me assure you," Koenig persisted, "that there was very little hope of preventing Jovan from getting visiting rights, especially since Sarah herself was trying so hard to make the separation an amicable one. And of course once Jovan denied in court that he had any intention of stealing Joey, that pretty well settled it."

"But he was lying."

"Of course he was. We know that now. But the judge believed him, and Sarah obviously wanted to believe him, too. Look, I don't mean to sound callous or uncaring, but that was Sarah's choice. She knew the risks and she was willing to take them."

"Sarah was confused. She didn't know what she wanted."

"Excuse me, Emma, but Sarah is a grown woman. She's capable of making her own decisions."

"And her own mistakes," Emma muttered ruefully.

"Yes, and her own mistakes. But if you remember when we were in court, it wasn't all that clear that it would be a mistake. Sarah was pretty certain that Jovan would not do anything that might cost him his degree, isn't that right? By the way, what happened with that? Ted? You still there? I thought he wasn't supposed to get his degree until the fall."

"October is what he told us. But he must have been lying. I don't know. Look, none of that is important now. The damage is done. What I want to know is, what can we do? What about extradition? Could we get Jovan back here for violating a court order?"

"I'll look into that and let you know, but I suspect that in a case like this, where you're dealing with a foreign government and so on . . . well, it's not going to be easy."

"But not impossible?" Emma broke in. "Is that what you're saying? It can be done?"

"Quite frankly, Emma, I have no idea whether it would be possible or not. Our firm doesn't usually handle this kind of thing. Never has. I wouldn't know where to begin."

"Christ on a crutch," Ted murmured. This was like pulling teeth. "Well, then," he said with forced patience, "what about another firm? Is there someone you can recommend who'd know how to go about this?"

"Offhand, ah, no, no, I really can't. But I'll certainly ask around and see what I can turn up for you."

"Good. Do that."

"Right," Koenig said with authority. "In the meantime, I'll go into court and get Jovan charged with violating the consent order."

"That's wonderful," said Emma, her voice thick with sarcasm. "We get a piece of paper saying that Jovan has been a bad boy. Just what is that supposed to accomplish?"

"You might be surprised. Getting charges filed would not be a solution, but it could be a useful tool. As a method of coercion, it might be all you need to turn Jovan around."

"You don't know Jovan," Emma muttered.

"In any case," Koenig went on, "a citation would make the offense a matter of public record. You'd then have an official declaration that under the law it was Jovan who violated Sarah's rights, not the other way around. That could be an important weapon in any future proceedings."

Now it was Ted's turn to interrupt: "What kind of proceedings? What do you have in mind?"

Paul Koenig was not about to let himself get pinned down. "Oh, nothing specific. At this point it's hard to predict what might or might not happen. But say you end up taking Jovan to court in Yugoslavia. Or maybe you get help from someone in the federal government—I don't know, from your congressman or somebody. You'll need that kind of documentation."

Ted jotted hasty notes on his legal pad. "Okay, let's say we get a citation against him. How soon does this happen?"

"I can be in court first thing in the morning."

"Sounds good. I have to be at my office then. Call me there and let me know how it goes, will you?"

"Sure thing, Ted. Will do. Take care now. You too, Emma. Oh, and Ted?"

"Yeah?"

"Tell Sarah how sorry I am that it turned out this way for her. Truly sorry."

Ed set the receiver back on its cradle. "Hell," he said. Talking to Koenig was like trying to hold water in your hand. Just when you thought you had something it dribbled away. He had been hoping that the lawyer would be able to offer some sort of simple solution. Obviously there was not going to be one.

49

He looked over the notes he had scribbled just now:

Coercion
Weapon
Crt in Yugo
Gov't contacts???
Congsmn

With his ball point he underlined the first word on the list. He liked the sound of it. It fit his mood.

CHECKPOINT
Saturday, April 23, 1:20 A.M.

"There!" said Hardy. "Is that 'im?"

Ahead, at the bend in the road, a mist of white light shone on the fir trees. As Sarah watched, the light grew brighter, then narrowed abruptly as a pair of headlights flared into the open: a big car rounding the bend, coming fast.

"That is 'im, i'n'it?"

"We'll know soon enough," said Wilkes.

None of them said a word as the car came barreling on. For a moment it looked as if it were going to ram straight through the crossing gate. But suddenly it veered, slowed, and came to a halt in the patch of light in front of the administration building. It was a large gray sedan with some sort of official-looking insignia on the front door. The headlights went out, the door opened, and a figure in a guard's uniform got out.

"Cor," breathed Hardy. "That bloke's a bloody giant."

Hardy was right. Even from this distance, the guard looked as broad as an ox and half again as tall. Pausing to cast an appraising glance in the direction of the crowded BMW, he turned and shambled none too steadily toward the administration building.

"All present and accounted for," Hardy murmured.

"Us or them?" asked Sarah's father.

"Both."

Again they watched and waited in tense silence. Sheila Hardy sniffled and blew her nose. The boy on Sarah's lap slept on.

Suddenly the door of the administration building burst open. The burly guard stepped out and came lumbering purposefully in their direction.

"Remember now," said Wilkes, "you're exhausted tourists, nothing more. Sarah, don't forget. If he wants you to get out of the car, stay put. I'll do the talking."

He rolled down the window. *"Guten abend,"* he said as the new guard approached.

"Guten abend, Mein Herr," the man growled, his breath steaming in the cold air. In one gloved hand he held the passports, level with the pistol on his hip. Bending to the window, he began speaking in animated German, his hands in constant motion, his head bobbing. Even in the backseat Sarah could smell the alcohol on his breath.

Whatever the guard was saying, he sounded very serious, very concerned, and as he went on talking and waving the passports around, Wilkes kept saying *"ja"* and *"danke."* Then, in the midst of his hand-waving, the guard handed Wilkes the passports. He did it so suddenly, so offhandedly, that Sarah almost missed it. Wilkes had them! He had their passports! But had they been stamped? Was the guard sending them back where they'd come from? It was impossible to tell, for the man was still talking and Wilkes was still nodding, agreeing, murmuring thanks.

Then, abruptly, the torrent of words ceased. Straightening

three

All that evening Sarah kept hearing their voices, the dissonant buzzing. Sometimes it was her father on the telephone, sometimes her mother, sometimes both, talking, talking, telling the story over and over, like actors rehearsing a play, going through the motions, while she sat curled up here on the sofa in front of the television, arms crossed, hugging herself and trying to think what the tune was that kept going through her head. A lullaby.

> *Hushabye, don't you cry,*
> *Go to sleep my little baby . . .*

The television flickered. Gunshots rang out. Tires squealed. A car chase. She almost jumped up to turn the sound down, thinking: Mustn't wake him, mustn't—But then remembered: he wasn't asleep. Not here. He would be asleep though, wouldn't he? Where he was it was the middle of the night. What was it, six hours' difference? Seven?

Over there.

On the other side of the world.

Dark. The room was so dark. It crossed her mind that maybe she should get up and turn on a light. *It's not good to watch television in a dark room, Joey.* Just get up and switch on the . . . But it didn't seem worth the effort. Maybe later she'd . . . What? What was it she'd been thinking about? Gone. Whatever it was. Didn't matter anyway. Nothing mattered except . . .

On the screen a man had just taken a drink of iced tea and was falling backward into a swimming pool. What she saw was a small boy on a diving board, suspended in midair . . . Just yesterday, wasn't it? When Jovan took him away. Or was it two days ago, on Saturday? When she'd last spoken to him on the telephone. *Do vidjenja, Mami.* Jovan could have done it right then. Could have taken Joey and been on his way to the airport as soon as he'd hung up the phone. Bastard. Liar.

The image on the screen changed again: the New York skyline at night. A disembodied voice intoned:

"It's . . . ten P.M. Do you know where your children are?"

Oh, God, she moaned, weeping again, tears flooding her eyes, her heart coming apart.

Why? Why had she trusted him? He'd been lying all along and she had trusted him. Why? Why had she refused to take his threats seriously? Why had she been such a fool to think he would let her go? Such a stupid fool she'd been. Right from the beginning. Yes, even then.

Except she'd been so much younger then. And driven by such need, such terrible longing. Wanting so much, dreaming . . .

In the beginning . . .

They'd met in Paris at a café on the Boulevard St. Michel. It was a warm night in the middle of July 1966. Out on the sidewalk, rivers of people swirled and eddied, soaked in the red and purple luster of neon. Now and then a few more strollers came spilling in through the open door. They came in twos and threes and fours, and nobody seemed to be leaving. The bar was shoulder to shoulder. Every table was taken. Waiters in black vests dodged up and back balancing trays over their heads. People kept coming and going. Motion everywhere. Voices. Laughter. Which was why Sarah didn't notice him at first.

She was sitting at a small table, sipping wine over the remnants of a late supper and telling Carole Hartman what a godsend her invitation had been and how exciting it was to be in Paris, and how happy she was to see her old roommate again.

Carole tossed her blond hair and laughed. "You're the godsend," she said. "And what a perfect time to arrive: on the eve of Bastille Day! There'll be dancing in the streets tonight."

Chattering away, high on wine and cigarettes and excitement, Sarah only gradually became aware of the two young men who had been working their way up and down the crowded aisle looking for an empty table. When she finally glanced up she found herself looking into a pair of yellow-brown eyes. Odd eyes, the color of—something familiar; she couldn't think what. The man had thick eyebrows and wavy dark hair that flopped over his forehead. And he was smiling at her. She looked away. The two men moved on. But then the couple at the next table got up to leave and the men came back and sat down.

It was awkward at first. The tables were side by side and jammed so close together that Sarah kept bumping elbows with him. He turned and smiled an apology, and for a moment she wondered if he hadn't been bumping her elbow on purpose. But his smile was gentle. A little impish, too. She smiled back.

The trip was a graduation present to herself: six weeks away while she tried to figure out what she wanted to do with herself now that she was almost twenty-two, now that she had her degree, now that it was all over between her and Rick, whom she might have married if things had worked out differently, if he and her father had been able to get along. . . .

Yes, Paris would be just the thing.

"I hope you can come," Carole had written. "I'm only taking one lit. course this summer so we'd have lots of time to do things together. And wouldn't it be fun to be roommates again! I've got a *petite chambre* at the back of a little pension on the Rue Jacob. It doesn't get much light, but it's cheap and it's right around the corner from just about everything."

Yes, it was perfect. By taking a charter flight, by sharing room and board with Carole and living frugally, Sarah guessed she could squeak by on the money she had saved up while working summers at Bamberger's—on that and the two hundred dollars her father had kicked in as a graduation present.

The waiters were turning the chairs up on the tables when Jovan poured out the last of the cognac, careful to see that each of them got some before letting the last few drops slide into his own glass.

He had been doing things like that all evening. Having pushed their two tables together, he had made himself the host of their little party. While he talked and laughed and listened attentively and lit one Gitane after another, he also made sure that the coffee and dessert arrived promptly, that the cognac was "three star," and that the check was taken care of before the rest of them were even aware that it had been presented. Sarah was impressed. None of the men she had ever dated could have managed it all so gracefully, so unobtrusively. Not even Rick.

Of course, Rick had been better looking, leaner, fine-boned. Jovan's face was broad, with Slavic cheekbones and thick eyebrows that came together over the bridge of his nose. And wasn't there a hint of something soft and fleshy there; along the line of his jaw, under his eyes? (Those strange eyes.) Still, he could be so unbelievably charming and considerate. He dressed well, too! A well-fitting corduroy jacket, a crisp white shirt open at the neck. And he did have the nicest smile.

He caught her watching him and there it was again.

What surprised her was how easy it was to talk to him, especially since neither of them spoke the other's language and they had to make do in French. His was thickened with a gutteral accent as well as with wine, and his syntax was sometimes confusing. Hers, learned in high school and college, was stiff with textbook formality. But he was patient with her and kind enough not to laugh at her mistakes—except once or twice, and then only because she started giggling first. He was as eager as she, it seemed, to understand. And to be understood.

He was leaning close, telling her about the work he did as a draughtsman in an engineering firm, drawing up plans for the heating systems of new buildings.

"That sounds like interesting work," she said.

"I hate it," he said, rolling the words deep at the back of his throat. "There is no poetry in it, there is no passion, no art."

"And you are an artist?" She heard the touch of awe in her voice.

He heard it too and grinned. "Artist of *science!*" he said proudly, raising a finger for emphasis. His passion was chemistry. It was his art, his poetry. It was why he had come to

Paris, why he was willing to spend evenings and weekends penned up in stuffy classrooms or buried in books at the library.

"I think it must be wonderful to have a dream like that," she heard herself saying. "Something to dedicate your life to." She sipped her cognac and felt it burn its way down her throat. "But why Paris? Why couldn't you study chemistry in Belgrade?"

"Why Paris? Paris is everything! Center of the world. You feel special just being here. It is true, Petor?"

Petor interrupted his quiet conversation with Carole. He paused to consider. He was thin and scholarly, with a high forehead, and wore wire-rimmed glasses; he measured his words carefully. "In a way perhaps yes. Being here changes one. One never looks at things the same way again."

"A lawyer's response," Jovan chided. "You see? I can always rely on my friend Petor to put such things into perspective."

Petor shrugged and turned back to Carole.

"Besides," Jovan went on, "in Belgrade I cannot study chemistry. It is not my training. When I am thirteen my mother enrolls me in state technical high school. Uncle Stefan tells her engineering is good profession. He tells her I will make money. I will support her."

"Your father couldn't support her?"

"My father is dead."

"Oh. I'm sorry."

He dismissed her sympathy with the wave of a hand. "There is no need. It was a long time ago. During the war."

"Was he a soldier?"

"He was with the Partisans. With Tito. He was fighting the Ustachi, the Chetniks."

"Who?"

"Our own Nazis."

60

She nodded, but still the names meant nothing. They only made her more aware than ever that he came from a place and a time so entirely different from her own as to be completely unimaginable—and absolutely fascinating.

"For my father to die that way," he said, "it was a noble thing."

The words sounded strangely ritualized, as though he had said them many times before. It occurred to Sarah that perhaps he had said them most often to himself.

"You must have been only a child then," she said gently.

"I was seven when he went away to the mountains. That was 1943. After that, I never see him again." He put his cigarette to his lips, inhaled deeply, blew the smoke out between his teeth. "And now I am engineer and they will let me do nothing else."

"Who? Your mother and your uncle?" Was she prying too much?

"Our government. The state. The state gave me education. The state has a right—of course—that I should give back in return something. For most people it is good system. Yes, of course. Why not? But for me, no. For me it is disaster!" He stabbed his cigarette into the ashtray and mashed it to shreds. "When I go back it will be as scientist," he said with a ferocity that alarmed her. "As *great* scientist!"

Petor, who had given up trying to talk to Carole over Jovan's rising invective, lifted his glass in salute. "And winner of *le Prix Nobel!*" he said.

"Yes, by God," Jovan said, missing the mockery. "And winner of the Nobel Prize."

"But not for peace," Petor added, giving Sarah a sly wink.

This time Jovan caught the tone—and the wink. Suddenly he was out of his chair and leaning over the table, flushed with rage. "What are you at?" he hissed in his friend's face. "You sneer at me? Eh? You mock me?"

Sarah held her breath. Carole sat frozen.

But all at once Jovan's fury went slack. His mouth open, his head cocked like a bird listening for a worm, he watched quizzically as the corners of Petor's mouth began curling into a puckish grin. He sat down. He wiped his forehead with a napkin. "No," he said sheepishly, "not for peace." Reaching over, he gave Petor a playful punch on the shoulder. Petor punched him back, and then they were both laughing.

"Not for peace," Jovan snorted, slapping the table. "It is a good joke, eh? Not for peace!"

Caught up in the spirit, Carole was laughing, too. So was Sarah. But when she stopped to take a last sip of cognac the glass was shaking in her hand.

———————

They walked on the boulevard afterward, past the cafés and the cinema marquees, and then along the river, away from all the lights and the people.

It was cooler under the trees. The lights on the opposite bank danced like fireflies on the dark water. Jovan was beside her, leaning close, talking, listening. Gone was the intensity that had so unnerved her a half hour before—yes, and excited her, too, in a strange way. He was quiet now, and calm, and attentive. It was very confusing.

Yet here she was, telling him all about herself; telling him more than she intended. Maybe it was a mistake. But she needed to. She told him about breaking up with Rick and the panicky way she felt wondering what she was going to do with herself now. And she talked about the longing she felt, a longing for—she didn't know for what exactly, but for something . . . *different*, something that would . . .

"Fill your life."

"Yes."

"Give it meaning. Give it a purpose, direction."

"Yes."

"So that when you are old and it all is behind you, you are not looking back and saying, Was that all there was? Did it amount to no more than that?"

"Yes, that's right."

"So that you do not regret forever all the things you could have done if you had not been always so afraid, always so ready to settle for a handful of crumbs off the floor when the whole loaf of bread was up there on the table and all you had to do was reach up and take it."

"You know, don't you? You know what it's like." She felt the cognac warming her insides.

"Yes, I know. Of course. It has been also for me like that. Growing up in war, afraid, always hungry. 'Lick salt,' my mother used to tell us, 'then you'll be mostly thirsty.' Yes, I have known. And then after the war, being put in state orphanage because my mother could not support me and my sister together and one of us had to go. I, I had to go. It was the only way. I was older and maybe to a boy it would not matter so much. Ach." He flicked his cigarette away, sending the glowing ash skittering into the gutter. "Enough. I am sorry. I speak too much. But listen to me: I do know what it is to be happy for the few crumbs. And also, Sarah," he said, turning to face her, "also I know what happens if you let it: you get so much used to the crumbs that after long enough you are even stopping looking up to what is on the top of the table. That is what you must fight against. Because if you stop fighting, if you stop reaching, you will have nothing. A few dirty crumbs and a hungry stomach."

They walked on, turned a corner. She was beginning to feel queasy.

"Ah," he said. "Here, this I want you to see. Look. Look."

They stood facing a broad esplande, which was bordered with parallel rows of trees and criss-crossed with broad walk-

63

ways. At the far end rose a domed building, a basilica with double tiers of columned porticos. Lit by floodlights, it lay upon the night like a jewel in a velvet case.

"Les Invalides," Jovan said. "Where Napoleon is buried."

"It is very beautiful," Sarah whispered.

"That was a man who was not afraid," Jovan said half to himself as he gazed at the monument. "Who embraced life, who took of life everything he could."

"Can we sit down for a minute? I feel . . . a little dizzy. The wind—" She could taste the bile rising in her throat.

"Yes, yes. Of course. Come. Over here."

Taking her lightly by the arm he led her to a bench in the lamplight. Leaving Carole and Petor to go on ahead, he sat beside her as she waited for her nausea to pass.

"You're right about what you said about being afraid," she said after a while. "I've been afraid for as long as I can remember. Always holding back, always letting someone else make my decisions for me. You know, I even gave up Rick because my father wanted me to and I was too afraid to stand up to him and say what *I* wanted. I guess I'm not very brave," she said.

Reaching over, Jovan touched her chin and gently turned her face toward him. "But that is changing now," he told her.

"Is it?" She was doubtful. "How? What do you mean?"

"But of course! You are here, aren't you! You came to Paris! You took this trip because *you* wanted it."

"Yes, I see," she said. "I guess that's true." Sitting there in the pool of light under the trees, she savored the revelation as if it were the tastiest of chocolates. Except that the pleasure began to melt away and she heard a small voice asking, "Then why am I still afraid?"

"You are afraid now?"

"I guess I am."

"Of me?"

64

"Yes. A little."

"But why?"

She tried to laugh. "Because you tell me I don't have to be afraid. And if I don't have to be afraid then I'll have to do all kinds of things that I've been too afraid to do."

He took her hand. "Like become in love?"

She let her hand rest in his. "It's late," she said quietly, looking at their hands together and not being sure for a moment which was his and which was hers. "We better go. Carole will wonder what's happened to me." She got to her feet. "I'll wonder, too," she added, managing the laugh this time.

Later, they stood together in the dark street outside the pension. Carole had gone in. Petor waited nearby.

"I want to see you again," Jovan said, without letting go of her hand.

"Yes," she said. "I'd like that."

"Tomorrow?"

"Yes, all right."

He lifted her hand and touched it to his lips. "Good night," he said.

"Good night."

Just then, as she looked up at him, his face was touched by a flicker of light from somewhere nearby and she realized what it was that those strange yellow-brown eyes reminded her of. They were almost exactly the color of the stone in a ring her grandmother had given her: a tiger eye. Warm and hard at the same time.

———————

They spent the Bastille Day holiday together and part of the next day and all of the next. They took a trip down the Seine in a glass-topped boat. At the Rodin Museum they took pictures of each other mimicking the poses of the nudes. For

65

lunch, they bought salami and bread and sat on a bench by the river. One rainy afternoon they went to see *Rio Grande*. His choice. John Wayne with French subtitles. Swagger and gunfire. He had seen it three times.

Another time he took her to a dark little Serbian restaurant in Montparnasse that was down a flight of steps, below the sidewalk. He spoke to the waiter in what must have been Serbian, the cadences rising and falling as if the words were being sung. The waiter brought a pungent cheese with a name she didn't catch, and lamb on skewers, and a red wine that Jovan said came from Dalmatia. They ate and talked and took their time. For dessert they had baklava and small cups of thick black coffee.

And all the while she kept being amazed at how easy it was to be with him—and not just because her French was improving either. At times he seemed to know her thoughts and feelings even before she did. Which might have been unsettling but instead felt comfortable and reassuring, as though they had known each other for years.

Afterward he invited her up to his room. "There is something I want to show you," he said.

"Oh? You do etchings?" she asked in English. He looked at her quizzically. "Never mind. Just a joke."

It was a small room on the third floor overlooking the Rue Rollin. There was the smell of cigarettes. There were books and papers everywhere: on the easy chair, on the table that he used for a desk, on the bureau, on the windowsill. Biology and chemistry textbooks, engineering textbooks, volumes of French poetry: Villon, Rimbaud, Verlaine, Baudelaire. The poetry surprised her.

"They're my favorites," he said. "Especially Villon." He cleared a place on the end of the bed. "Here. Please. Sit. One poem I would like to read to you."

"By Villon?"

66

He grinned. "No, no. A modern poet." He picked up a typewritten sheet. Leaning an elbow on the bureau, a cigarette cocked between two fingers, he began to read. The poem, in French, was about a girl with brown hair and brown eyes, a beautiful girl who laughed and dreamed and longed for something to fill her life, and about a man who hoped he could be everything to her, as she had become everything to him.

When he was finished she didn't know what to say. No one had ever written a poem for her before. "Thank you," was all she could manage. "Thank you."

"Do you like it?"

"Like it? Jovan, it's beautiful."

He came and sat next to her. "Because you are beautiful you make my poem beautiful," he whispered.

They made love that night on the narrow bed, books and papers strewn on the floor around them, the room lit only by a crooked window of light thrown onto the ceiling by the lamp in the street below. Afterward he found her face salted with tears.

"What is it?" he whispered. "What is it?"

She shrugged. She could not stop the tears.

"Sarah, Sarah. I'm sorry, Did I hurt you?"

She shook her head. "No, no. It's all right. Just hold me." And she cried and felt all the loneliness and sadness and longing welling up in her and overflowing like a pond in a summer rain.

———————

She let it happen, let Jovan wrap the summer days around her like a down comforter, ignoring any thought of where she might find herself tomorrow or the day after, only wanting the time to slow down, slow down, stop rushing by so fast.

She neglected Carole, stopped writing to her parents.

Jovan, who had promised to visit his mother in Belgrade, decided to stay with Sarah instead. They were together constantly. But then, too quickly, the summer was almost over, only a few days left.

"Stay," Jovan whispered as she lay beside him on top of the sheets, her head cradled in her favorite place under his arm. "Don't go back." He traced a finger around the pathways of her earlobe. "The visa you can get extended, yes? And money you could get from your father."

"You know I can't. We've been over that before." It was crazy. No matter how often she told him otherwise, Jovan could not seem to get the idea out of his head that just because she was an American her father must be wealthy. Which of course was ridiculous; her father had been complaining about how tight things were for as long as she could remember. Anyway, that was not the point. Visa or no visa, money or no money, she needed to get back home.

He did not understand. If she loved him she would stay. No reasons, no excuses.

It was so unfair. He always left her with such awful choices. There was never any middle ground with him. It was either all love or all hate, all loyalty or all betrayal, all his way or not at all.

She tried to explain. She needed time to think, she said, time to catch her breath. Everything in the last few weeks had been so new for her, so full. How long could it go on that way before something happened?

"What would happen?"

"The summer will end. The seasons will change."

"They always do."

"You will find out that you don't like me as much as you thought you did." Or I will get in too deep, she thought, and then discover that it's all been a mistake.

He shook his head. He was still puzzled. And annoyed now,

too. He got out of the bed and went looking for his cigarettes. "You talk like a child," he said. "You are talking foolishness."

But she knew she wasn't. She knew that as much as she loved being swept along by his dreams, by a sense of vision and purpose that she could not find in herself, she also felt overwhelmed by him sometimes, as if her own life could be swallowed up by his: by those fierce outbursts, that voracious will.

"I'm sorry," she said. But she held firm. She had to slow down, had to give herself space. Later, she could come back, she told him. In the spring, perhaps, after she had had a chance to work for a while and save up some more money. Yes, in the spring.

———————

On the morning that her flight was to leave, he came with her on the bus to Orly. He did not let go of her hand the whole time. His anger at her leaving had turned to grief. He looked absolutely miserable.

At the check-in counter, he helped her with her bags, then went with her to the gate.

"Will you write to me?" she asked, her hands in his.

"I'll write to you every day," he said gravely.

She smiled. Sometimes his "all-or-nothing" could be very touching. "And send me poems?"

"Ah, Sarah." He pulled her to him. "Yes, my love. And send you poems."

———————

His letters began dropping through the slot in the front door almost as soon as she got home: thin, blue airmail envelopes bearing beautiful French stamps and the Paris postmark; three and sometimes four of them a week. The letters were written in French and were full of longing. Letters telling her how much he missed her. Letters with poems enclosed. One

69

letter came with a snapshot of him (taken by Petor?) posed in a way that made it look as if the Eiffel Tower were balanced on his head.

Wonderful letters. But also confusing. Sarah was having a hard enough time getting used to being back. Arriving home, she had walked into a job in the children's room at the public library and had settled once more into her old room upstairs in her parents' house on Mercer Street: the red-brick Dutch colonial with the pillared front porch and the heavy-lidded dormers—comfortable, maple-shaded, hedged in. Her room was a little girl's room with frilly white curtains and a white chenille bedspread; the room where she had lived all through high school and during semester breaks from college. The neighborhoods she drove through every morning on her way to work were the same neighborhoods she had driven through for years, with the same neat rows of houses, the same stolid churches, the same stores and factories. Passing the great square clock tower of the Eberhardt factory, she checked her watch as always against one or another of its four gigantic dials. Each clock face was eight feet high; each kept perfect time, scarcely deviating for even one erratic second on any given day; each, in its huge, its awful precision, regulated people's lives for miles around. No, nothing had changed. Nothing would ever change. At times, in fact, she found it hard to believe that she had been gone at all, or that the summer had ever happened.

Except she knew it had happened, because *she* had changed; because she had had a taste of what her life could be, separate from the life she had known before; because here were Jovan's letters to remind her. When she was reading them, she could almost imagine him again on one of those shimmering summer mornings, when the rain-wet pavement steamed in the sunlight and when she kept smiling all the time because she was sure that everyone she passed—the old women with their string bags, the smart young women hurrying to the Métro, the taxi drivers, the indolent young males lounging in the cafés—everyone could tell that she had just come from her lover's bed, and everyone was as happy for her as she was.

But then the letter would end and there she would be again, back in her room, wondering how or if ever she could make the two parts of her life come together in her head.

It was very disorienting, like looking through binoculars and not being able to get the two lenses into focus at the same time.

And still the letters kept coming.

By November he was pleading with her to come back to Paris, and she was beginning to think it might be a good idea. At least if she saw him again she might be able to get things settled in her mind.

"Settled?" said her mother, pouring dressing on her salad. Ted peered at Sarah over the tops of his horn-rimmed glasses. "What do you mean, 'settled'?"

Sarah's younger brother, Richard, who was a gangly nineteen-year-old, glanced quickly at each of them, but kept eating and said nothing.

They were sitting at the kitchen table having supper: roasted chicken, mashed potatoes, a garden salad, and, for Sarah, a glass of wine—a habit she had brought back from Paris. She took a sip. "I think he wants to get married," she said, trying to sound nonchalant.

"Married," her father repeated.

"Are you sure, dear?" said her mother.

"No, but . . ."

Her father glared. "She's not sure."

"He hasn't actually said so, but I think he does."

"Well, of course. What could be more natural. They've known each other for all of three or four weeks. Why shouldn't he want to marry her?"

"Six."

"What?"

"Six weeks. We were together for six weeks."

"Oh, oh. Pardon me. That makes a big difference."

"Ted, please."

"For God's sake, Emma, they don't even speak the same language."

Neither does anyone in this house, Sarah thought, but she kept it to herself. She had long ago given up trying to bridge the distance between herself and her parents. "We manage okay in French," she said.

"Oh, in French! Very nice. Very romantic," her father said sarcastically.

Richard, who had stopped eating, quietly put down his fork and excused himself. Sarah would have left too, but she knew if she did it would only be worse the next time.

Her father had many questions. He wanted to know what she was going to do about her job. It was, he reminded her, the first real career job she had ever had. Did she think she could just waltz out of one job and into another whenever she felt like it? Where was the future in that? Or maybe she thought that making a living was beside the point? Also, what about cultural differences? What did this Joe-vahn know of her way of life? What did she know of his? Did she think she could live with a man whose background was so totally different from her own?

"It's Yo-vahn," she corrected.

"What?"

"His name. In Serbian, the *J* is pronounced like a *Y*."

"Whatever," he said.

It wasn't that she was trying to shut her father out. It was just that to Sarah the kinds of issues he was raising simply did not matter. The important thing was how she *felt*. And whether she would have a life of her own.

72

It was her mother, finally, who asked the only question that made any sense at the moment: "Do *you* want to marry *him?*"

"I don't know," she said. "I really don't. Sometimes I'm absolutely sure there's nothing else I'd rather do in the whole world. And other times—I get scared. I think of all the differences. That's what I have to get settled. That's why I have to go back and see him again."

Instead, he came to see her.

The visit was a compromise: her mother's idea. Rather than jeopardizing her new job, Sarah could invite her "friend" to be a guest in their house over the Christmas holidays. That way, he would have an opportunity to meet the family and to see something of what life was like in America. More to the point, of course, the family would have a chance to meet him.

Sarah wrote to Jovan that evening, to pass on her parents' invitation. His reply arrived a week later:

Tell your mother and father for their generosity I thank them. I will like very much to be the guest in their house. But the cost of tickets is too expensive. I cannot afford.

Fortunately, because she was living at home, Sarah had managed to keep her expenses low and to save a good portion of her take-home pay, so she was able to send him the fare.

———

On the day Jovan was to arrive, Sarah and her parents drove to Kennedy Airport to pick him up. That was the worst time: wondering if he would be different from what she remembered, if her parents would like him, what she would do if the whole thing turned out to be a mistake, a summer fantasy gone to pieces. By the time they got to the airport and found their way to the waiting area in the international arrivals building, Sarah felt so jumpy she could hardly stand still.

From her position behind the barrier that separated the spectators from the customs area, she searched the lines at the customs counters. She found her gaze settling on what looked like a familiar figure, except for an instant she wasn't sure because the man seemed shorter than she remembered, the hair thinner. But then she was certain. "There! There he is." Hair rumpled, eyes searching. A bag in one hand.

"The one in the hat?"

"God, mother. No, not him. The other one. In the sport-coat. With the collar turned up."

Sarah waved, trying to catch his eye. If only he would look her way. When at last he spotted her, he threw up a hand, waved, grinned happily, blew her a kiss. And then he was through customs and she was in his arms and she wished she could stay that way. But it was awkward because he hadn't put down his suitcase; it was banging against her hip, and when he bent to put it down her parents were there waiting.

He had brought gifts for everyone. For her father there was a fine leather wallet; for her mother, a ceramic brooch, hand-painted with tiny flowers. Her brother Richard got a pen and pencil set in a case lined with velvet. And for Sarah? For Sarah he had brought not just the anthology of French poetry or the yellow and black Saint Laurent scarf, which she loved, but the wonder of his actually being there, of being able to see and touch him again and of knowing for certain that the summer had been no illusion, that it really had happened, that Jovan Stefanovic was real and whole and would make her that way too.

With her parents, he was at his most charming: bowing slightly from the waist when he was introduced; deferring

74

respectfully to her father who seemed impressed; bestowing bouquets of compliments upon her mother, who blushed and did not know what to do with her hands.

Grandma Helen—her mother's mother and Sarah's own most loyal ally—was enchanted when she finally had a chance to meet Jovan. "Oh, Sarah, he's a real gift horse," she gushed, displaying her usual talent for mangling clichés. "He's *so* good-looking. And *so* charming. If you don't grab him, you're just plain crazy."

Once the introductions were over, however, the visit turned awkward. Not everyone was cordial. Sarah's father was hearty and jovial—the way, Sarah guessed, he was with his customers: "Have a drink. Have a cigar. Sit down, sit down. Make yourself at home." He even offered the use of his bathrobe when he discovered that Jovan—who would be sleeping on the living room sofa—hadn't brought one of his own.

Richard, meanwhile, kept a shy distance and dodged quickly past when he met Jovan on the stairs or in the hall. But Sarah also noticed that Richard took to wearing a sportcoat over his scarecrow shoulders and to walking around with one hand thrust into one of the coat pockets, the way Jovan did.

Sarah's mother, for her part, tried hard to make Jovan feel welcome. She served supper in the dining room instead of the kitchen and insisted that the table be set with linen rather than placemats. She began baking pies and cookies, which she hadn't done in years. All of which would have been very nice except that she went too far, tried too hard. At supper she served things like goulash and stuffed cabbage. The recipes, she explained, had come from Mrs. Ruschak down the street, whose parents or grandparents—she wasn't sure which—had come from somewhere in Eastern Europe: "Hungary or Rumania or one of those places."

Sarah wasn't sure whether to feel grateful to her for making the effort or whether to crawl into a closet and never come out.

"She means well," Jovan told Sarah later, when she tried to apologize. But Sarah knew he was just being kind. Her mother's efforts at making him welcome succeeded only in making him feel more like a stranger than he already was.

Nor did Sarah's father help matters, for despite his efforts to appear a generous and good-humored host, Sarah sensed that he was in fact struggling against a contrary impulse. She noticed it one evening at supper when he began interrogating Jovan—there was no other word for it—about his background, his education, his jobs, his goals. Coming from a prospective father-in-law, the questions themselves were natural enough. But his abruptness, the hard edge on his voice, made him sound less like a concerned parent than like a TV detective grilling a burglary suspect.

Puzzled, Sarah thought at first that it might be only the language barrier—having to wait for everything to be translated—that was making them all so uncomfortable, their attempts at cordiality so awkward, so clumsy.

But gradually she realized that the trouble was something more than language. She saw it in the look of disgust that passed over her father's face whenever Jovan began heaping garlands of praise on her mother for the way she was dressed or the way she had prepared a meal. She saw it in the patronizing skepticism with which he greeted Jovan's fervent declaration that he would one day win a place of honor in the annals of science for himself and his country. "Sounds good," her father said blandly, but it was obvious that Jovan's ambitions were not to be taken seriously.

Sarah discovered, in fact, that all the things she found so appealing about Jovan were the very things that her father seemed to trust the least. Jovan's charm he regarded as an

76

affectation. Jovan's vision, his dreams of brilliant success, were just that: dreams, irrelevancies. What mattered to Ted Novack was how this Jovan was going to support himself and Sarah if and when the two of them did decide to get married. And where would they live? And when was Jovan going to finish school?

"Come to think of it," he said one evening over coffee, "why is he still in school anyway? He's thirty years old. He should be out making a living by now."

Should? Whose *should?* What *should?* In her father's mind there seemed to be some sort of timetable for how people were supposed to live their lives: a preplanned schedule complete with a chronological listing of stops along the way and estimated times of arrival. And whatever did not conform to his scheme of things—such as Jovan's change of heart about an engineering career; such as Jovan's daring to break the mold and start anew—all that, in her father's eyes, was somehow irresponsible, untrustworthy.

Well, that may have been her father's idea of how a life should be lived: by schedules and timetables. But it certainly wasn't Jovan's. And Sarah did not want it to be hers, either.

Years later, looking back, Sarah sometimes wondered if it wasn't her father almost more than Jovan who induced her finally to make up her mind about getting married: whether it wasn't her father's mistrust of her judgment, his insistence that security and certainty were the only things in the world that mattered. For what Sarah feared at the time was that secretly those things mattered as much to her as they did to him, and that if she did not grab the chance to break free the way Jovan kept urging her to do—take her life in her own hands and make of it as much as she could while she could—she might very easily let herself coast along and coast along and not realize until too late that the great iron hands on the

77

Eberhardt clock had traveled too many times around that monumental dial and that she had missed her chance of ever finding out all that her life could have been.

They were married at the end of March, by a Paris magistrate. Though her parents were both convinced that she was making a mistake, they flew over with her for the ceremony.

"You're twenty-two years old," her father had told her. "You know how we feel. Now it's up to you. But if you decide to go ahead with this thing, I just want you to know that we'll stand by you."

Sarah was grateful to them for that. Still, it would have been nice if they could have mustered a few good feelings for her once she had made her decision. But on the flight over—their first trip abroad, the European vacation they had never before been able to give themselves—they were grim and subdued.

The ceremony was a simple one. Sarah, Jovan, and her parents took their places in line with a dozen other wedding parties in an ornate courtroom, with sunlight slanting in from the high mullioned windows and with a black-robed magistrate presiding in a powdered wig from behind a high wooden bench. Petor was there, serving as Jovan's best man, and so was Jovan's mother, who had flown in from Belgrade.

When it was their turn, Sarah and Jovan stepped forward. Only then, and then only for a moment, did Sarah feel a stab of panic. Jovan's hand was in hers, the magistrate was reciting the terms of the marriage contract, when it suddenly occurred to Sarah that maybe her parents were right, that maybe she was making a mistake, and that she had no idea who the man was to whom she was about to give the rest of her life. But then the magistrate was asking her if she, Sarah Novack, accepted Jovan Stefanovic as her husband from this day forward, and she was saying yes, and then Jovan was kissing her and the thought was gone, and there were kisses and handshakes and congratulations all around.

Afterward, her father invited everyone to an elegant Right Bank restaurant for a champagne lunch, with crepes and salad and a wedding cake festooned with bows of white frosting. Whatever his feelings about Jovan and the wedding, he did not stint. After the cake was cut, he even presented Sarah and Jovan with a check for five hundred dollars "to help the two of you get started."

But later, when he and Emma were about to leave for the airport for the trip home, he slipped Sarah an envelope containing a special present for herself alone. Inside the envelope was a one-way airline ticket back to the United States. "In case you change your mind," he told her.

"Sarah? Are you up? Sarah?" It was her mother, calling from downstairs.

"Yes?" What time was it? Morning? From beneath the bottom edge of the window shade a blade of sunlight slashed across the room. Thank God. As least the night was over. The odd thing was that she could not remember turning off the television and getting into bed.

"What is it, Mother?"

"It's Jovan, dear. He wants to talk to you. He's got Joey on the phone."

Her heart lurched. She came suddenly awake. Joey. She jumped out of bed and rushed to her parents' room. She picked up the phone in time to hear him ask, "How is she?" and to hear her mother reply: "Oh, she's just fine. She's just wonderful. She's singing and dancing. You bastard, how do you expect her to be?"

"Mother!"

"You've got some nerve asking how she is. After what you've done."

"Mother, please. Get off the line."

"Sarah?" Jovan sounded as though he was speaking through a pipe. She waited until she heard the phone click off downstairs. Then she said: "I want to talk to Joey." She would not get angry. She would not cry. He would not hurt her anymore.

"Yes, he's right here. He wants to talk to you, too. And I wanted to—"

She cut him off. "I have nothing to say to you. Either you put Joey on right now or I'm hanging up."

"Yes, yes. All right. Don't hang up."

A murmur of voices on the other end, then: "Mama?" His small voice was somewhere between a squeal and a shriek.

"Joey. Oh, Joey." Tears flooded her eyes but she fought them back. She did not want to worry him. "How are you? Are you all right? Where are you staying?"

"I'm ok-k-kay. I'm at B-b-baka's house. It's n-neat. There's an outhouse, l-like on a f-farm. And there's a w-w-well where we g-g-get w-w- . . . where we g-g-get w-w- . . ." He could not finish the word.

"Water," she said, to relieve him of his agony. God, she thought, his stutter was worse than ever. He wasn't okay. He wasn't okay at all.

"Why d-d-didn't you c-come like D-daddy said you would?"

"Like Daddy—?"

"He said you'd be c-coming on the next airp-plane. Why didn't you c-c-come, Mama?"

"I'm sorry, Joey, I—" She groped for words. What was Jovan trying to do to him? How could she tell him the truth: that his daddy had lied to him, that his daddy was using him to hurt her. Jovan was all he had now. He would need to trust him more than he needed to hear the truth. "I—I got delayed. I'm sorry. I won't be able to come right away."

"Why c-can't you c-come now? I miss you, Mama. I want you to b-b-be here, t-too."

She thought her heart was going to come apart. "I miss you, too, Joey. I miss you very, very much. And I'll see you just as soon as I possibly can."

"But when, Mama?"

"Please, Joey. I'll be there." Would she? What was she saying? It was impossible. "I don't know when yet, but I'll be there very soon. Okay? Joey?"

There were some scuffling sounds, then Jovan was on the line again. "You see? You see what you are doing to him? He wants you here with him. Can't you see how you are hurting him by staying away? You belong here with us, Sarah. Sarah! Listen to me!"

He was still shouting at her when she dropped the receiver back into its cradle.

four

Just before noon on Tuesday, September 7, Ted finally heard from Bob Koenig. By then, Ted had been at his office in downtown Sommerton for almost four hours.

"Sorry it's taken so long to get back to you," the lawyer told him. "Your case had priority but so many other things came first."

"How's that again?"

But Koenig went barreling on without a pause. This morning, at his request, he told Ted, the Family Court of Sommerton County, New Jersey, in and for the county of Sommerton, had issued a contempt citation charging Jovan Stefanovic with violating the custody provisions of the Consent Decree issued by the court in June. Accompanying the citation was a warrant for the arrest of Jovan Stefanovic, age thirty-nine, height unknown, weight unknown, eyes unknown, hair unknown, employed by New York University, New York, New York, Social Security number unknown.

"Don't worry about the missing information," said Koenig. "We can fill in the details later."

Ted was elated. It was the first good news he had heard, the first positive step. They had a weapon now, the legal amunition Koenig had been talking about. Besides, there was a certain vindicative appeal in the thought of Jovan going to jail —expecially after what he had done to Sarah on the telephone this morning. Vicious bastard, using Joey like that, to twist the knife.

The warrant, Koenig continued, commanded "the Sheriff of the county aforesaid" (and here he read from the document): "to take Jovan Stefanovic so that you may have him before the Judge of the Family Court forthwith, to answer all such matter and things as shall be charged against him, to wit, that he did neglect and refused to comply with said Consent Order."

"That's terrific," Ted said, when Koenig finished.

"Well, ah . . ." He heard the lawyer cough, clear his throat.

"It is, isn't it? Isn't that what you were hoping for?"

"As I said yesterday, Ted, the citation and the warrant will strengthen your hand in your negotiations. But beyond that . . . Look, Ted, I'll be frank with you. There's really no way the warrant can be applied unless your son-in-law decides he wants to return to New Jersey."

Ted felt his elation slipping away. "But what about extradition then?"

"Not much chance, I'm afraid. I did some checking on that. Turns out that in New Jersey it's not a felony for a person to steal his own child. It's only a misdemeanor. Which means it's not an extraditable offense."

"I see," Ted said grimly. He swiveled his desk chair toward the window. Outside it was another beautiful day: sunny, dry, the sky a faultless blue. The street below was busy with traffic, the sidewalks crowded with shoppers, loungers, lunchtime strollers. Everything back to normal. As if the weekend had never happened. As if Joey were safe at home and Sarah weren't going to pieces and Emma hadn't been doing the dishes at three o'clock this morning, the way he'd found her when he'd been awakened by his own restless dreams.

"Look, Ted," Koenig was saying, "I've done what I can for you as far as the courts go. I've also got calls in to several colleagues who are familiar with international law. One of them might be able to offer some suggestions."

"Good," Ted said, without enthusiasm.

"In the meantime, I've also spoken with a friend of mine who's a private investigator. He's handled a number of cases like this before. Tracks the kids down. Gets them back to the rightful parent. He's willing to talk to you if you'd like, give you some tips."

"Wait a minute, Bob. I think you're misunderstanding something. We don't need someone to track Joey down for us. We *know* where Joey is."

"I know that. I just mention it as something to keep in mind. As an alternative."

"Alternative to what? What are you getting at? Am I missing something?"

"Ted, you've got to be realistic. Under the circumstances there may be no other way. If negotiations and legal routes don't work out . . ."

Ted felt a sudden chill run through him. "Why shouldn't it work out? We've got the law on our side, don't we? Isn't that what you've been telling me?"

"Yes, yes, of course. But there's still the matter of . . ."

"And now we've got documents to prove it."

"Yes, and that should help. But it may not be that simple. You're going to be dealing with foreign courts, a foreign government. An Iron Curtain government. You can't expect those people to be very sympathetic."

"I'm not asking for sympathy. I'm asking for Jovan to honor his legal obligations."

"Fine. That's all well and good. All I'm saying is . . ."

84

"Well, dammit, I'm not going to be pushed into something like that—a counterabduction or whatever it is you've got in mind. This is my family we're talking about, not some characters in a TV thriller."

"Ted, listen. Nobody's saying you have to do anything, okay? I just thought you should know what the alternatives are, that's all. That's part of my job. That's what I'm here for."

"Well, thanks, but you can just forget about anything like that. I don't want any part of it."

The call left him depressed and annoyed. For the first time he felt a morose dread gnawing at his insides.

He was still mulling, uncertain what to do next, when the phone rang. Business this time.

It had been that way all morning: constant interruptions. One minute he'd be worrying about Joey; the next, he'd be answering a call from a customer or touching base with one of his district salesmen.

Whenever he had a chance he had been stealing quick looks at his file of index cards. The two long metal boxes, which did double duty as bookends at the back of his desk, contained the names, addresses, and phone numbers of hundreds of people with whom he'd done business over the last thirty-odd years. The odds were good that somewhere among all those cards were buried at least a few useful leads: the state official who knew the right man in Washington; the marketing executive who did business overseas. . . .

If only he could drop everything else. If only he could concentrate his time and energy on getting Joey back. Already he had put off many of his business appointments. Getting Joey back, that was what mattered now. The rest would just have to wait.

Joey. His beautiful boy. Gone.

A part of himself gone, too: torn away like an outstretched

arm in some freak accident. Except that the part that had been torn away was infinitely more vital than any limb. It was the childlike, playful, loving part that he had somehow never allowed himself to share with anyone, not even his own children—the part that even he had forgotten had ever existed, until Joey came along and teased it out of hiding.

"I'm glad you came with me today," Ted said.

"Thank you," Joey said matter-of-factly.

They were bicycling together on the towpath that ran along the old canal down by the river. A bright summer afternoon, just a month ago. The river the blue of crystal, the shade of the trees deliciously cool. Joey, in red shorts and a T-shirt, kept racing ahead, falling back. He was growing so fast these days that he complained about his legs hurting.

"You're good company," Ted said, trying again. What he longed to hear was that Joey was enjoying the outing, too, that he was not bored; that he would happily come bicycling with Grampa again and again. "The best company ever," he persisted.

"That's what I'm here for," Joey piped up cheerfully. "If I weren't here you'd be very lonely."

Ted had to laugh—at himself as well as at Joey. "Pretty sure of yourself, aren't you?"

Joey grinned. "Yup," he said. Then he stood on his pedals and took off down the path. "Beat you to the big tree, Grampa," he called back over his shoulder.

"Probably," said Ted.

The trouble, Ted knew, was that he had never had the same kind of time with his own children that he'd had with Joey. Always too busy earning a living. Days at a time away from home, or home so late that the kids were already in bed when he got there. But that's what the job had demanded—at least at first, when the kids were little and he was just starting out.

Hardware and general housewares had been his line then, back in the forties. Eventually he had begun specializing in paints and finishes, including all the related solvents, binders, adhesives, removers, deglossers, applicators.

Having the answers. Helping people. In Ted Novack's book, those were the important things. Not just making a sale but performing a service. Figuring out what people needed, and then showing them how his products would fill those needs.

It was gratifying work. And always, added to the satisfaction he felt, was the piquant thrill of wondering whether the next sale was going to be the big one, the one that would bring the orders—and the commissions—flowing in for months and maybe for years to come. It did happen now and then. That was the beauty of the job, the payoff for all the hard work.

In fact, he had done quite well over the years. By living modestly, by saving and investing, he had managed to put two kids through college and could now look forward to retiring early and comfortably.

Yes, he had come a long way.

And yet . . . And yet . . . During all these years there had been that one big drawback, the price he'd had to pay, the thing that always nagged at him: having so little time for the family trips and the school plays and the picnics after work.

It was all kind of too bad. They had never had a chance, Ted and his kids, to get to know each other. Which was why Joey had come as such a blessing. It was as if Ted had been given a second chance to catch up on all he had missed: the bike rides, the afternoons of swings and seesaws and sandboxes, of building towers out of blocks on the living-room rug and drag-racing toy cars up and down the hallways. Nor did Joey need to settle for hand-me-downs. Crib, carriage, blocks, pull-toys, dump trucks, the bicycle—his Joey got whatever he needed. Ted made sure of it.

Indulgent? Jovan thought so, or pretended he did. "You are going to make him spoiled," the guy would growl, putting on a big show of indignation. As if he weren't delighted to have all that stuff for Joey—and at no expense to himself. Damned phony! If Jovan had really been so worried about his pride he would have given everything back. Which, of course, he never did.

"Sure, I'm spoiling him," Ted would reply, brushing aside his son-in-law's objections with a wave of his cigar. "That's what grandparents are for."

"It is not good. He will be expecting always such things."

"Don't worry. He won't be expecting them from you."

Cheap shot. Ticked Jovan off good. But hell, it served him right. If Jovan wasn't able to give Joey the things he needed, it was his own damn fault. With his grants and his government loans, he and Sarah should have been able to manage just fine. But to Jovan, of course, managing was not living. Wine on the table every evening, that was *his* style. And a trip to Yugoslavia every year. And expensive gifts for all the folks back home so they could see what a great success he was making of himself in America, while every other month Sarah was calling home in a panic because the power company had turned off the lights, or the rent was overdue, or the Falcon had broken down again: *Could you please help us out, Daddy. Please. I'm sorry to be asking again, but please. I don't know what we'll do otherwise.*

And, Ted always gave in, though he knew perfectly well he was making a mistake. What was it he had once heard a psychologist call it: feeding a weakness instead of encouraging a strength? But what choice did he have? Sarah was his only daughter, Joey his only grandson. How could he have turned his back on them? How could he have lived with himself knowing they were in such trouble?

And that, of course, was exactly what Jovan had always counted on.

It was probably what he was counting on now.

Now that he had Joey.

Now that he had a way of getting Sarah back, too.

Except that this time it wasn't going to work. The games were over. This time the bastard wasn't going to have it his way. Because they *were* going to get Joey back. Somehow.

———

By late afternoon, Ted had a splitting headache and was ready to call it quits for the day. Outside his door the office had pretty well emptied out and the phones had finally stopped ringing. He swiveled his chair away from the desk, and got to his feet. Standing, he began straightening his desk.

Whether he had made any headway or not he was not sure. So far his card file had yielded half a dozen new leads but most of them were pretty tenuous: the head of an aeronautical research firm in Connecticut, who might or might not have government contacts; a Newark importer who might or might not still be in business. . . .

But there were some plusses, too. From an old contact at Union Carbide he'd gotten the name of a New York businessman who was involved in promoting trade between Yugoslavia and the United States. The man's name was Steve Kobelec. "Feel him out," Ted had been told. "Find out if maybe American cooperation in some Yugoslav business venture couldn't be tied in with getting back your boy." Ted had made the call and the man had agreed to see him in New York on Friday.

Another friend had given him the name of a Yugoslav émigré in Hartford, a former government official of some sort who might be able to offer advice on how best to approach the Yugoslavs for assistance. So far, Ted had been unable to reach the man, but the lead seemed a promising one.

Meantime, Ted had also set up a Thursday afternoon appointment with an aide in the local office of Congressman Michael Vanderbeck. The congressman himself had returned to Washington after the summer recess, but his aide would no doubt know how to get help from the proper authorities: the State Department, the Yugoslav Embassy perhaps.

So, some progress, Ted told himself as he arranged his notes and slipped them into his briefcase. No need to be discouraged. These things took time. He'd been in business long enough to know that.

He was looking over his desk one last time when the telephone rang. It was his stockbroker friend, Sherwood Brice, on whose answering machine he had left a message the night before.

"Ted? Sorry I couldn't get back to you sooner. I've been just too swamped. There's been a lot of heavy trading today. Now that August is over everyone's gearing up again. What can I do for you? You want to get in on the action?"

"No, thanks, Sherwood. Not today. I'll tell you why I called . . ." For what must have been the hundredth time that day, Ted went through the story. By now he had pared it down to the essentials: the custody issue, the weekend kidnapping, the apparent legal difficulties. . . .

Sherwood's response was as forceful and unequivocal as ever: "What you need is a lawyer in Washington."

"I do?"

"Absolutely. You're talking international, right? Government pressure? Legal avenues? You need someone who knows the ropes. The ins and outs of the bureaucracy. You see what I'm saying? Someone who knows who to talk to, who not to talk to, what kind of legal steps are feasible. That kind of thing."

"Isn't my congressman supposed to help with problems like this?"

"Is he a personal friend?" Brice asked.

"No."

"Friend of a friend?"

"Not that I know of."

"Then you can forget it. Now don't get me wrong. He's important, sure. He'll write letters and maybe talk to a few people for you. And that may help. But what you really want is someone on the scene who'll keep after the congressman and the bureaucrats. Someone who'll be doing nothing but looking after your interests. You see what I'm saying?"

"Yeah, I get the point." Ted took a long breath before venturing his next question. "These Washington lawyers, they cost quite a lot, right?"

"Oh, sure. Eighty, a hundred per."

"Per?"

"Hour."

"I was afraid that's what you meant."

"You get what you pay for. You know that."

"Yeah. I know. I know." But he also knew that Sherwood Brice could afford to be unperturbed; it wasn't his money they were talking about. "Okay, listen, say I want to sit down with one of those people—you know, just for starters, to try to get some idea of what our options are. Do you know anybody I can talk to?"

"Matter of fact, I do. Man's name is Stevenson. Colonel George Stevenson. Ring any bells?"

"Wasn't he a White House adviser under Eisenhower?"

"That's the man. He's now the head of one of the top firms in Washington. He also happens to be a close friend of my family. I'll give you his number. Tell him I told you to call, then explain your situation. If he can't help you he'll certainly know who can."

When Ted hung up, he felt exhilarated. By God, it was finally beginning to happen. He was finally making headway; first the Yugoslav-American trade man, then the congressional aide, and now this Washington lead! Of course, there were no guarantees that any of those leads were going to pay off. But at least there was some hope now—the kind of hope he felt when he telephoned prospective customers: hope that one call or another would eventually hit the jackpot. Not immediately perhaps, but eventually, if he just kept at it— kept talking, probing.

Persistence.

Tenacity.

Those were his best weapons. Always had been.

He picked up the phone again and dialed the Washington area code, then the number of Colonel Stevenson.

CHECKPOINT
Saturday, April 23, 1:45 A.M.

Once they got beyond the checkpoint, the road descended the mountain fast, looping and turning and doubling back on itself and dropping so steeply that Sarah's ears kept popping. A snow bank flashed white in the headlights as the car pitched around a sharp bend. Sarah clutched the back of her father's seat. Her stomach was in her throat.

"Do you have to go so fast?" she asked through clenched teeth.

They swung around another bend. A rock wall loomed ahead. Wilkes missed it by inches.

"You didn't imagine this was going to be a pleasure trip, did you?" Wilkes replied. He did not slow down. He gripped the wheel hard as he headed into another turn.

"If you want to kill us all," Sarah snapped back, "you should have done it on the other side of the border and saved us all that trouble at the checkpoint."

"Can we stop, please?" asked Sheila Hardy in a small voice. "I need some air."

"You'll have to wait."

"Bloody 'ell," said David Hardy. "If you don't stop, this one's gonna upchuck all down your bloody back."

Wilkes said, "Oh, shit." But he slowed down and pulled over onto the shoulder the first chance he got. He was just in time. Sheila Hardy was barely out of the car before she was spewing the contents of her stomach onto the pavement.

"Come on, Adam," said Sarah, slipping the drowsy boy off her lap. "Let's go for a walk."

She helped him out of the car. The gravel on the shoulder crunched under their feet. She took deep breaths. The cold night air was rich with the smell of fir trees—at least, as long as she stayed upwind of where Adam's mother was still retching. She felt bad for the woman; a little while longer and it would have been she being sick.

While Adam relieved himself against a tree, Sarah walked a little further up the road, glad of the chance to stretch her legs and get away from everyone for a few minutes. Overhead, the sky was filled with stars. They were very bright and distinct and it was somehow comforting to see them there, so clear and steady when everything else in her life was in such turmoil.

"I'm coming, Joey," she said, sending the words up to the sky. "I'm coming."

"Is me mum going to be all right?" Adam asked, standing beside her.

"She'll be fine in a few minutes," Sarah said, taking his hand. "She just needed some air. We all did. Come on. Let's go back now."

Soon they were heading down the mountain again, but at an easier speed. Wilkes was subdued; the break had done him good. And Adam was back with his parents now, which meant Sarah no longer had his weight pressing on her—only his feet jabbing at her every time he moved.

After a while, the road broke out of the forest and they

94

found themselves driving down the main street of a small town, following the trolley tracks past darkened houses, shops, hostels, ancient churches. The town, Wilkes said, was called Kranj, a ski resort. It was apparently a prosperous and busy place in the daytime, but at two in the morning the streets were deserted.

"Any chance of stopping for coffee?" Sarah asked.

"It doesn't look too promising," her father said.

Wilkes cruised slowly down the street, peering to the right and left. "Keep your eyes open," he said.

Finally, on a back street, they came upon a café that had its lights on. Wilkes pulled up in front and turned off the engine. For a moment no one moved. Wearily, they sat savoring the silence: no tires humming, no engine throbbing, no wind rushing past the windows.

The café, which was next door to a small hotel, was a drab, low-ceilinged place, with a small bar, a few tables covered with red-checked oil cloths, and dingy curtains across the bottom half of the windows. On one wall hung a black-and-white portrait of a glowering Marshal Tito.

Three burly men huddled shoulder to shoulder at the bar. They glanced up as Wilkes led Sarah and the others to a table in one corner. The only other customers were a couple drinking beer at one of the tables against the wall: a middle-aged man and a girl in a too-tight blouse. The man was playing with the buttons on the blouse but the girl was either too bored or too drunk to care.

As Sarah, Ted, and the Hardys arranged themselves around the table, the barman came over and Wilkes began speaking to him in German.

"He says there's no food," Wilkes reported.

"Good," said Sheila Hardy.

"He says he'll make us coffee if we'd like."

"No tea?" asked Hardy.

"Don't push your luck."

Wilkes ordered a soda for Adam and his mother, coffee for the rest of them. When the barman was gone, the Hardys got up and went looking for the restrooms, taking their boy with them.

Wilkes adjusted his glasses and lit a Marlboro. Smoking was a good sign for him, Sarah decided. He smoked when he was relaxing; back at the border, when the danger was greatest, he hadn't smoked at all.

"Look," he said, turning away from Sarah and addressing himself to her father, "I've been thinking about what happened at the checkpoint. I don't trust it."

Ted lit up a cigar. "You mean about the guard being on his break?"

Wilkes nodded. "I'm still not convinced that wasn't a phony story. If it was, they could be on the watch for us right now."

"But what could they do to us?" Sarah protested. "Our papers are in order."

Wilkes spared her hardly more than a condescending glance over his shoulder. "If those chaps at the border put out an alert for us," he told Ted, "and if we get pulled in, all they have to do is start questioning the Hardys and their lad and it will be all over for us."

He stopped talking as the barman came and set Joey's soft drink on the table.

"What do you have in mind?" Ted asked when the barman was gone.

Wilkes leaned closer. "I want to get the Hardys out of this as soon as we can," he said in a low voice. "For their protection as well as for ours. We've got the visa stamp now, that's the main thing. And you've seen how much help Hardy's been with the driving."

"Yes? So?"

Wilkes blew smoke through his nostrils. "There's an airport in Zagreb. We'll be there around dawn. Instead of taking the Hardys on to Belgrade with us, we'll put them on the first flight back to the West."

"Right. I agree," said Ted.

"That means I'll need your help with the driving from there on."

"But what if we're stopped?" Sarah asked. "The police will have a record now, won't they? They'll know I came in with a child. If Adam isn't with me—"

But just then the Hardys reappeared and Wilkes was on his feet. "Me next," he said, and ignoring both her and her question, he strode off toward the restroom.

Angrily she watched him go. "Creep," she muttered.

five

The odd thing, Sarah realized, was the way she kept expecting every minute to hear Joey or see him. As if he were just in the next room, or out playing in the yard.

Late in the morning, when she was lying in bed not wanting to get up, not wanting to do anything, she'd find herself listening, waiting to hear—*some*thing: the TV blaring, or the back door slamming, the sound of his feet running up the stairs, his voice calling, "I'm back, Mama. Daddy brought me back. I'm home, Mama. I'm home."

She was doing it now. Lying there. Listening. But there was nothing. Just the awful quiet permeating the house, filling every room, seeping into every corner. Downstairs the clock ticked quietly on the mantelpiece. Beneath her open window, the lawn sprinkler pattered briefly on the ivy, moved off, pattered back again.

Lost. She felt so utterly lost.

Waking or sleeping, the pain was always there, a fist pressed against her heart.

And always she was so tired. Her body so heavy. Unable

to move. Always so ready to sleep, terrible sleep, like falling down a well . . .

What made it all worse were the reminders she kept finding everywhere: one of his miniature toy cars poking out from under a sofa cushion when she went to sit down; his toothbrush in the holder over the bathroom sink, the bristles cemented together with layers of toothpaste; his Mets jacket hanging on the hook inside the back door, as if he'd left his shadow behind.

She picked up the book she'd been reading before she dozed off: *Shogun* in paperback. Twelve hundred and eleven pages. She'd been working on it for months. But the words ran down the page like water. She could make no more sense of it than she could of the images on the TV screen.

Just then she thought she heard something. She sat up. Yes, there it was again, growing louder. A familiar squeaking out front on the sidewalk. A tricycle for sure. She ran downstairs to look. Was it possible? Was he really there?

She threw open the front door, peered through the screen. Her heart sank.

Pedaling up the front walk was a small boy, but it was not Joey.

"Hi," said the boy, stopping at the bottom of the steps. "Can Joey come out to play?"

Not Joey. Of course not. Joey was gone. It was only Robert from down the street; poor, slow Robert, with his T-shirt hanging half out of his dirty jeans, his face smudged with grime as usual. Didn't his mother ever give him a bath?

"Can he?"

She stood looking at him through the screen door, not comprehending. "Can he what?"

"Come out and play?"

"Oh. No. Not today. I mean, no, Joey's not home."

"Where is he?"

"He's . . . away." Her evasion surprised her. Who was she trying to protect? Him? Or herself?

"Away where?"

"Just *away.*" This was crazy. Why was she standing here letting this child ask her all these questions?

"When will he be back?"

"I'm not sure. I don't know."

"Can he play tomorrow?"

"Robert, I said I don't know." But then she realized what she was doing. She was keeping him there on purpose. She was trying to keep him there as long as she could so she could keep looking at him and listening to his five-year-old chatter.

She came to her senses. "Joey's gone away, Robert," she explained. "I don't know when he'll be back. Okay?"

"Oh," he said. The idea seemed to puzzle him, but only for a moment. "Okay," he said. Then he turned his tricycle around and pedaled away down the sidewalk. "Bye," he called cheerfully over his shoulder.

"Bye, Robert," she called, realizing with an aching heart how much she envied the mother he was going home to.

She turned back into the house just as the phone began ringing in the kitchen. Sarah ignored it. Her mother would get it. Sarah did not want to go near the thing. During these last days, the phone had become a hateful intrusion on her life. Nothing good came over the phone. Unless it was hearing Joey's voice. But then she'd have to talk to Jovan first.

The phone was still ringing.

"Mother?" she called.

No answer.

Reluctantly, she edged toward the kitchen where she stood watching the insistently ringing instrument. Then she remembered. Earlier this morning, before she fell asleep again, she had heard her mother say something about going out to do the grocery shopping. There was no one in the house now but her.

Sarah waited through one more ring, then finally lifted the receiver. "Hello?" she said tentatively.

"Well, there you are. I was just about to hang up."

To her relief, Sarah recognized the voice of Grandma Helen. She said, "Hello, Gran."

"I didn't wake you, did I, dear?"

"No, Gran, you didn't wake me. Not this time. I—I was out front. I didn't hear the phone."

"Well, better late than never, I always say. How are you holding up, dear?"

"Not too well, I'm afraid."

Sarah pulled out a chair from the kitchen table, sat down, and lit a cigarette from the pack her mother had left behind. It was going to be a long phone call, and there was no one else —aside from Joey—whom Sarah would rather be talking to. Ever since Sarah was a child, Gran had been one of her best friends: trusted and trusting confidante; fun to be with on shopping trips; loyal and supportive whenever Sarah needed her help or a sympathetic ear, as she did now.

Grandma Helen Heilicki, who lived in Cherry Hill, down near Philadelphia, could be a difficult and domineering woman. When her husband, Harry Heilicki, died after being married to her for over fifty years, the doctors attributed the death to cancer. Sarah's father, however, maintained that the real cause was all those years of having to put up with Grandma Helen.

Gran was insufferably vain. In her younger days she had been a dancer and a fashion model, and she never let anyone forget it. She was always well dressed and still carried herself with what Sarah's mother tactfully referred to as "flair." Although her figure now reflected total surrender to her passion for cakes and chocolates, in her own mind apparently she was still a coquette. Over her voluminous hips she wore skirts that showed off plenty of leg. And to conceal her too-wide feet, she insisted on wearing shoes that were a size or two too small, with the result that most of the time she was hardly able to walk, so deformed had her feet become.

None of this mattered to Sarah, however. On the contrary, she enjoyed most of Gran's quirks and foibles, even admired them. For Gran always seemed to say and do exactly as she pleased, in a way that Sarah had never felt free to do. Gran, for her part, seemed to delight in being part of Sarah's life, as if through Sarah she was somehow reliving her own youth. They shared a special bond, the two of them, and to Sarah there was never any doubt that she could always count on Gran to be there for her, a willing ear and a generous heart.

"I don't know what I'm going to do," Sarah told her now over the telephone. "I just cry all the time and it never seems to stop. And when I'm not crying I'm sleeping."

"I know, dear. I know. It must be so terrible for you, darling. But don't forget, if it gets too bad, you just take one of those pills I gave you. The little white triangular ones will help you stay awake if that's what you want."

"Yes. And I take the red capsules if I want to sleep, is that right?"

"That's right, darling."

During Grandpa Harry's fatal illness, Gran had acquired a fair amount of knowledge about pharmaceutical remedies. A brother who was in the business kept her well supplied. Sarah's father referred to her as the "family dope pusher."

Sarah and Gran talked for over an hour, Gran listening, encouraging, offering advice. She also gave Sarah the name of a man she knew: the owner of a big tow-truck operation in

Philadelphia who had offered to use his contacts with the mob to get Joey back.

"Thanks, Gran, but no thanks," Sarah said. Even if the man's offer was for real, which Sarah doubted, there was no way she wanted to get involved with such people.

Talking to Gran, however, did give her the strength she needed to make the call she had been putting off all morning. Her father had insisted that she call Jovan's adviser at the university.

"Try and find out if he knew anything ahead of time about Jovan's intentions," Ted had instructed her. "And while you're at it, see if he knows anything about the status of Jovan's degree."

But even thinking about making the call had been agony for her. She hated having to talk to strangers about what had happened to her. How could they possibly understand. *Hello, this is Sarah Stefanovic. My husband just stole my son and I don't know what I'm going to do.* It made her feel ashamed. Made her feel like one of those bag ladies in the subway, showing off her sores in public, begging people for help when all she really wanted to do was to run away and hide, to curl up in her bed and not have to talk to anybody, to see anybody. Or be seen.

But now, buoyed by Gran's call—and calmed by one of Gran's little red capsules—she dialed the university. And somehow managed to speak clearly to the professor, whose name was Dr. Knight. And somehow managed to take in what he had to say.

———

"He was surprised when I told him that Jovan was gone," she reported to her parents that evening over dinner. "He said Jovan was supposed to have come in to see him the day after Labor Day to talk about job prospects. But then he didn't show up and nobody knew where he was."

103

Her mother shook her head sadly as she passed Sarah the salad bowl. "What a waste," she said. "I can almost feel sorry for him. All that struggle he went through to get that degree, and then he gives it up on a whim."

"Oh, but he didn't give it up," Sarah said. "That's the other thing Dr. Knight told me. Jovan handed in his dissertation last month and had his orals last week. He finished his work. He's graduated."

"Oh, no," Sarah's father groaned, a forkful of salad halfway to his mouth.

Emma said, "I guess that explains why he left when he did."

"Well, he's almost graduated anyway," Sarah went on. "Now he's just waiting for his grade and then he'll get his diploma. There's going to be some sort of presentation ceremony in October. That's when it becomes official."

Ted set his fork down. He was suddenly alert. "You mean he doesn't have the diploma yet?"

"Not the actual piece of paper, no. Why? Does it matter?"

"It might. How do you suppose he's going to get his diploma if he's not present at the ceremony?"

Sarah shrugged. "I don't know. I guess he must be having it mailed to him."

"Exactly what I was thinking." Ted wiped his mouth with his napkin and pushed back his chair. "And that diploma might be just the weapon we're looking for. If we can stop the university from sending it to him it might just give us some leverage. Without that diploma the bastard can't get the kind of job he wants, can he? He'd have to kiss all his dreams good-bye, wouldn't he? The status, the big money, the whole works. He'd be stuck right where he started five years ago."

Sarah exchanged glances with her mother. Was her father suggesting what she thought he was? She felt an odd surge of excitement in the pit of her stomach. "So what do we do?" she asked cautiously.

Ted's eyes shone bright and hard. "If we can get our hands on that diploma, we can arrange it so that Jovan has to come to us for it. Then we trade. He gets his diploma if we get Joey."

"But what if he comes back for the diploma and leaves Joey over there?"

"Then no diploma. That's the deal."

So it was true! Her father *was* talking about blackmail. He was talking about doing the same thing to Jovan that Jovan had done to her. And the amazing thing was that Sarah realized she didn't mind a bit. On the contrary, instead of shocking her, the prospect of getting back at Jovan, of just this once turning his own wicked games back on himself, positively filled her with elation.

On Friday morning, Ted and Sarah drove to New York, where Ted was to meet with the head of the Yugoslav-American trade office. They left home early so that they'd have time to stop at the university on the way. It was Ted's hope that taking Sarah along, getting her more involved, might just help to pull her out of the depression that kept dragging her down. That's what he had been hoping for when he first insisted that she call Dr. Knight. It had helped then and it seemed to be helping now. As they drove toward the city, he was pleased to see that she seemed more alert and less down-at-the-mouth than he had seen her in days.

Arriving at the university, he and Sarah found their way to the office of Martin Zinkler, whose name Ted had found in the university directory.

Zinkler was the university's chief counsel. A man of late middle age, with a gaunt face and rimless spectacles perched on the end of his long nose, he had the lean look of someone who played tennis at least twice a week and ate nothing but fish and salads and drank Perrier instead of cocktails.

"I doubt that there is any legal precedent for withholding a student's degree on the grounds you're suggesting," Zinkler told them after Ted had explained the situation. "If you'll give me a couple of days I'll look into it for you, but I'm afraid I cannot hold out much hope. As far as the university is concerned, a student's personal life really has no bearing upon his or her academic standing."

"I see," said Ted, not bothering to hide his disappointment. "Well, whatever you can do, we would certainly appreciate it." He got up to leave, but then, as if in an afterthought, he turned back. "Look, ah, there is one other thing maybe you could help us with."

"Yes? What's that?"

"Let us have a list of the university's board of trustees."

"The trustees?" Zinkler raised an eyebrow. "May I ask what you want it for?"

"Oh, I'm just curious. I thought there might be someone on the list that I might know."

"Going to pull a few strings, is that it?"

"Something like that."

Zinkler shook his head. "I'm sorry, but I really cannot condone that kind of intrusion into the university's affairs."

"No, of course not, it's just that—"

"The answer is no, Mr. Novack. Now, if you will please excuse me . . ."

Ted let out a deep breath. Clearly there was no point in arguing. He was beaten, at least for the time being. He extended his hand. "Thanks anyway."

Zinkler reached across his desk for the handshake. "I'll let you know as soon as I have some information for you."

He was about to show Ted the door when his telephone rang.

"We'll find our way out," Ted said. "Come on, Sarah."

Leaving the man to answer his phone, they stepped out into the reception area, where Zinkler's secretary was busy at her typewriter. By the lighted button on her telephone console, Ted could see that her boss was still on the phone. It gave him an idea.

"Excuse me, miss," he said, stopping at the secretary's desk.

The young woman looked up from her typing and smiled with the wide-eyed squint of someone whose contact lenses do not fit quite right. "Yes, sir? May I help you?"

"I hope so. Mr. Zinkler told me that I could have a list of the university's board of trustees. I forgot to get it from him before I left and I hate to trouble him again. You wouldn't have a copy by any chance, would you?"

She hesitated. "Well, yes, I do. But I don't know if I really should—"

"Oh, it's perfectly all right. As I said, Marty was going to give it to me himself but we both got so involved it just slipped our minds."

"Well . . . I guess if Mr. Zinkler said so . . ."

Ted left with the list tucked in the inside pocket of his sportcoat. As he hurried down the corridor and out into the street, Sarah had to run to keep up with him.

"Do you do that kind of thing often?" she asked.

They were at the car now and he had his key in the lock. "What kind of thing?" he asked.

"Lying to people."

He glanced up to see if she was serious. She was.

He opened the car door, got in, and reached across to open her side. "Before you get too judgmental," he said as she slid in, "you might think about just how scrupulous Jovan was being when he left the country with Joey."

She had nothing to say to that, of course, but he wished she had. Maybe he'd have felt better. That was the trouble with

107

raising kids to be upright and moral: they had a way of holding you to your own standards.

"Now let's see what we've got here," he said as he unfolded the paper and scanned its contents.

All it took was a quick glance to see why the university was so reluctant to give out the list. It included the names, addresses, and private telephone numbers of some of the top executives, financiers, politicians, and social figures in the country. If some kook ever got his hands on this he could make life very unpleasant for a lot of important people.

Halfway down the list Ted stopped. "Here we are, just what I was looking for."

The name he had come to was that of Charles Kogan, a senior vice-president of one of the world's largest banks. Ted had known Kogan for years, ever since the two of them had worked together on a fund raiser for the Sommerton Lion's Club. They had gotten on well and since that first meeting they had had numerous encounters at club events, serving often on the same committees and even lunching together occasionally.

"What can he do?" Sarah asked.

"Maybe put some pressure on the university administration."

"To withhold the diploma?"

"You've got it."

"Are you going to call him?"

"Later." He tucked away the list and started the car. "Right now we've got to get downtown."

———

By the time Ted had negotiated the city traffic and found a place to park in the garage of the World Trade Center he was already five minutes late for his appointment with the head of the Yugoslav-American Trade Association.

108

"Going to come up?" he asked Sarah as they hurried through the lobby.

"No, thanks. You go ahead. I'll wait for you down here in the coffee shop."

There was no time to argue. "Have it your way," he said and headed for the elevator.

Steven Kobelec had a corner office on the forty-sixth floor. Two walls of windows displayed a panoramic view of New York harbor, where myriad spots of sunlight glinted on the water like diamonds strewn on a blue cloth. To judge from the setting and the room's luxurious furnishings—all sleekly modern wood and muted fabrics—trade relations between Yugoslavia and the United States were going very well indeed.

"I have grandchildren of my own," Kobelec was saying. "I can imagine what you must be going through and I can sympathize, of course."

"Of course," Ted said dryly. He was not deceived. He recognized the man's expressions of sympathy for what they were: a polite prelude to rejection.

Kobelec, a man of considerable girth, leaned back in his thickly padded chair with his pudgy hands folded comfortably across his ample belly. "As I am sure you can appreciate, however, my personal feelings are irrelevant in such circumstances."

"No. I'm sorry. I don't appreciate it," Ted said grimly.

Kobelec frowned, leaned forward, pressed his fingertips together. They looked, Ted thought, like a set of sausage links, ready for the frying pan. He wished he'd never come.

"Mr. Novack, allow me to be frank with you. To imagine that any business concern is going to jeopardize its profits or trade agreements for the sake of a purely personal matter such as this—Well, I think that's being just a trifle naive, don't you?"

"Obviously I don't or I wouldn't be here."

Kobelec sighed heavily. "You're a businessman yourself. I'm sure you can understand my position."

"Oh yes, I understand completely. Business first, isn't that the way it goes? Well, that's not the way *I* do business. In my book, it's people that come first. Always have and always will." Ted got to his feet. "Thanks for taking the time to see me. I appreciate it." He turned and started for the door.

"Just a minute. Please," Kobelec lifted himself from his chair and came around the desk. "Before you go storming out, I'd like to make one suggestion."

Ted waited, his hand on the doorknob. "I'm listening."

Kobelec placed a beefy hand on Ted's arm. His florid face, with its baggy jowls, was just inches from Ted's nose. His gravely voice was low, confidential. "As you may imagine, I know the Yugoslavs pretty well, and it has always been my experience that the best way to deal with them is by being as direct as possible."

Ted would have backed off but with the fat man so close on one side and the door so close on the other, he had no place to go. "What do you mean?" he asked.

"I would suggest that you find yourself a lawyer in Yugoslavia."

Ted was taken aback. He already had a lawyer in Sommerton and he'd soon be seeing Colonel Stevenson in Washington. How many lawyers was he going to need?

"I give you this advice," the man continued, "because I suspect that eventually your daughter is going to have to go to Belgrade and work out some arrangement with her husband through the Yugoslav courts."

Ted shook his head. "You don't know my son-in-law. He's not the negotiating type. He wants it all."

The man raised a finger and an eyebrow. "Perhaps," he said, "that's all the more reason for you to engage the services of a Yugoslav lawyer. Now, one more thing." Kobelec stepped away. Ted felt like a wall had been removed.

Returning to his desk, Kobelec flipped through his Rolodex with his pudgy fingers. He found the name he wanted, and jotted it down on a piece of paper, then came over and handed it to Ted. "This is the man who heads up the Yugoslav desk at the State Department. I've dealt with him often. He's a good man. He won't give you the bureaucratic runaround. I'm sure he'll be able to advise you on how best to proceed. Probably he'll also be able to get you the name of a lawyer through our embassy over there."

"A CIA man?" Ted asked, only half joking.

Kobelec smiled. "I think, my friend, you've been reading too many spy novels."

———

That evening, Sarah telephoned Baka's number in Belgrade. She couldn't help herself. She had to talk to Joey again. She had to let him know that she had not abandoned him, that she still existed.

"Joey? Hello, it's Mama," she said when Baka brought him to the phone.

"Hello, M-m-mama." His sweet small voice sounded so strange over the six thousand miles of telephone cable, more falsetto than she remembered.

"How are you, lovey?" She tried hard to sound calm, casual, tried to control the tremor in her voice.

"I'm f-f-fine, Mama."

"Are you being a good boy for Baka and Daddy?" Stupid question. It wasn't at all what she wanted to say.

"Yes, Mama . . . M-m-mama, I m-m-miss you."

"I miss you, too, Joey. And Gramma and Grampa send you their love, too."

Silence. She hurried to fill it.

"Robert was here asking about you the other day," she said. It was a reminder. She wanted him not to forget that his home was here, his friends were here. Love was here.

"Joey? Are you still there?"

"Yes."

"Did you get the package I sent? Did you get Mr. Monkey?"

"Yes."

"Now you've got Mr. Monkey to keep you company. Did you notice I fixed his mouth and his eye? He's just like new."

"Yes, M-mama."

Why was he talking to her that way, in monosyllables? Was Jovan or Baka standing at his elbow?

"Mama . . ."

"Are you all right? You sound funny."

Silence, then an odd sound, a kind of moan and she could hear him sobbing.

"Joey, what is it? Don't cry. Tell me what's the matter."

"I want you, Mama. I don't want Mr. M-monkey. I want you."

She felt a stone shift in her chest. "Oh, Joey. Don't cry. Please don't cry." But she was crying herself now.

"Please come, Mama. Will you c-c-come?"

God, she thought, why did I call? Why did I stir it all up again? But I had to. He has to know I'm here. He mustn't forget.

She wiped her eyes with the back of her hand. "I don't know when I can come. I'll have to see. I'll—"

"Sarah, you are coming?" It was Jovan's voice, eager and hopeful. He must have pulled the phone away from Joey. "Are you really coming?"

"Where's Joey? I want to talk to Joey."

"He's too upset now. He's crying again, like last time. See what you do when you talk to him? You turn him into a crybaby."

"He's only five years old. Please. Bring him back."

"So he can live in America? So you can turn him against me, you and your father?"

"But that's so wrong. Don't you understand yet what happened?"

"I understand everything. It is you who do not understand."

"Jovan—"

"No, Sarah. That is all. Finished. He is going to live here now. You want to see him, you come here." As always when he got angry, his English was getting more thickly accented.

"America is his home. He was born *here*. This is the only place he knows."

"Now he will know this place. He will learn. Already he is learning. New words every day." .

"Jovan—" she pleaded.

He cut her off. "No. You have had your turn. You and your parents. Now it is *my* turn. *Mine*. You run from me, you take my son from me. You think I will stand and do nothing? If you think so, you are stupid foolish woman."

"Yes," she shouted back. "Yes, I am a fool. I was a fool to ever trust you. But that has nothing to do with Joey. Don't hurt Joey to get back at me."

"*I* hurt him? It is you who hurt him. He wants you here to be his mother but you do not come to him."

"He's only a child. Don't you think about what all this is doing to him? Why do you think his stuttering has gotten worse?"

"He was stuttering before."

"It's worse now. I can hear it. You've torn him away from

everything he knows. From me, from his friends, from his home."

"He will get over it. I know what it is like. I was torn away too at his age, remember? He will get over it just the way I did."

"Did you, Jovan?" she asked, her voice thick with sarcasm. "Did you ever really get over it?"

"You," he growled. "Always you twist what I say."

But she would not be put off. Now that she had started she could not stop herself. "Tell me about it," she spat at him. "I want to hear about how well you got over being separated from *your* mother."

He answered with a snarl. "You think you are the smart one, eh? You think you have the answers. Smart American woman. I tell you something now, you woman. You listen. My father went away to fight when I was the same age as Joey is now. I told you once. You remember? My father went away. Captured. Dead, maybe, we never knew. All I knew was he never came back and I never saw him again. But I never forget either. And now for my son it will be different. Joey will have *his* father. This new place, new friends, it is not so big a thing to get used to. A few weeks, a few months, he will learn the new things. It will be for a while hard for him, yes. But he will have at least his father. Do you hear me, Sarah? *My son will have his father!*"

She heard. His anguish and his hurt. Once it might have moved her to pity. But no more. Not now. It was too late.

"You didn't answer my question," she persisted. "What about your mother? You talk about forgetting but you don't want to remember how you felt when your mother left you in that orphanage. How you cried yourself to sleep for her and dreamed about her at night. How you dreamed that she was an angel coming to take you home again. What are you

114

trying to prove? Must Joey suffer the same way you did? Is that what you want?"

For a moment she heard nothing but the hollow-tube gurgling of the transatlantic cable. When he finally spoke, his words chilled her heart. "That, my darling, is something you must ask yourself. Because the answer is all up to you."

six

On Saturday, September 11, Sarah drove to Yonkers with her parents to close up the apartment. Left to herself, she would never have gone near the place again. The books, the clothes, the furnishings—it could all rot for all she cared. But going along was better than staying home alone in an empty house, which was why she now found herself back in the apartment, sitting on the living-room couch and watching indifferently as her mother packed books into cartons collected from the A&P. Across the room her father was busy at the desk, opening drawers and leafing through the papers Jovan had left behind.

"Maybe we'll find something we can use against him if we have to go to court," he had said on the drive up the turnpike. And the way he was now poring so avidly over the desk's contents made Sarah realize that part of him was enjoying all this. Relishing it. Just hoping for a chance to get even with Jovan. To screw him good.

They had already ascertained that the photo album was gone. So were the linens—not only the living-room draperies, but also the kitchen curtains, the towels, the tablecloth Sarah had made when she and Jovan had first moved into this place. Jovan had taken it all. But for whom? His mother? His sister? Not that Sarah wanted any of it for herself. No reminders, please. Take it all. Dead is dead. Except for all those pictures of Joey that she had pasted in the photo albums. Why couldn't he have at least left her the pictures. . . .

"There," her mother said, folding down the flaps on another carton. "That's about it for the books." She leaned back on her heels and surveyed the living room. "What about the paintings? Do you want those?"

"Give them to Niki," Sarah said. "He can always find someone who'll want them."

Niki Djordjevic was the building superintendent. By an odd coincidence, he was another displaced Yugoslav. He was also a sharp operator when it came to making a dollar on other people's castoffs. Old furniture, applicances, rugs—everything had a way of ending up in Niki's storage area in the cellar, to be sold off to any tenant willing to pay his price. Over the years, in fact, Sarah and Jovan had found themselves indebted to Niki more than once for the bargains available in his bargain basement. Now Sarah could only wonder what hopeful newlyweds would be furnishing their first apartment with *her* castoffs.

Sarah and Jovan were not exactly newlyweds when they moved into the apartment. It was the spring of 1968 and they had already been married for over a year. Jovan had passed his final exams at the Sorbonne that December and had agreed to try living in America, where he thought it might be easier to get a job. They had moved into her old bedroom in her parents' house, and within a short time Sarah had landed a job as a substitute teacher in the Sommerton public schools. But finding something for Jovan proved more difficult, especially since he seemed to be having such a hard time adapting to the new world in which he found himself.

"It is hard thing being foreigner in this country," he told her one night after another unsuccessful round of interviews. "People hear you talking English not so good, they think you are stupid."

When finally he did find work—as a lab technician at a small pharmaceutical company in New York City—it was far from the kind of exciting research work he had envisioned for himself. He spent his days running tests on pills and medicines, making sure they came up to legal standards. "Shit work," he called it.

Still, it was about as much as he could hope for without an advanced degree and a better command of English. And it was a beginning, as Sarah hastened to remind him whenever he got too depressed about it. Besides, it enabled them to get a place of their own. And that *was* something!

True, the apartment they found in Yonkers was no more than an impersonal set of rooms in a featureless high rise. But it was cheap, it was close to the city, and it was *theirs*. Finally they could come and go as they pleased, keep the hours they pleased, fill up the space the way they wanted to, without worrying about impinging on her parents, or being impinged upon.

As soon as they moved in, Sarah set about trying to give the apartment some of the hominess it lacked. She found cheerful blue-flowered curtains for the kitchen and hung spider plants in the window over the sink. The dining-room table and chairs were a house-warming present from Gran, and to liven up the room Sarah bought bright-colored fabric and made a tablecloth, with color-coordinated napkins. To cover the secondhand club chair that Jovan had bought from Niki, she found a sturdy green-corduroy throw. She worked hard to make it all feel right.

And yet none of her efforts added up somehow. The paintings on the walls, the books on the shelves, the music on the stereo—most of it was Jovan's, and in a language of which she knew only fragments. Oh, she understood well enough what Jovan was doing. He was building himself a refuge from the alien and seemingly hostile world outside. The trouble was, that in the process of shutting out the world around him, Jovan was also shutting her out of his life.

One evening she tried to explain this to him. "Don't you see?" she said. "Don't you see what you're doing? I'm not the enemy."

It had been another difficult day for him at the hospital: a day of meaningless drudgery and of being ignored by his coworkers. He had come home tired and angry. Pouring himself a glass of slivovitz, he had put an album of Serbian folk music on the stereo and turned up the volume.

Sarah, sitting beside him on the floor, pleaded with him. "Don't close me out. This is Sarah. Your wife. I love you and I want you to be happy."

Suddenly misty-eyed, he put an arm around her and kissed her. "You are my only friend," he said, stroking her hair tenderly.

Yet nothing changed. The longer he was in America and doing work he despised, the more he seemed to isolate himself. His friends—the few he had—were fellow Serbs whom he had met at the Yugoslav consulate downtown, where he sometimes went to read Serbian magazines and to attend concerts and lectures. He made it plain early on that he was not interested in spending time with *her* friends, who were mostly colleagues from the Yonkers high school where she was now a teaching assistant. On the rare occasions when she did invite someone over, he would spend the evening closed up like a clam.

"I do not understand these people," he would say afterward if she commented on his rudeness. "They talk only foolishness."

"How do you know that if you don't understand them?"

"I know. I understand enough. They are foolish people."

Eventually she simply stopped inviting anyone to the apartment. It was not worth the arguments—or the embarrassing apologies she felt obliged to make to her guests the next day.

The single exception to this rule were the Markovics, Elena and Marko, who were both of their friends, and as such were welcome company at any time. Elena was a teacher at Sarah's school, which was where they had met; Marko was a doctor. Together they had emigrated from Yugoslavia and together they had achieved the kind of professional and material success in America that Jovan aspired to. They drove a Mercedes, owned their own apartment, traveled, went to the opera, were respected in their community. Most importantly, they had offered their friendship at a time when both Sarah and Jovan were very much in need of friends.

To Sarah, Elena was an especially rare kind of friend, because she alone understood what Sarah was up against where Jovan was concerned.

"You must only be patient," Elena told her one afternoon over tea, when Sarah confided her despair of Jovan ever finding his way in the States, of his ever ceasing to yearn for home, for Belgrade. "We all sometimes miss the old country. But it passes. Wait. Give him time. He will learn more English, he will become used to the life here. You must understand, everything here is still new and strange for him."

"But he's been here for over two years," Sarah protested.

"For such a large change that is not so much time. And when the new life is so difficult it is natural for a person to cling to what is past and what is familiar. He needs only time. You will see. It just takes time."

Sarah hoped Elena was right. She wanted more than anything for Jovan to stop turning his back on her world. The question was, how long would she have to wait?

And when would he start writing poetry for her again?

———————

In the spring of 1970, Sarah discovered that she was pregnant. The prospect was frightening. She could not imagine herself being a mother. What did she know about caring for an infant? Most of the time it was all she could do to take care of Jovan's and her own needs. Besides, she and Jovan had come to rely on her paycheck as a supplement to his meager income; she wasn't sure they could get by without it.

But when she thought of waiting, of not having the baby, her mind and her body rebelled. She didn't want to wait for another time. She wanted *this* child, the one that was growing inside of her now, a new life, a part of herself. And she would love it and care for it and maybe, just maybe, its coming would fill the aching, empty place inside her.

"A son!" Jovan rejoiced when she told him the news. "I am going to have a son!" He immediately ran to the kitchen and opened a bottle of slivovitz. He poured a glass for each of them and made a toast. "To my son," he said, and drank it down in one gulp.

She laughed and took a sip from her glass. "It might be a girl," she cautioned. "There are no guarantees."

"No, no. It will be a son. I am sure of it." He came and kissed her. "Today you have made me the happiest man alive."

"I'm glad," she said.

For herself, she knew she would be happy whether it was a boy or a girl. Either way, it would still be her child, her own heart's love.

Jovan telephoned his mother in Belgrade immediately with

the news. Sarah waited until after five, when the phone rates were lower, and then called New Jersey to tell her parents. They were delighted. The baby, when it came, would be their first grandchild.

Planning ahead, Sarah's parents offered to hire a nurse to help her at home during the first few weeks after the baby was born.

It was a wonderful and generous offer and Sarah was grateful. But Jovan refused to consider any such arrangement.

"I will not have a stranger in my house," he stormed. And he was adamant about it. If Sarah needed help, he would ask his mother to come and stay for a few weeks.

"But that's impossible," Sarah said. "We've only got the one bedroom. Where will she sleep?"

"I will talk to Niki. Niki always has something. Maybe an extra bed we can buy. It will be crowded a little, yes, but we will manage for short time."

So it was arranged. The money Sarah's parents would have spent on a nurse would go instead to pay for bringing Jovan's mother to the States. And Niki, as hoped, came up with the necessary accommodations: someone's cast-off convertible sofa that he let Jovan have for sixty dollars.

Jovan was happier than Sarah had seen him in months. His mother would be coming and his child, his son, was on the way! Finally something was going right for him.

Sarah's labor pains began two days early. It was the middle of the afternoon and she was home alone. She telephoned the lab but Jovan was unavailable. She left a message for him, then called a taxi to take her to the hospital.

She was in labor for seventeen hours. And she was alone. Where was Jovan? She had no idea.

Now and then a nurse took her temperature and offered her a cool cloth for her forehead. Once, a doctor looked in to tell her she was not working hard enough.

At times, lying there alone with the pale walls swimming before her eyes, she thought she was going to die. The pain was unbearable. She tried not to cry out, but could not help herself. An impatient nurse looked in, then hurried away.

Somewhere during a lull in the cycle of pain, Jovan appeared at the door to her room. He looked frightened and as pale green as the wall. "Poor Jovan," she said, reaching for his hands as he came and sat down beside her bed. It was clear that he did not want to be there. Clear, too, that the shock she saw in his eyes was an accurate reflection of the way she looked. She was about to tell him how happy she was to see him when another wave of pain engulfed her, causing her to cry out again, despite herself. Jovan turned white and hurried from the room. Desperately she made an effort to call to him. "Come back. Don't leave me alone." But the only sound that came out was another strangled cry and then a nurse was looming over her with a needle and the pain was awful, the thing inside of her was ripping her apart and all she could think about was the pain and wishing it would stop, please God, make it stop.

Later, under the bright lights of the delivery room, when she finally pushed the baby out and the nurse flopped the wet, red lump of squirming flesh upon her breast, she was too exhausted to feel anything but relief and an all-consuming desire to sleep. Except that there was an elation, too, a sense of triumph. She had done it! On her own. She had overcome fear and pain and had brought her baby into the world healthy and alive. She had found a strength she did not know she had and she had survived. She and her son. The two of them. Together.

Voices. She was still half asleep, but she heard the voices near her, hushed voices, speaking in a strange language. No, not so strange. Some of the words she knew. *Lepo, dobro.* Beautiful, good. Without moving—she was too tired to move—she opened her eyes halfway. She found herself in a bed in a large room. She was vaguely aware of other beds nearby, of other women in the beds, of flowers and the smell of hairspray, and the two hushed voices. Turning her head slightly, she saw Jovan and his mother hovering over a plastic bassinet. Jovan was beaming.

"*Dobro, da,*" his mother was agreeing: "Beautiful, yes. And look at the eyes. He looks like one of us."

One of you? No, Sarah protested soundlessly. He's not one of you. *You* had nothing to do with it. It was me. I carried him around all these months. I gave him life. He is my son. *Mine!*

But she was too tired to tell them. She could not keep her eyes open. Without a word she drifted off again.

———————

The next day, her parents came to the hospital during visiting hours to see their grandson. Jovan and his mother were already there.

Though she was still feeling weak, Sarah had made the effort to fix her hair and put on a little makeup, and when Jovan brought them all to her bedside they greeted her happily with kisses and hugs and told her how good she looked.

"A little thinner than the last time we saw you," her father joked.

Jovan grinned. "Eight pounds thinner."

"Eight pounds, three ounces," Sarah corrected.

Jovan translated all this for his mother, who smiled and nodded appreciatively.

"Where is he?" her mother asked, glancing around. "Do we get to see him?"

"Yes, yes. He is in nursery," Jovan replied. "Come look. Come, come."

Excitedly he led them down the hall without waiting for Sarah. Don't mind me, she thought, getting out of bed. I just work here.

Shrugging into her bathrobe and scuffs, she shuffled down the corridor after them.

There was a crowd at the nursery window when she got there. Jovan and his mother and Sarah's parents were surrounded by strangers: the husbands, friends, and relatives of other new mothers, the mothers themselves looking as tired and stiff as Sarah herself felt. There was a good deal of pointing and cooing and twisting of heads this way and that as everyone tried to get a better look into the room on the other side of the window.

What they saw through the window were a dozen infants displayed like loaves of bread in a bakery, each in its own see-through bassinet, with pink labels for the girls and blue for the boys. Most of them were asleep, and most were bundled so tightly in their blankets that only their heads stuck out. But one was crying lustily and two or three were squirming.

Joey was one of the squirmers. Twisting and turning, he kept wriggling out of his blankets and peering vaguely at the world around him through eyes that still looked puffy and bruised from the ordeal he'd been through. The hair on his head was no more than a light brown haze, and his pink fists waved in the air as if he were ready to start crawling the minute someone flipped him over on his stomach.

Watching him, unable to take her eyes off of him, Sarah wanted to fix him in her mind forever just the way he was now, so pink and healthy and new, still untouched by failure or disappointment, still so full of—*possibilities.*

A nurse, a large black woman, came into the nursery just

125

then. Pretending annoyance she redid Joey's blankets for what must have been the dozenth time. Winking at Jovan through the window, she crooked her arm and made a fist, miming a muscle man.

Jovan grinned and hugged his mother.

Sarah's father laughed out loud. "He's going to be trouble, that one."

"He's beautiful, just beautiful," said her mother, her eyes glistening.

She put her arms around Sarah and hugged her, and Sarah remembered later that for that brief moment they were all happier together than they had ever been.

The moment passed almost at once, for it was just then that Jovan chose to announce that he had paid a visit to the Yugoslav consulate that very morning and had obtained a Yugoslav birth certificate for Joey. He repeated it for his mother in Serbo-Croatian, and was rewarded with a shriek of delight and a kiss on the lips.

"I don't understand," said Sarah's father. "He'll have a New York City birth certificate. Why does he need one from Yugoslavia?"

"Why?" Jovan looked surprised. "He is my son! He is Yugoslav!"

"Partly he is," Ted corrected with an indulgent smile. "Partly."

"A birth certificate makes it official." Jovan thrust out his chin. "He is Yugoslav citizen now, like his father."

Sarah saw the smile fade from her father's face. "Wait a minute. Are you telling me you've made Joey a citizen of Yugoslavia?"

"Of course. Yes." Jovan said it proudly, as if it were the most natural thing in the world to tell a man that his new grandson was now a citizen of a foreign country.

126

Ted scowled darkly. Anxiously, Sarah sought to reassure him. "I think it's supposed to be like a gift to his mother," she said.

Ted looked at her, then at Jovan's mother, then at Jovan again, as if unwilling to accept what he was hearing. "But why?" he asked again.

"Why not?" Jovan spat back. "He *is* citizen. It is the fact. He is my son."

"He's Sarah's son, too," Ted growled.

"He is Stefanovic," hissed Jovan.

"Stop it, you two," Sarah whispered fiercely. "Will you stop it."

Around them, people were staring: nurses, pregnant women in bathrobes, a young father in a blue hospital gown. For a long moment more the two of them stood glaring at each other.

Which of them would have backed down first no one ever found out, for suddenly Sarah's head was swimming and her legs were buckling under her. She reached for the window frame to keep from falling.

At once Jovan was at her side. "Sarah, Sarah, you are all right?"

"I'm fine. I'm—"

Hands reached for her. A nurse appeared with a wheel-chair. Sarah was taken back to her bed.

Her recovery was difficult. She could never seem to get enough sleep. The nurses were forever waking her up for food, for pills, for diapering lessons and breast-feeding lessons and infant-care lectures. She couldn't wait to get home to her own room, her own bed.

But when she finally did get home, she wondered if she hadn't been better off in the hospital.

The crib was set up in the living room and Jovan's mother had taken up residence in the bedroom.

"And just where are we supposed to sleep?" Sarah protested the first chance she got—in whispers in the kitchen, so the old woman wouldn't hear them arguing.

Jovan looked surprised. "On the sofa bed, as I told you. What did you think it was for?"

"That's *not* what you told me. The sofa was going to be for her."

"But what an idea! *She* is the guest. *She* must have the bed."

"But with the baby—"

"In the bedroom there is no place for the crib. This way you can be right with him in the night. It is better."

They were interrupted by his mother's husky voice calling from the next room. "*Gde se,* Jovan?" she sang out. "Where are you?"

He poked his head around the corner. "I am here, Mother."

"*Dogi ovano. Dogi i sjedni sa mnom,*" Sarah heard her cajoling. "Come in here. Come sit with me."

"Yes, yes, I am coming."

But before he went, Jovan turned back to Sarah. "It will be all right," he said. "It is better she has her own room to be in. Now, be a good wife and make us coffee and do not talk more about this thing. The way it is, is the way it is going to be."

Sarah was able to put up with it for a total of four days. How she managed that long, she had no idea. With the crowding in the apartment, the lack of privacy, and the baby waking up every two hours in the night, she was more exhausted and irritable than ever. And Jovan's mother—or Baka, as she wanted to be called now that she was a grandmother—did little but complain of being ignored and neglected. Her Royal Highness, the Queen of Sheba. Did she know that she had been invited to help, not to be waited on? Had she forgotten so soon what it was like to be a new mother, to be tired all

128

the time, to be hurting all over, to wake up in the middle of the night listening for your baby's breathing and being sure that he was dead in his sleep until—thank God!—he took another long breath and slept on.

Some nights Sarah was so exhausted, her breasts so sore, that when the baby began crying, she didn't know how she was going to get up and let him chew on her again with his bony gums. But then there the old woman would be, wrapped in Jovan's bathrobe, wearing Jovan's slippers, nudging Sarah awake.

"Get up. Your baby is crying, don't you hear? Your baby is hungry. How can you lie there like that, you lazy thing, and not go to him? What kind of mother are you, eh? What kind of woman? Get up! Get up!"

Sarah was hardly fluent in Serbo-Croatian, but the gist of the old woman's words was clear enough.

There was no relief. The old woman was there with her all day long. She never went out. In the evenings, when Jovan was home, the two of them would sit huddled together on the sofa, mother and son, like two conspirators hatching plots, chattering away in Serbian, totally ignoring Sarah and the baby. If Sarah had earlier felt like an intruder in her own house, she felt even more so now.

"Jovan, don't you see what's happening to us?" she whispered to him one night when they lay awake on the sofa bed. "I have no place here anymore. Everything is for her now. Her schedule, her food, her needs. When it's not Joey, it's her I have to cook for and clean for and make room for. I can't do it all. I just can't."

"Yes? And what am I to do? Send her away?"

"Would you, Jovan? Please? For me? For us?"

"No. I will not. She is my mother. She will stay in my house as long as she wants."

"Then I will go. I mean it. If she doesn't go soon, I will."

He laughed contemptuously. "Do not talk such foolishness. Where will you go? Home to your mama and papa? Hah! You think you have no life of your own here, you will have even less with them."

"Jovan, don't. This isn't a contest between you and them. It is you and me I care about."

"Baka will go when she is ready to go, not before."

Sarah left the next morning, after Jovan went off to the lab and while Baka was still in bed. Taking Joey with her, she got in the car and drove to Sommerton.

As soon as Jovan heard she was gone, he called, full of apologies. "I love you. Please come back. I need you." Her leaving had shaken him badly. He had never imagined she would ever actually do it.

But Sarah refused to give in. Not until two days later, when he called from the apartment to assure her that his mother was gone, did Sarah go back.

Jovan made a big show of welcoming her and Joey back: a bottle of wine, an "American" dinner of fried chicken on the table, fresh sheets on the bed.

But the damage had been done. From that time on, there existed between them a depth of bitterness and mistrust that was never overcome. Sarah had forced him to choose. She had forced him to plead, even to beg, and finally to back down. And for that she would not easily be forgiven.

———————

"Look at this!" exclaimed Sarah's father. "Here's another one. That makes two thousand six hundred and fifty-five dollars worth so far."

"Of parking tickets?" asked her mother.

"You've got it. And that's in less than a year."

Having emptied Jovan's desk drawers of their contents, he had been arranging the various pieces of paper in small piles.

Mostly they were overdue bills: telephone, electricity, credit cards. But there were also dozens of unpaid parking fines and unanswered summonses.

Her mother went to look. "That's incredible," she said. "How did he get away with it for so long?"

"He didn't, at least not all the time. Master Charge canceled on him in June. He owed them eighteen hundred dollars. He seems to have kept the phone company and Con Ed at bay by making minimum payments."

Sarah shrank further into the sofa, where she had been sitting for the last two hours. Each new bill was like a slap in the face. She could imagine Jovan sneering as he stood there at the desk opening the bills and tossing them aside: screw you, Sarah. Screw your rules. Screw your America.

And somehow her father's attitude made it worse. He was positively gloating in triumph. To him, the overdue bills and summonses would give them an advantage if they ever succeeded in taking Jovan to court: "Clear evidence of a disreputable character," the lawyers would call it; "clear evidence of a long-term pattern of fraud and deceit." Never mind what it told the world about Sarah and what a fool she'd been for ever having loved him once, for having cared. . . .

Still, a few minutes later, when her father turned up a different kind of paper, Sarah herself felt a twinge of excitement, almost despite herself. The paper was a notice of default on a student loan for $25,000, issued to Jovan through the university by the National Institutes of Health.

"This should make those dummies at the university think twice about handing him his diploma," Ted crowed.

"But won't that give Jovan even less reason to come back here?" asked Emma. "He could be arrested for violating the court order *and* for defaulting on the loan."

Ted stared thoughtfully at the document in his hand. "You've got a point," he said.

"Maybe there's another way," offered Sarah.

Both Ted and Emma turned to look at her. Absorbed as they had been in the papers on the desk, they had all but forgotten she was in the room with them.

"Well," said her father.

"What if we try making a bargain with Jovan?" she said.

"What kind of bargain?"

"If the university decides not to give him the diploma until his loan is paid off," she said tentatively, "maybe we could offer to—"

"To pay off the loan if he gives Joey back?" her father interrupted.

"That's what I was thinking," said Sarah.

"That's crazy," her mother said. "Where are we going to get twenty-five thousand dollars?"

"Not all at once, hon," Ted said. "We'd pay it in installments, just the way he would." He turned to Sarah, beaming. "You know," he said, "you're one clever cookie."

Sarah smiled. "I'm glad you noticed."

CHECKPOINT
Saturday, April 23, 5:15 A.M.

How Wilkes was managing to stay awake Sarah had no idea. Probably it was his endless cigarette smoking and the quart of coffee he had swallowed in that dismal little café where they'd stopped after crossing the border.

Sarah did not even try to keep her eyes open. Speeding toward Zagreb in the early-morning hours, they had the highway almost to themselves. The night slid by on a lulling drone of tires and wind and the throb of the engine. Jammed in her corner of the backseat, Sarah drifted into a fitful sleep, disturbed by images of flashlights shining in her eyes, of policemen with machine guns, of Peter Wilkes' face lit by a sickly green light.

She came out of it when she felt the car rolling to a stop. It was just before dawn. In the east the sky was turning a milky gray.

"Here we are," Wilkes said.

"Is this Spine?" the boy asked sleepily from where he lay sprawled in his father's arms.

"Not long now, lad," Wilkes said.

Coming awake beside Sarah, Sheila Hardy extracted a tissue from her purse and blew her nose loudly.

Sarah, still half asleep, peered out the window and saw that they were in a parking lot in front of the passenger terminal of Zagreb Airport—a building that looked hardly bigger than the terminal at the county airport back in Sommerton.

For a moment she had to stop and think what they were doing here. But then she remembered. They'd come to put Adam and his parents on a plane.

Wilkes turned in his seat. "You may as well bring your bags along," he told the Hardys. "We'll check them right through."

"Should we come too?"

"Better not," Wilkes told Ted. "No point in attracting any more attention than necessary."

Wilkes got out. He helped the Hardys with their bags, then led them toward the terminal. He was back ten minutes later to get Sarah and her father.

"The coast is clear," he said. "If there *is* an alert out for us, it's not evident here."

As before, he addressed himself to her father exclusively. To Sarah he paid no attention whatever, except to absent-mindedly hold open the door to the terminal for her.

"Oh, thank you," she said, stepping past him. "How very courteous of you."

He either missed her sarcasm or chose to ignore it.

"I got the Hardys on a flight to Rome," he told Ted as he led the way through the lobby. "From there they'll go to Madrid for their holiday."

"What time is their flight?" Ted asked.

"Seven. They board in forty-five minutes."

Sarah said, "Do we wait and see them off?"

Wilkes spared her hardly a glance. "That's the idea."

What was it with this man? Why did he dislike her so? Or was it just the way he treated all women? Sarah pitied whoever had married him. Someone had. He wore a wedding band.

They met the Hardys in the airport café, where they had coffee and bread beneath yet another portrait of President Tito; in this one he was wearing a uniform.

When it was time for the Hardys' flight to begin boarding, Sarah, her father, and Wilkes were at the gate to see them off. They all shook hands warmly, as Wilkes had directed. The two women embraced. If any policemen were watching, they were getting the show that Wilkes intended: a typical farewell between good friends instead of the distant parting of strangers who had known each other less than twenty-four hours and who were unlikely to ever meet again.

"Aren't you coming with us?" little Adam asked as Wilkes offered his hand.

"I'm afraid not, son. I've got some things to do here." His voice was so tender, so full of warmth, that it took Sarah by surprise. For the first time, she wondered if he had children of his own.

The boy looked up at Sarah with his big eyes, then turned back to Wilkes. "Is the nice lady coming with us?"

Sarah was touched. She lowered herself to one knee. "I have to go with Mr. Wilkes," she said, giving him a hug. "I hope you have a nice time in Spain."

"I will."

"It was fun playing make-believe with you last night. You did a really good job."

He grinned, gave her a quick kiss, then went with his mother toward the gate. But a moment later he turned and

135

ran back to Sarah. "I hope you get your little boy back," he said earnestly.

She felt a sudden catch in her throat. So he had known all along what the game was about; he hadn't been fooled for a minute. "Thank you, Adam," she said. "I hope so too."

seven

When the alarm went off, Ted flung out an arm and slapped the thing to silence. And lay there, arm outstretched, eyes shut, legs tangled in the summer blanket.

It had been another bad night, his sleep disturbed by restless dreams . . . which he could not quite remember . . . which were . . . slipping away. . . .

He opened an eye, peered at the clock's glowing digits: 7:16 A.M. Time to get moving. Lots to do. Paperwork to catch up on, calls to make . . .

Lord, when was it all going to end? When would things start getting back to normal? When would he start getting enough sleep?

Still Ted lay there, weighted down, his temples throbbing with the beginnings of a headache. And there was a tightness in his lower back that hadn't been there the day before.

Finally he got out of bed. By the time he had finished his calisthenics, his blood was pumping nicely. The tightness in his back was still there but not as bad as before, and his headache had receded. He hurried through a shower, then

137

plugged in his razor and turned to the mirror. He was startled by the face that confronted him: pasty flesh, purple rings under the eyes, jowels sagging. He knew he was feeling run down—but not *that* bad!

Have to watch it, he told himself as he patted on the aftershave. Can't afford to get sick now. Not when there was so much to do. Not when there were so many people counting on him.

As soon as Ted got to his office, he telephoned the dean of Jovan's university. The man may have been unmoved by pleas for human sympathy, but this time Ted would be making a solid dollars-and-cents argument for cooperation: Jovan had defaulted on his loan; surely the university would not want to send him his diploma before he had fulfilled his financial obligations. It was simply good business.

To Ted's disappointment, however, even this argument cut no ice. The dean—a raspy voice on the other end of the line —seemed not at all perturbed to hear that Jovan had received a notice of default.

"When was the notice dated?" the man asked.

"August third."

"Mr. Stefanovic could very well have cleared it up since then."

"Cleared it up?" Ted said. "We're talking about getting twenty-five thousand dollars from a guy who's dead broke."

"Most students are," the man replied dryly. "All that is usually required in such cases is that the student resume making payments on the loan. In certain cases, a simple written statement of good faith is sufficient."

"Well, did he make such a payment? Did he submit a statement?"

"I have no idea," said the dean. "But even if I did, I would not be free to divulge that information. The financial status of our students is a matter of strict confidentiality."

That's what you think, Ted thought as he slammed down the phone. There were ways of prying loose such information. For starters he'd have Sarah's lawyer subpoena the university's records.

First, though, he'd have to do something about the headache that was continuing to plague him. That and the tightness in his lower back.

He went and got a couple of aspirins from Marie, then washed them down with a cupful of water from the office cooler.

He was just getting back to his desk when his intercom buzzed. He hit the button hard. "Yes, Marie? What is it?"

"Mr. Hoyt on the line, sir."

"Thank you." He hit another button. "Hello, Ray, how are you?"

Ray Hoyt, Jr., was Ted's boss, the president of Paintex. Having inherited a struggling little company from his father, Hoyt had turned it into a multimillion-dollar enterprise, with sales nationwide. Ted had played an important part in the company's success, opening first the New Jersey and Pennsylvania markets and then spreading the company's products across the whole Northeast. Although he and Hoyt had never become close friends, they shared a mutual respect for one another's professional abilities.

"I'm fine, thanks, Ted," Hoyt replied. "How's the detective work coming? Any progress on getting your grandson back?"

"Not much, I'm afraid. We're still plugging away."

"It's a rotten shame what's happened. Sally and I are rooting for you, you know."

"I appreciate your concern, Ray."

"And I *am* concerned. I'm deeply concerned. I know how much that boy means to you. But look, I have to tell you, I

139

am also concerned about our business here. I ran into Tony Gardello from Nationwide Hardware on the golf course this weekend and I was embarrassed to hear that you haven't been returning his calls."

"Gardello? Oh, hell, that's right. Sorry. I'm afraid it's been pretty hectic around here lately. I'll call him right away."

"I think that's a good idea. I don't have to tell you that Nationwide is one of our biggest accounts. Now, I know what you're up against with your family situation and I don't for one minute think that it's been easy for you. But we can't let our personal affairs get in the way of business interests. I'm sure you understand that."

"Of course. I'll get right on it."

"Appreciate it. I know I can count on you."

"Absolutely."

"Good, good. Take care now. Talk to you soon."

"Right, Ray. Thanks for calling."

Ted hung up. "Damn it," he muttered. Being called on the carpet like a delinquent schoolboy was the last thing he needed, no matter how justified Ray may have been.

He pressed the button on his intercom. "Marie, get me Tony Gardello at Nationwide, will you?"

Once that was out of the way he'd call Sarah's lawyer about the subpoena. Then he'd try Charles Kogan at Federal National Bank, whose name he had found on the list of university trustees; maybe Kogan could persuade the university to withhold the diploma. With any luck, Ted thought, he could still get away by noon to make another trip to Yonkers, where he and Sarah would—

"Mr. Gardello on the line, sir."

"Thank you, Marie. Hello, Tony? How're you doing? Listen, I'm sorry I haven't been able to get back to you sooner, but . . ."

Later that afternoon, Sarah and her father drove to Yonkers to pay a visit to the post office there. The idea had been her mother's: if none of their other efforts worked, perhaps they could intercept the diploma in the mail. Since Sarah was still officially Mrs. Stefanovic, she might just be able to have Jovan's mail forwarded to her in Sommerton.

"Good idea," Ted had said at the time.

Sarah had been doubtful. "I just hope we're not too late. He may already have had his mail forwarded."

"Aw, come on," Ted had replied. "Don't be such a pessimist."

But now, talking to the black woman behind the counter in the Yonkers post office, he and Sarah found that Jovan had done just that.

Ted, discouraged, turned away. "Looks like you were right, kitten," he said.

But Sarah wasn't through. "Can you tell us the forwarding address, please?" she asked the woman.

"Same address but a different apartment number. The name is—well, here, you look at it. I can't tell you how to say it."

Sarah looked at the card. She could not have been more astonished. The name was that of Niki Djordjevic, the superintendent of the building where she and Jovan lived. Her father had questioned Niki closely on the morning that they had discovered Joey and Jovan were gone. To all of Ted's questions Niki had had nothing but negative answers. No, he did not know where Jovan was. No, he did not know when they had left.

Sarah turned to her father. "I thought he told you he didn't know anything."

Ted glowered. "Obviously he was lying."

"But why?"

"That's what I'd like to find out. Come on."

A half hour later they were winding their way through the dimly lit cellar of the apartment building, where they had been directed by Niki's wife. Everywhere were piles of old furniture: sofas, tables, desks, lamps, bedsteads, bureaus, credenzas. The place looked like a used-furniture warehouse. Sarah glanced around but could see none of her own things amid the dusty piles. Had Niki already disposed of them? she wondered.

They found the man himself back in a corner where, under the light of a single bare bulb, he was busy gluing a leg on a battered old dining-room chair.

"Jovan Stefanovic is my friend," he told them defiantly when Ted confronted him with the evidence of his deceit. Far from offering any apologies for having lied to them, he seemed proud of what he had done. "My friend asks me as favor to say I know nothing. I say I know nothing." He stood facing them, with his fists planted firmly on his massive hips. His fat jowls were shadowed with their usual day-old growth of beard and from deep within the folds of his face his tiny black eyes gleamed with hostility.

Ted glanced at Sarah, then turned again to Niki. "I'm sure your loyalty is commendable," he said. "But now that you've fulfilled your obligation, maybe you can help us by answering some questions."

Niki shook his head and bent over his work once more. "I am busy man, mister. I do not have time to answer questions."

The sight of a twenty-dollar bill in Ted's hand quickly changed his mind. Yes, he told them, he had already sent Jovan some mail. Yes, there had been a large envelope from New York University. He remembered it because Jovan had asked him to watch especially for such an envelope. It had arrived two days ago, maybe three. "I know he wants it quickly so I send it right away. It is the favor he asks of his friend Niki." He thrust out his stubbled chin as if daring Ted to challenge his loyalty to a fellow countryman. "Now, you have maybe other questions? Or can I go back to my work?"

Ted glared at him a moment in disgust, then shook his head. "No, no more questions. Come on, Sarah, let's get out of here."

So, they were too late. The diploma was already gone. They had been robbed of their only weapon before they had even had a chance to get their hands on it.

"I guess there's no point in trying to subpoena the university's records, now," Emma said gloomily as she sat over coffee that evening with Ted and Sarah.

Ted rolled the end of his cigar along the rim of the ashtray, then tapped off the loosened curl of an ash. "No," he said. "There's no point."

"Or following up with that trustee?"

"Afraid not."

Ted watched as Emma stared into her cup. He wished he had been able to bring her some good news. Like the rest of them, she could use it. She had spent a long, tiring afternoon on the telephone, calling, among others, the telephone company and Con Edison, making sure that service to the apartment was turned off and that Sarah would not be billed for any charges. Dealing with the parking tickets was going to be more complicated. The car, an aged Ford Falcon that Ted had passed on to Sarah and Jovan, was still registered in Sarah's name, meaning that she would be held liable for the tickets. Obviously another call to the lawyer was in order.

What had happened to the car itself they had no idea. With any luck Jovan had abandoned it on the street somewhere,

where vandals could be counted on to strip it to the axles. It was certainly not worth even a fraction of what it would cost to reclaim it if the police picked it up.

"So, I guess that's it then," Emma said. "Jovan's got everything he wants now and we've got a pile of his bills."

Gone from her voice was all the force and resolution of the last few days. Ted ached for her. For one vivid moment he saw her not as the woman who nurtured the plants on the windowsill and worried about her diet, but as the bright, dark-eyed girl he had met at a dance—what was it, thirty-six years ago? thirty-seven?—when he had nothing and their whole lives were ahead of them and neither of them could have imagined being parents much less grandparents.

He reached out a hand to her. "No, he doesn't have everything. Not quite."

Emma looked puzzled. "What do you mean?"

"He hasn't got Sarah," he said, nodding in their daughter's direction. He was pleased to see a flicker of a smile cross Sarah's face.

"That's true," she said quietly. But the smile faded almost as soon as it had appeared. "The trouble is, Joey doesn't have me either."

For a moment the three of them sat in silence.

Finally Ted said, "Anyway, I guess we still have a few options left."

"The lawyer in Washington, you mean? Colonel Stevenson?"

"I'll be going down to see him on the twenty-eighth."

"I'll come, too," Sarah said.

"Are you sure? You don't have to, you know."

"I want to. It's my son you'll be talking about."

Ted nodded. "Good. It'll help if you're there."

Emma looked up. "What about what that man at the Yugoslav-American trade office told you, Ted? About getting a lawyer in Belgrade and taking Jovan to court over there?"

"That's one of the things we'll be talking to Colonel Stevenson about. I also want to talk to Senator Case's office again. Congressman Vanderbeck's, too. One of his aides said he'd be getting in touch with the Yugoslav ambassador for us."

"And don't forget about the man at the State Department," Sarah added, "the one whose name you were given by the man at the trade office."

"His name is Jack Traymore," said Emma. "I tried to reach him this morning. He's supposed to be getting back to me."

Ted smiled. He was pleased by their renewed spirits. "There, you see!" he said. "We're not finished yet, by God."

September 16, 1976

Hon. Michael Vanderbeck
Rayburn Office Bldg.
Washington, D.C. 20515
Att: Mr. George Roberts

Dear Mr. Roberts:
Persuant to our telephone conversation of this morning, I am enclosing copies of documents, including an outline of events up to the abduction of our grandson to Yugoslavia, by my son-in-law.

Needless to say, anything your office could do for us beyond the usual bureaucratic channels, or any suggestions from you, would be deeply appreciated.

Yours very truly,
Edward H. Novack

145

September 20, 1976

Mr. Jack Traymore
Room 5219, EUR/EE
Department of State
Washington, D.C. 20520

Dear Mr. Traymore:
Thank you very much for your kind concern with
our delicate family problem.
Pursuant to our telephone conversation of this
morning, I am enclosing copies of documents,
including an outline of events up to the abduction of
my grandson to Yugoslavia by my son-in-law; custody
and visitation agreement, and a copy of a warrant for
Jovan's arrest for violation of the court order.
Needless to say, any assistance from you in
expediting return of Joey to his mother would be
deeply appreciated by a family now experiencing a
horrible nightmare.

Sincerely,
Edward H. Novack

September 21, 1976

Honorable Clifford Case
315 Senate Office Building
Washington, D.C. 20510
Attention: Mrs. Wendell

Dear Mrs. Wendell:
Pursuant to our telephone conversation of this
morning, I am enclosing copies of documents,
including an outline of events up to the abduction of

our grandson to Yugoslavia by my son-in-law. Also enclosed is a copy of warrant for Jovan's arrest.

Is it possible for your office to get some cooperation from the Yugoslavian Embassy in Washington in view of the manner in which the child was taken to Yugoslavia?

Is it possible for your office to explore the availability of funds if it becomes necessary to go to Yugoslavia to engage an attorney and fight the case in their courts? We provide Legal Aid for foreigners here.

Needless to say, anything your office can do for us beyond the usual bureaucratic channels, or any suggestions from you, would be deeply appreciated.

Very truly yours,
Edward H. Novack
Sarah Novack Stefanovic

United States Senate
Washington, D.C. 20510
September 23, 1976

Mr. Edward H. Novack
15 North Mercer Street
Sommerton, New Jersey

Dear Mr. Novack:

I have been advised of the phone calls from you and Mrs. Novack and your letter has now been received at the office. I was sorry indeed to learn of your daughter's difficult situation.

As a member of my staff indicated to you, the State Department has earlier advised that questions of child custody are considered private matters that can only be resolved by a court of competent jurisdiction in the country where the child is physically located. However, in accordance with my policy of longstanding to deal with foreign governments on such cases only through the State Department, I was glad to ask the appropriate officials there about any possibilities of assisting you and for information on the questions you have raised. Just as soon as a response is received, I will let you know.

Best regards,

Sincerely,
Clifford P. Case
U.S. Senator

Congress of the United States
House of Representatives
Washington, D.C. 20515
September 27, 1976

Honorable Dimce Belovski
Yugoslav Ambassador
Yugoslav Embassy
2410 California Street N.W.
Washington, D.C. 20008

Dear Mr. Ambassador:

I am writing you to ask for your personal intervention in a matter of tragic consequences involving a Yugoslav national, Mr. Jovan Stefanovic. Mr. Stefanovic married a U.S. citizen in 1967 and became a permanent resident alien of the United States. He pursued a Ph.D. course of study at New

York University through financial assistance from the National Institutes of Health.

Early this month, Mr. Stefanovic visited his wife from whom he was legally separated and without permission took the couple's five-year-old son and departed for Yugoslavia. Needless to say this most deplorable act has caused tremendous grief for the son's mother and grandparents.

Aside from the horrible act of spiriting away this child, Mr. Stefanovic has left behind serious financial obligations owed to the United States Government.

For these many reasons I would urge that you lend your kind offices to contact Mr. Stefanovic in an effort to bring about the reunification of the son with the mother in whose custody the courts had placed the son and under whose custody the child could secure the wholesome upbringing and love he deserves.

The child's remaining family would be forever grateful to your Government for any help rendered in this grave matter.

Sincerely,
Michael Vanderbeck
U.S. Congress

While the letters and phone calls were going back and forth, Ted's headaches and the pain in his back were getting progressively worse. He did his best to hide his discomfort from Emma and Sarah; he saw no point in burdening them with yet another worry. But pushing himself through his calisthenics in the morning had become an agony and at times it was even difficult for him to sit for very long. Steambaths at the health club and long soaks in the Jacuzzi brought him little relief and visits to the chiropractor didn't help much either. He finally called his regular doctor, Ben Larkin. But Larkin, who had heard about Joey's abduction through the grapevine, was more interested in talking about that than he was in hearing about Ted's symptoms.

"Sounds like stress," he said, almost as an afterthought. "I'll phone in a prescription for you for a pain killer. In the meantime, try to get more rest and take it easy."

Take it easy! Ted almost laughed out loud. How in the hell was he supposed to take it easy when there was so much to be done?

The next day, Saturday, September 24, he went to his office early to catch up on his paperwork. What with everything else going on, weekends were now about the only time he had to keep his business affairs in order. And in a few days he would be going down to Washington to see Colonel Stevenson, which would further cut into his time.

He had just sat down at his desk when he suddenly felt an unbearable stab of pain in his spine. Doubled over, he managed to hobble out to the water cooler, where he downed one of Larkin's pain killers. Then, thinking to further ease the pain, he lowered himself carefully to the floor in his office and stretched himself out full length on his back.

It was when the telephone rang on the desk above him that he discovered he could not get up again.

Fighting excruciating pain, he managed to raise himself up on an elbow, dislodge the receiver, and bring it down to his ear.

"Ted? This is Ben. Ben Larkin."

"Ben, am I glad you called."

"Listen, I had dinner last night with a Yugoslav friend of mine and told him all about your situation."

"Ben—"

150

"He says what you've got to do is get right over there to Belgrade and get a lawyer and take the boy's father to court."

"Ben, will you shut up for a minute and listen to me. I'm not going anywhere. I'm flat on my back on the floor. I can't move."

Then everything went dark.

Sarah and her mother arrived at Memorial Hospital ten minutes after the ambulance brought Ted in. They had been told only that he was unconscious and that tests were being conducted to find out what was wrong.

"It may take a while," Dr. Larkin told them. "If you'd like to go back home, I'll call you as soon as we know anything."

Emma shook her head. "Thank you, Doctor, but we'll wait here."

The wait was interminable. After what seemed like hours, the doctor finally returned. A surgical mask dangled around his neck and sweat beaded his forehead. His expression was somber and, at the sight of him, Emma reached out for Sarah's hand and gripped it hard. As if through a fog, Sarah heard the doctor's diagnosis: "spinal meningitis . . . bacterial variety . . . unpredictable . . . touch and go for the next twenty-four hours . . . depends on whether we caught it in time. . . ."

With a low moan Emma sagged against Sarah's shoulder.

Numbly Sarah put a protective arm around her. Oh, God, don't let him die, she prayed. Please, God.

"When can I see him?" her mother asked. "I want to see him."

The doctor did not try to discourage her. "He's still in quarantine, so I can't let you into his room. You'll have to just look in from outside his door."

"Just so I can see him."

Dr. Larkin led them to an elevator and rode with them to the third floor, where they passed through a door labeled Intensive Care.

"I have to warn you, he doesn't look very pretty right now," the doctor said.

He led them down another hall. At room 317 he stopped. The door was closed but it had a glass window in it. They looked inside. What they saw made Emma gasp. Sarah felt her own breath catch in her throat. Her father was as pale and still as a corpse. He was lying on his back with the blankets pulled up to his armpits. His hair was plastered to his head and only the slight movement of his chest showed that he was even alive. There was a tube running up into his nose and another taped to his wrist. A third led from a nearby machine to somewhere under the covers, chest high.

"His body signs have stabilized," the doctor was saying. "That's a good sign, but it's going to take a while before we know anything definite."

"He will get better, won't he?" Emma asked.

"We're doing everything we can. We'll be monitoring him closely. The best thing you can do now is go home and get some rest. If there's any change we'll call you immediately."

Shaken and depressed, Sarah and her mother drove back to the house, silent except for Emma's quiet weeping.

At home, Sarah helped her mother prepare a light supper and sat with her for a while before seeing her off to bed. Afterward, she sat alone at the kitchen table, sipping coffee and leafing aimlessly through the piles of notes her parents had made over the last few weeks: notes scrawled on legal pads in her father's broad, confident hand and on steno pads in her mother's neat, orderly script. There were messages jotted on the backs of envelopes; tallies of people called, leads followed. Useless now, because her father was the only one who knew how all the pieces went together. What would happen if he

152

didn't get better? she wondered. What would happen to her? To Joey?

Should she call his secretary, tell her to cancel his appointments? Maybe she should call the lawyer in Washington, too. Even if her father got better, he would certainly not be able to go down there anytime soon. It could be months before he was well enough to pick up where he'd left off.

Oh, God, she prayed again, please help him. Please help all of us.

eight

It was two days before Sarah's father was removed from quarantine and pronounced out of danger.

"It's a good thing we got him here when we did," Dr. Larkin told Sarah and her mother in the corridor on the way to Ted's room. "The infection was starting to move up his spine. If it had reached his brain it would almost certainly have been fatal. He's had a very close call."

"But he is—" Sarah's mother faltered, as if afraid there might yet be bad news. "He is going to be all right?"

"I don't see why not. Fortunately he kept himself in good shape. That's going to help a lot in his recovery."

"How long will it take?" Sarah asked.

"It's not the kind of thing that can be hurried," Larkin replied. "Complete recovery could take four or five months."

Sarah's heart sank. Months! Not weeks but months! But that meant that— She forced the thought out of her mind. Her father had to get well. That was the important thing. Joey, everything, would just have to wait now. Except, how could it? How could she put Joey out of her mind for as long as that?

But then they were at her father's door and donning surgical masks.

Inside, the curtains had been pulled back and sunlight was streaming in. Her father lay as he had before, with a tube still attached to his wrist and another running up under his blanket. But Sarah was relieved to see that the tube in his nose had been removed. He still looked very white and weak, but he opened his eyes when they entered. He smiled faintly when he saw them. Almost immediately he closed his eyes and slept again. But Sarah's mother felt reassured.

"He recognized us, didn't he?" she asked. Sarah led her back to the car. "He knew who we were."

"Yes, Mother. I'm sure he did." But her own relief was mixed with despair.

Ted improved steadily and by the end of the week he was sitting up in bed and was well enough to carry on a whispered conversation, though his throat was still sore from the tube that had been run from his nose to his stomach.

Sarah and her mother visited his room every day. Sarah's brother Richard flew in for a few days from Berkeley, and even Grandma Helen came to pay Ted a visit, though she complained the whole time about how much she hated hospitals and how dreadful the food was in the cafeteria.

Ray Hoyt, Ted's boss, also came by, bearing a basket of fresh fruit and the assurance that the company's health insurance plan would cover almost all of Ted's medical and hospital bills. "Of course, there's also disability income for as long as it takes you to recover. So you just take it easy and get yourself better. We're all rooting for you, Ted."

After Hoyt left, Sarah's father turned to her with a mischievous gleam in his eye. "What did Larkin say was the normal recovery time for meningitis? Four or five months, wasn't it?"

155

"About that."

"See if he'll stretch it to six."

"Ted!" Emma looked appalled. "What a thing to say!"

"Look, Larkin knows all about Joey. He wants to help. If he agrees and we can stretch this thing out long enough, I'll have just that much more time to concentrate on getting Joey back without having to worry about the office, too."

Sarah felt tears of gratitude welling up. Despite everything that he had been through, he hadn't stopped thinking about Joey.

"What you need to spend full time doing is getting rest and getting better," Emma said sharply.

Sarah followed her mother's lead. "That's right, Dad. The main thing is for you to get well. I've canceled all your appointments and there's nothing for you to do now but rest and take it easy."

Suddenly he looked alarmed. "You didn't cancel the trip to Washington, did you?" he whispered hoarsely.

Sarah took his hand. "Dad, that appointment was for two days ago. There was no way you were going to make it. All that is just going to have to wait for now."

He gripped her hand hard. "It can't wait," he said, his words ragged with emotion. "You know damn well how it's hurting Joey. Every day he's over there he's growing farther away from us. From you, Sarah."

It was true. When she spoke to Joey on the phone these days, he offered little more than monosyllables: "Yes," "No," "I'm ok-k-kay." His voice sounded dead, anesthethized, as if he were resigning himself to the fact that he was never going to see her again. Jovan's taunting and badgering she could handle; *that* she was used to. But this distance of Joey's, this sense that he was removing himself from her—this was new. And it hurt more than she could bear.

"We heard from Mr. Traymore at the State Department the

156

other day," Emma said, trying to console Ted. "He says the embassy in Belgrade sent someone to check on Joey. He seems to be doing okay. He's not sick or anything."

"Emma, that's only what they can *see*. What's going on in his head, that's what I'd like to know. Have they listened to him talk? Have they heard him stuttering? Have they heard him crying for his mother at night?"

Emma shrugged helplessly. She had no answer.

"Look, you two," Ted said. "You don't have to play the dutiful wife and daughter and hang around my bedside. The best thing you can do for me is make that appointment again and go down to Washington and see Colonel Stevenson. I can't get there myself, but there's no reason why you two can't go in my place."

Emma shook her head. "I'm not leaving you," she said emphatically.

"That's ridiculous," Ted said. "There's nothing you can do for me while I'm in the hospital."

"You'll be out of the hospital in a few more days. You'll need me at home. I don't care how much you object, I'm not going."

"God dammit, Emma," he said in a strained whisper. He swatted at the bedclothes in frustrated rage. "Maybe I'll just divorce you. Then you'll have to leave me."

Sarah swallowed hard. While her parents argued she had been struggling against doing what she knew she must do. But now she had made up her mind. "Don't worry, Dad," she said. "I'll go down there myself. I'll see Colonel Stevenson."

Both of them stared at her.

"Are you sure you're up to it, dear?" her mother asked.

She wasn't but she lied and said she was. "Anyway, Dad, you certainly don't need both of us here to look after you. And this way we won't have to wait until you get better."

He squeezed her hand. Tears flooded in the corners of his eyes. "Thank you, Sarah," he said, "you've just made your dad very happy."

The offices of Stevenson, Davis, Russell & McLean were located on the top floor of an elegant gray-stone office building in downtown Washington.

"Colonel Stevenson will see you in a few moments," the receptionist said in a voice that was as silky and soft as the blouse she wore. "Won't you make yourselves comfortable." With a wave of a well-manicured hand, she directed Sarah and Grandma Helen toward a deep plush sofa.

Gran's loud "Thank you, dear," made Sarah wince. Although Sarah had been fully prepared to make this trip on her own, she had been relieved and grateful when Gran had offered to come along for the ride and keep her company. But in these hushed surroundings, amid all this muted elegance, Gran's natural volume seemed to blare like a trumpet. And her flamboyant clothes—maroon jacket over a floral-print dress—were decidedly out of place.

While they waited, suave men in white shirts and charcoal-gray pinstripes came and went across the thick carpet, speaking in muffled tones. Smart women in tailored suits glided past on their way, no doubt, to important conferences. In the background, the receptionist's IBM Selectric tapped faintly, discreetly.

Although Sarah had dressed herself neatly in a plaid skirt and sweater and had touched up her hair in the taxi while riding over from the station, she felt mousy and drab. And Gran's irrepressible "flair" did not help her feel any more at ease in this oh-so-proper setting.

"The colonel will see you now," purred the receptionist at last.

"Well, that's more like it," Gran declared, hoisting herself to her feet.

Following the receptionist, Sarah and Gran passed along a carpeted hallway, then through a pair of massive walnut doors, which opened into a high-ceilinged room that looked like a library in a stately home. The walls were richly paneled and the shelves were lined with books bound in leather. Heavy drapes framed the rain-streaked windows. In the center of the room, a polished walnut conference table gleamed softly in the golden light of an ornate chandelier.

"Now, *this* is classy," Gran exclaimed. "Look at those drapes! Oh, and look! That's a real painting over the mantel."

Before they could take it all in, a side door swung open and through it strode a lean, gray-haired man in pinstripes, his hand outstretched in greeting.

"Sorry to have kept you waiting, ladies. I'm George Stevenson. Welcome to Washington."

The man's voice, deep and mellow, slid mellifluously in a soft Southern accent, and his elegant movements reminded Sarah more of a concert pianist than a lawyer.

"I'm sorry we couldn't arrange better weather for your visit," he drawled. "Early October is usually *the* most beautiful time of year for us. Have a seat, won't you?"

With a languid wave of a long-fingered hand, he indicated the leather-backed chairs around the conference table. "May I provide you with some refreshment? Coffee, perhaps?"

"Yes, thank you," said Sarah.

"And you, ma'am?"

But Gran did not hear. Still preoccupied with the elegant furnishings, she was veering from one attraction to the next, now peering at the dour portraits on the walls, now running a palm over the rich upholstery of a wingback easy chair.

"Gran?" Sarah caught her attention. "Some coffee?"

"What? Oh, why yes. Thank you."

Far from being put out, the colonel merely smiled benignly and stepped to a side table, where he poured coffee from a gleaming silver pot into two delicate china cups.

All at once, from over by the window, Sarah heard Gran utter a gasp of astonishment. "Well, for heaven's sake," she exclaimed. "Will you look at that!"

Curious, Sarah stepped to the window. There, six stories below and less than a block away, was the White House itself, with its columned portico and its spreading lawns. Parked in the great curve of the driveway, a line of black limousines glistened in the rain.

"Pleasant view, isn't it?" said the colonel, handing them their coffee cups. "On a sunny day it can be quite spectacular."

"It's quite spectacular now," said Sarah. "I didn't realize we were this close."

The colonel chuckled amiably. "I dare say we are a good deal more comfortable up here than the President is down there. If the polls are correct, this coming election is going to be a close one."

Just then a door opened behind them.

"Ah," said the colonel. "Here's Bill. Come in, Bill. Come in."

Turning to follow the colonel's gaze, Sarah found herself facing an earnest-looking man who was carrying a manila folder in one hand and a pack of cigarettes in the other.

"Ladies, may I present my colleague, Bill Borden. Bill, this is Mrs. Sarah Stefanovic and this is her grandmother, Mrs. Helen Heilicki."

"How do you do," Borden said, giving a little bow. Quickly depositing his cigarettes and folder on the conference table, he offered each of them his hand. He had fair hair and serious gray eyes. He was shorter than the colonel and considerably younger—probably in his late forties, Sarah guessed.

160

"Bill will be handling your case if you decide to come with us," the colonel said.

Sarah was puzzled. "I'm sorry, Colonel Stevenson, but I don't understand. I thought you would be representing us."

Borden cleared his throat. "There are, ah, a number of partners in the firm, Mrs. Stefanovic," he explained patiently. "Each of us takes on different kinds of cases. However, we do consult with one another as circumstances require and each of us has the full services of the firm at our disposal."

"I see."

The colonel smiled warmly. "You will be in excellent hands with Bill, I can assure you. Now, if you'll excuse me, I'll leave you people to get acquainted. I know you'll have a lot to talk about."

Sarah felt disappointed to see him go. She liked his stately manner, his grandfatherly charm. And this new man seemed so serious, so remote.

"Wonderful old gentleman," Borden said as soon as the colonel had left the room. "Brilliant lawyer. Of course, he takes on only a few cases himself these days, but his name still carries a good deal of weight around Washington. With the colonel's help, there isn't anyone in this town we can't reach if we have to. And that," he added, nodding toward the window, "includes the occupant of the house down the street."

"If you're trying to impress us, Mr. Borden," Gran said, "you're certainly doing a good job of it."

Borden smiled for the first time, the corners of his eyes crinkling into friendly crow's-feet. "As a matter of fact, I'm trying to do just that, Mrs. Heilicki. I want both of you to know that we are prepared to bring considerable resources to bear on your behalf. Besides"—he turned to Sarah—"once I began reading the background material on this heartbreaking case, I discovered that I very much wanted to do whatever I could to help you to get your boy back."

161

Sarah felt her reserve melting away. Somehow this man managed to be both personal and businesslike at the same time. The combination was reassuring.

After offering them seats at the conference table, Borden took his own place across from them. Methodically he laid a yellow legal pad on the table in front of him and uncapped a felt-tipped pen.

"Now, Mrs. Stefanovic, perhaps you'll tell me about yourself and Joe-van. Am I saying that right, by the way? So far I've only seen the name in writing."

Sarah smiled. "It's *Yo-vahn*. The Serbian *J* is pronounced as a Y."

Over the years few people had ever bothered to ask about the correct pronunciation. That Borden had done so made her like him even more. Soon—and more easily than she had anticipated—she found herself telling him her story. She would rather not have had to. She would rather have put the past behind her and gone on with her life. But it was not yet time for forgetting.

With Borden taking notes and Gran sitting quietly at her elbow, a comforting presence, Sarah talked about how she and Jovan had met and how he had courted her with love and dreams and poetry; about how she had finally agreed to marry him—despite—or perhaps because of—her parents' suspicion that she was making a mistake; about coming with him to live in America; about how difficult that change had been for him, and how, since that time, she could remember only one brief period when she and Jovan had been really happy.

It was 1971, the year just after Joey was born. Jovan had not forgotten that Sarah had walked out on him or that she had forced him to choose between her and his mother. But as the weeks passed, he seemed anxious to put the bad times behind them, to make a fresh start. And for a while it looked as if that might be possible. He spent more time at home and was more attentive to her. He even began writing poetry again: verses about the delights of fatherhood and about the small miracle that was his son. He bought toys for Joey and played with him on the living-room rug. And when friends came to visit, Jovan loved nothing better than showing off Joey's latest accomplishments.

"Look! See how well he crawls! Strong legs. A soccer star when he grown up, eh?"

There was a new calmness in him, a sense of contentment that Sarah had never seen before. And when, during that summer, he received the news that he had been accepted at NYU graduate school in chemistry, it was like icing on the cake. He was ecstatic. The brilliant scientific career that he had envisioned for himself was finally about to begin.

Of course, going back to school would mean having to quit his job at the drug company, and what with the extra expense of the baby it might be a little harder for them to make ends meet. But Jovan was not concerned. There would be grants, he explained; loans from the government, from banks.

"There is not problem," he told Sarah confidently. "Do not all the time be so worried. Everything will be good now."

And indeed, Jovan's high spirits and self-assurance made a wonderful change. During that summer, he and Sarah were happier together than they had been since those first days in Paris. There were picnics, sunny afternoons at the beach, walks in the park with the downy-haired boy asleep in his nest in the stroller, one chubby fist lying open on his pillow like a blossoming rosebud.

Those special days ended abruptly in September when classes began and Jovan discovered that the work load was going to be far more demanding than he had imagined. And the language barrier did not make it any easier. Although his command of English had improved considerably, the linguistic subtleties Jovan encountered in the classroom and in his textbooks made his studies all the more frustrating, while the sheer volume of work was overwhelming. Between attending classes, reading, and doing research, he had hardly a free moment. Coming home in the evening, he would rush in like a freight train, grab a bite to eat, then take himself over to the desk in the corner and bury himself in his books for the rest of the evening. Sarah's nights became as empty as her days, with the deadening routine of child care and house care unbroken by adult conversation. And Joey, who had so recently been Jovan's darling and delight, was now little more than an irritant in his life.

"Dammit, can't you make him stop that!" Jovan would demand if Joey's crying went on too long. "How can I think with him screaming like that!"

"We live here, too," Sarah would protest. But that only made Jovan angrier and after a while Sarah simply retreated to the bedroom with the baby and closed the door behind her. Often the only time she and Jovan shared together from one week to the next were those occasions when he asked her to help him decipher some scholar's garbled English. At such times she used to pray that the baby would not wake up crying or the telephone start ringing, for those moments together were too rare to be interrupted.

How they made it through that first academic year, Sarah had no idea. Jovan pushed himself mercilessly, driven almost to desperation by the fear that he might yet fail to realize his dream. But as difficult as it made their life together, Sarah was proud of his efforts, nonetheless. His success was her dream, too; she wanted it for him as badly as he did.

The school year was not quite over when Jovan's sister, Myra, sent word from Belgrade that Baka was seriously ill. Pneumonia, the doctor said. And at Baka's age it could be especially dangerous.

Jovan did not hesitate. "I must go to her."

"Of course," Sarah said, seeing the anxiety in his eyes. Then, hesitantly: "But where will you get the money?"

The meager grants and loans that he had managed to obtain gave them hardly enough to buy groceries, let alone a plane ticket to Belgrade.

Jovan brushed the objection aside. "We can borrow."

"From who?"

"Your father. He has plenty."

"You think he's rich or something? You're wrong. Anyway, I just borrowed from him to have the car fixed. I can't ask him again. Not so soon."

"Then I will find someone else."

"But how will we pay it back?"

He flared up. "Enough! We will talk no more about this." His face contorted with rage. "You think I can worry about a little money when my own mother is maybe dying?"

"No, of course not. It's just that—"

"A year and a half now I do not see her. For you I send her away. And now you wish me not to go to her when it might happen she will not live even until tomorrow. No! I will go!"

Somehow—he never told her how—he found the money for the air fare. He packed a few clothes and a suitcase full of books; final exams were less than a month away and he could not afford to ignore his studies.

Sarah drove him to the airport, then took Joey and went to stay with her parents.

———————

When Jovan returned ten days later, he brought word that Baka was on the mend. She had begun to improve, it seemed, almost from the moment he'd appeared at her bedside.

"Myra was not believing the change. Like a miracle, she said."

"I'm really glad," said Sarah.

But the news made her uneasy, though she wasn't sure just why. In the weeks that followed, however, it became clear that something in Jovan had changed. The trip to Belgrade had unsettled him. He was more harried and irritable than ever, and she sensed that it wasn't just because he had lost so much time from his studies. Difficult and frustrating as the past year had been, there had never been any doubt that he was where he wanted to be, doing exactly what he wanted to be doing. Now he seemed unsure of himself again, discontented and disagreeable in a way that Sarah had not seen for a long time. And when he finally took his exams and then did poorly on them, his depression and his temper only got worse. He began to sink back into his old isolation. He would go out for long walks by himself and not come home for hours. He would sit for entire evenings listening to his Serbian folk records and staring off into space. And before long he began talking about going home to Belgrade for another visit, this time taking Sarah and Joey with him.

Perhaps he needed such a trip in order to put the pieces of his life together; that was what Sarah's friend Elena suggested. Perhaps he needed to separate his past from his present—or to unite them in some way. Perhaps he just needed to escape from his pressures for a while. It didn't matter. Whatever his motivations, there was simply not enough money for all of them to go to Europe and back.

"If you want to go I guess you'll find a way," Sarah told him. "But I'm not going with you and neither is Joey."

"I tell you, I can get money. I did it last time."

"Where? How? We're already so deep in debt we'll probably never get out."

"Excuses. It is only because you do not want to visit Baka and you do not want me to visit her. Go on, admit it. It is the truth."

"No. It is not."

But it was. She did not like what happened to him when he was with his mother. His last trip had somehow undermined everything he had accomplished for himself: his independence, his confidence. If he saw Baka again, Sarah feared that he would come back to her even more divided and confused than ever.

He made the trip anyway: a three-week excursion fare, the cheapest he could find. But he went alone. As before, Sarah and Joey stayed with her parents while he was gone. It was better than staying alone in the apartment. At least in Sommerton Joey had a backyard to play in and grandparents who could afford to spoil him. Besides, it gave Sarah a break as well: a chance to get away from the apartment for a while— away from cleaning and cooking and fending off the dunning phone calls from the pediatrician and the supermarket and the credit-card companies. Even so, Sarah did not realized just how much she enjoyed being home until the three weeks were almost over and she found herself dreading Jovan's return.

And she had reason to dread it, as she discovered when she went to pick him up at Kennedy.

"Where is Joey?" he snapped as soon as he was through customs. "Why isn't he here?"

Sarah tried to ignore his testiness; he was tired, she told herself; it had been a long flight.

"Joey's home with Mom and Dad," she told him. "They want us all to have supper with them before we go back home."

"Oh? And why do you not ask me first if this is okay?"

"I'm sorry, Jovan. I just thought—"

"You did not think. You thought what you wanted, not what I wanted."

He kept at her all the way to Sommerton. It was as if he had been storing up his grievances for days. "You spend too much time with your parents," he complained. He was driving fast, jumping lanes, cutting in and out of traffic. "I do not like it. It is going to change. You are my wife, you will do things my way, not theirs."

"Slow down, Jovan. Please."

"Baka was very angry that I did not bring you and Joey to see her. Very angry. And what could I tell her? That my wife does not do what I say? What kind of man does that make me, eh? I will not be made a fool. It changes now. It will be different. You will do what I say. It was not good the way it was. Not good. But it is over now. No more."

They sailed onto the Verazano-Narrows Bridge doing seventy. Abruptly Jovan cut around a pickup truck. Swinging back, he came dangerously close to sideswiping the bridge railing. Sarah dug her fingers into the armrest. "All right, Jovan. All right. Just please slow down. I want to get there in one piece."

Silence and depression settled over her. What was it that these visits did to him? It was as if going home reminded him of all the roles he had forgotten, parts he should be playing. As if all that he had accomplished, all that he had come to value—his family, his work, his home—was suddenly no longer good enough. As if he was somehow afraid that he would fail to live up to someone else's twisted idea of the kind of man he should be. But whose idea? His mother's? His country's? His dead father's?

When they got back to Sommerton, Sarah apologized to her parents for not staying for supper, then began getting ready to leave. She packed the last of Joey's things into a carry bag while Jovan took her suitcase out to the Falcon, which he had left in the driveway back by the garage. She said good-bye to her parents, then carried Joey to the car. Still dazed by Jovan's tirade, she began buckling Joey into his car seat.

Jovan was behind her, holding the door open. "Come on,

get in," Jovan prodded. "What are you waiting for? I want to get home. I have work to do."

He had touched the wrong nerve. Into Sarah's mind leaped a single word: *no.*

She backed out of the car and turned to face him. "No," she said.

Jovan looked surprised. "What do you mean, 'no'?"

"I mean I'm not going back with you."

"What kind of bullshit is that? Get in the car."

"No, Jovan. No more. I can't go through all that again."

"What are you talking about? You're jabbering like an idiot."

"Your work! Your needs! What about me? What about *us?* I can't do it anymore, Jovan. I won't."

His arm flew out and for a moment she thought he was going to hit her. But he grabbed her by the wrist. "You will do what I tell you to do," he snarled.

"Let go of me."

He was squeezing her wrist hard now. His mouth was twisted into an ugly slash. His eyes flared dangerously. "Maybe you think I become like American husband and let my wife tell me what to do, eh?"

"Let go. You're hurting me."

"It is them. Your goddamn parents. They turn you against me."

"You're wrong. They have nothing to do with this."

"I should never let you come here. Get in the car. Now. Go on. Or I throw you in."

Twisting her arm up behind her, he tried to force her through the open door. But she jammed her free arm against the frame. "Stop it," she shouted. "Let me go!"

In the backseat, Joey began screaming.

Then, from somewhere behind her came another sound, a throaty growl: "You son-of-a-bitch."

It was her father's voice. Suddenly the pressure on her arm was released and she was falling backward, catching herself in time to see her father jerking Jovan around and away from her. Jovan's fist came up. Ted blocked it. Then his own fist shot forward: a blow to the stomach that doubled Jovan over and left him gasping for air.

"No!" Sarah ran to her father, pulling him away.

He shrugged her off. "Take Joey and get in the house. Lock the doors."

"Don't hit him again, Dad. Please don't hit him."

Behind her, her mother had come around to the other side of the car, where Joey was shrieking hysterically. She pulled him out of his car seat and ran with him toward the house.

But now Jovan was up again and stumbling after her, clawing at her as he fought to pull Joey from her arms. He was yelling like a crazy man. "Give him back, you bitch. You can't have him. He's mine. Give him back."

Emma screamed and then Ted was moving again, plowing into Jovan shoulder first, knocking him off his feet and sending him sprawling.

This time Jovan did not try to get up. While Emma hurried inside with Joey, Ted stood over Jovan, ready to knock him down again the minute he got to his feet.

"Get in the house, Sarah," Ted commanded again. "Go on."

Choking on tears, torn between shock and guilt and confusion, she stood rooted where she was, staring in disbelief at the scene before her: her husband stretched out on the grass where he had fallen, tears streaming down his face; her father looming over him with clenched fists.

"Dammit, Sarah, move!" Ted barked. "Go on. Get the hell out of here."

With an effort she forced her legs to carry her up the back steps and into the house. Inside, she found her mother waiting to lock the door behind her and Joey crying so hard he could not catch his breath.

———————

It was Gran, of course, who suggested that they break for lunch. For Gran, days were measured by the distance between meals.

Across the gleaming conference table, Bill Borden slipped the cap back on his felt-tipped pen and pushed back his chair. "Excellent idea," he said.

Sarah was grateful. Dredging up that horrible afternoon had left her emotionally drained. She wasn't sure she could give any more. Not right now.

Borden took them to an elegant French restaurant, where he and Gran chatted amiably about food and wine. Sarah realized they were giving her a chance to collect herself, and she took the opportunity to do just that, letting the conversation drift along without her. Thanks to the wine and to the tranquilizer she had gulped in the ladies' room, she was contentedly oblivious. She only wished she could stay that way.

Later, back in the conference room, they found that someone had set out fresh coffee and clean ashtrays for them. They settled themselves in their chairs once more and, with Borden's prodding, the interview resumed.

"How long ago did that happen—Jovan's fight with your father?"

Sarah shrugged. "I don't know. Three years ago, I guess."

"And Joey was how old?"

"Two and a half. Almost three."

"And it was after that that you left your husband?"

"Oh, no."

"No?"

Sarah studied her hands, the nails bitten to the quick. "I—kept hoping things would get better."

"Did they?"

"For a while, yes."

That was just the trouble, of course. That was what had kept her hanging on for so long. For Jovan had been as shocked and bewildered as any of them over what had happened that afternoon.

"What have I done?" he had moaned as he lay on the lawn where he had fallen, his head buried in his hands. "What have I done?"

He did not resist when Ted sent him home alone to cool off. And when he reappeared the next day he brought apologies and gifts for each of them: flowers for Emma, earrings for Sarah, a bottle of bourbon for Ted. For Joey, there was a blue hippopotamus bath sponge. What he had done was awful, terrible, he told them. He didn't know what had come over him. He had certainly not meant to hurt anyone. Yes, of course he would agree to visit a marriage counselor if Sarah thought that would help.

In the days and weeks that followed, he went out of his way to make up for what had happened, being as considerate and caring as he could be.

But with the new academic year, the pressures began mounting again: he got behind on his research; inflation began cutting into his grants and loans and there wasn't enough money to pay the bills. On top of that, Joey was sick with a cough and a fever, which kept Jovan awake at night when he needed his sleep. As for the marriage counselor, Jovan went with Sarah to only one session before deciding the man was a quack. If there was a problem with their marriage it was Sarah's fault, not his.

And so it went. The rows never again reached the point of physical violence, but they were destructive enough, poisoning what was left of love and trust.

What hurt Sarah most of all, though, was seeing what their

172

quarreling was doing to Joey: the fearful silence that came over him the instant he heard his father's key in the door at the end of the day; his stutter, which was always worse when Jovan was home. It made Sarah want to weep every time she heard that painful, fearful groping for words.

That, if nothing else, should have forced her to make a move. She knew perfectly well that things could not go on the way they were. But still she did nothing.

"Why not?" Borden's voice was not unkind. "What held you back?"

Sarah squirmed, said nothing, looked down at her hands again.

Gran intervened. "Mr. Borden, is it really necessary for you to go into all this? Can't you see how hard this is for her?"

Sarah shook her head. "It's all right, Gran." She made a move toward the pack of cigarettes before her on the table, then changed her mind. She'd already had too many; if she had another now she would probably be sick. She made an effort to reply. "I—was afraid of the alternative."

"Which was?"

"Being alone. Admitting it was over. Admitting that I had failed."

"When did you decide you'd finally had enough?"

"Last year. Just before Christmas. When Jovan's mother came to live with us again."

Borden looked up from his notepad. He did not bother to conceal his astonishment.

"It was supposed to be temporary," Sarah rushed on, feeling suddenly defensive. She knew how it sounded: how foolishly self-destructive she must have been to have allowed that woman back into her home. Except it had made such sense at the time—or seemed to. "The thing is, we needed someone to look after Joey," she said, trying to explain. "I was going to have to start looking for a job, you see. We needed the money.

173

But there was no way I could do that until we had someone to stay with Joey."

"Why didn't you just hire a sitter?"

"I told you, we didn't have any money."

"But having your mother-in-law living with you—Wouldn't that have added to your expenses even more than a sitter?"

"Yes, I know. But—" She was getting confused. Maybe there was no way to explain. Maybe none of it made sense after all. "I don't know. It was just such a difficult time. And Jovan was so insistent."

"About his mother coming, you mean?"

She nodded. "He said it would be the best thing. He didn't want me leaving Joey with some stranger. But I think really he just wanted her to be there. Or maybe she wanted to come and he just couldn't say no. I'm not sure. But I knew that having her there would at least give me a chance to get out and start looking for a job. So finally I gave in. It seemed like a good solution."

"You sound as if you were looking forward to going to work."

"Oh, I was. I'd been thinking about it for a long time. I thought that if things with Jovan got bad enough and I had to leave him, at least I'd be able to support Joey and myself. I didn't want to have to go running home to my parents again."

"Did Jovan know you were thinking that way?"

"I don't know. He may have suspected. He certainly put up a fight every time I talked about going out and getting a job. 'A mother belongs at home,' he always said. But finally the money got so tight that we didn't have any choice. If we were going to keep eating and paying the bills I had to go out and find something."

"So having Jovan's mother there was a good opportunity for you, too."

"Yes, I guess that's true. I knew I couldn't make a move until I had a job and I couldn't look for a job until I had someone to take care of Joey."

"I see."

Borden was about to go on when Gran interrupted. "Excuse me, dear," she said, laying a hand on Sarah's arm, "but something just occurred to me. Maybe Jovan wanted his mother there as a kind of insurance policy."

"I don't understand."

"Well, Baka was really the only person he could trust to look out for his interests once you went to work, which meant guarding Joey to make sure you wouldn't run off with him. He knew that if Baka was with Joey, he could count on you always coming home again."

Sarah said nothing, only stared blankly at a spot of light reflected on the polished surface of the table. She remembered well enough how trapped she had felt once Baka began taking over again: how Baka was always there watching everything she did; how either Baka or Jovan always went with her whenever she went outside with Joey, until finally she began feeling like a prisoner in her own house, hating to stay in but hating even more to go out to look for a job because it meant leaving Joey cooped up with that sour old woman, who spoke no English and who spent her days posted like a sentry in the corner of the living room sofa, as mute and ungiving as a stone, her hands busy with their crocheting, her little black eyes busy with their own work, watching, watching. . . .

"Is that right?" Borden prompted. "Joey was their hostage even then?"

Instead of answering, Sarah told him about the day last December when she was finally driven to leave Jovan for good. She had been in the bedroom while Joey slept and was quietly talking on the telephone to her father, who was urging her to come home for a visit.

"It's been weeks since we've seen you and Joey," he was saying. "How about it, hon? Come and spend a few days. I'll come and pick you up if that's easier."

"I'd love to, Dad. So would Joey."

But Jovan had been listening on the living room extension, and suddenly he was shouting into the phone.

"Sarah stays here, damn you. You come near here, Ted, I will kill you. I have a knife here and I will use it if you make me."

"Jovan, for God's sake."

"Shut up, Sarah. Just shut up and get off the phone. And you, Ted, you listen. Stay away from here. I warn you. Stay away."

But Sarah did not hang up. Something had just snapped, and she realized with a cold certainty that she had finally reached the end, that she was not going to take any more.

"Jovan," she heard her father saying, "listen to yourself, son. You're talking crazy."

"You come near this place, goddamn it, I'll show you how crazy I get."

"Sarah," Ted shouted. "Are you there?"

"I'm here, Dad." But now Joey was up and crying beside her on the bed, clinging to her in terror at the sound of Jovan's rage, which came in loud and clear from down the hall. "Look, forget about us visiting for now, Dad," she told him, trying to end it, trying to just get it over with. She was shaking so badly that she couldn't hold the phone still. But her voice was strong and firm. She knew now what she had to do. "Okay, Dad? Just forget it. We'll be okay. Just don't worry."

"Sarah," Jovan shrieked. "I told you to get off the phone."

176

"Honey, look. Don't—"

"Dad, please. Not now."

"Mama, Mama," Joey cried.

"Goddamn you, Sarah, do what I say."

"Dad—"

"All right, honey," said Ted. "All right. I'll talk to you later."

He had no sooner hung up than Sarah heard Jovan slam down the phone in the other room and come storming down the hall toward the bedroom.

"Damn you, you bitch," he was yelling. "You go plotting behind my back with him, I'll take care of you—"

But she leaped for the door and had it slammed and locked before he got there.

Jovan was livid. He cursed and shouted and pounded on the door.

"Get away," she shouted. "Just get away."

For one terrified moment she thought he was going to break down the door. But finally he backed off.

"All right, you stay there," he bellowed. "You just fucking stay there all day. And you better not come out while I'm gone. Because if you do, Baka will be here to take care of you."

He went away then, leaving Sarah to try to comfort Joey and to quiet his hysterical crying. For a while she heard Jovan banging around in the living room and venting his rage to his mother, whose sympathetic murmurings were clearly audible in the bedroom.

At last Sarah heard Jovan go out, slamming the door behind him. He was on his way, she guessed, to his Saturday class. When she was sure he was gone, she quietly picked up the phone and dialed. Her insides hurt: for herself, for Joey, for all of them. But she was clear now. She would do what she should have done long ago.

"I'll be there as soon as I can," her father said when she asked him—coolly, calmly—to come and take her and Joey home.

"Be careful," she warned. "He may have given Baka the knife."

While Sarah waited, she got the suitcases down from the closet and packed clothes for herself and Joey. Eventually the doorbell rang. Cautiously she turned the bedroom lock.

"You stay here," she told Joey. "I'll be right back."

She stepped out into the hall. She came around the corner just in time to see Baka backing away from the front door, a hand to her mouth in fright. In her other hand, waist high, she held a long carving knife, its blade thrust before her as she backed into the living room.

And then Ted was coming through the door. In the corridor behind him stood two burly Yonkers policemen. The words *Yugoslavia* and *Police State* leaped into Sarah's mind and she realized that Baka must be terrified of the police.

"Come on, Sarah," her father said. "Let's get you and Joey out of this loony bin."

Sarah did not know whether to cry with relief or laugh with delight. "Rescued by the cavalry," she remembered thinking giddily as she hurried to collect Joey and the bags for the trip back home.

"Rescued by the cavalry," Borden repeated, grinning. "I like your dad's style."

Sarah smiled. "When he sets his mind to it, he usually gets what he goes after."

"And what about you?"

"My problem is figuring out what it is I want."

Quickly, then, she told him the rest of the story: Jovan's rage when he discovered that she had fled with Joey; her eagerness to placate him; her blind, foolish will to believe that she could still somehow make everything all right between them. They would remain separated, yes; she would never live with him again. But she didn't want him to hate her forever. Or to take some awful revenge . . .

"Is that why you went along with his having visiting rights?"

"Yes, that. And, well—"

"And what?"

"I wanted Joey to have a father. I thought maybe if the two of them had time together, just the two of them, then maybe things would be all right between them. They'd have a chance to be father and son, despite our separation. I also hoped—it was stupid but I hoped that if I let Jovan see Joey whenever he wanted, he'd be satisfied. I guess I was wrong." She paused, took a deep breath. She had been talking all morning and well into the afternoon and she was exhausted. "Can you help me, Mr. Borden? Do you think we can get Joey back?"

The question seemed to surprise him. "Why, of course we'll get him back," he said, as if there were no doubt at all in his mind. "I won't settle for anything less."

nine

"Ted, did you ever miss a treat!" exclaimed Gran the next morning when she and Sarah joined Emma at Ted's bedside at Memorial Hospital. "You should have seen that conference room! Thick carpets, beautiful furniture, paneling everywhere. Honest to God, I have never in my life seen anything like it. Like a palace it was. And the White House right there, just outside the window. It was amazing."

Ted, who was propped up on his pillows, rolled his eyes to the ceiling. "I've been in fancy offices and I've been in broom closets and believe me, it's not the office that makes a guy a prince or a bum. What I want to know is, can he do the job?"

"I think he can," Sarah said. "I liked him very much. And I got the feeling that he's probably very good at what he does."

"Good. I'm glad to hear it. What's he asking?"

Sarah took a deep breath. "A lot. Three thousand dollars as a down payment and three thousand when he gets Joey back."

Emma shook her head. "Six thousand dollars! Can you imagine!" She had heard the figure from Sarah the night before and she was still shocked.

"Plus expenses," Sarah added hesitantly.

But Ted dismissed their reservations with a wave of his hand. "Hell, do you really think I give a damn about a few thousand dollars?" All at once he raised himself off his pillow and shook a fist in the air. "I don't care what it costs. I don't care if it takes every goddamn penny and every drop of energy I've got. We're going to get Joey back and that's all there is to it."

Sarah saw tears glistening in his eyes. She had to fight hard to choke back her own.

"Ted, please," Emma said, rushing to his side. "You're getting yourself all worked up."

He allowed her to ease him back against his pillows. He closed his eyes for a moment, then reached out for Sarah's hand.

"Borden said *when* he gets Joey back?" he asked weakly. "He didn't say *if* but *when*?"

"He said *when*."

Ted nodded. "Well, then, what are you all standing around for? Get on the phone and tell the man his check is on the way."

————————————

Sarah and her mother made the arrangements that afternoon. Two days later, Bill Borden called to let them know that he was already at work on their behalf.

"I just spoke with Jack Traymore over at State," he told Sarah. "He's been very helpful. I think we've got a strong ally there. Usually it's like pulling teeth to get any cooperation from those people, but Traymore is really going to bat for you. I'm very encouraged."

"That's very nice," interrupted a third voice. It was Sarah's mother, talking over the upstairs extension phone. "I'm glad you're encouraged. But what is the man actually *doing*?"

181

"That's one of the things I'm calling about, Mrs. Novack," Borden continued, unruffled. "Traymore has heard from the American Embassy in Belgrade. The counselor officer over there is going to be sending us information about Yugoslavian legal precedents in cases like this. I've also done some checking myself regarding the possibility of extradition. Unfortunately, under the terms of America's treaty with Yugoslavia, civil cases are not subject to extradition. However, if we can prove that Jovan committed a felony, we might have a chance."

"He hasn't committed robbery or anything, if that's what you mean," said Sarah.

"No, but what about fraud? When you were down here you mentioned something about his having defaulted on a loan from the National Institutes of Health. I'd like to pursue that. I'll want whatever documentation you can send me. Even if we can't get him extradited, the loan default will certainly help your case if you end up having to take him to court in Yugoslavia. It does not reflect very well on his character."

"Is that a possibility? Going to court, I mean?"

"I'm hoping we can avoid it. Courts are too unpredictable. We'll take it to court only as a last resort."

"Well, what do we do instead?"

"We try to persuade your husband that it's in his best interest to cooperate. We let him know that if he doesn't want to play ball he faces some pretty serious consequences. Prosecution for fraud. A suit for breach of contract for violating the custody agreement he made with you. I'm sure we can come up with a few more."

"I see."

"That's why I'll need all your documents—anything relating to your separation, to Jovan's education, and to his debts."

"Yes, all right."

"I also want you to be prepared to go to Belgrade."

182

His words brought her up short. So, the time had finally come, as she knew it would.

"Why?" Sarah's mother asked. "What could she do over there?"

"Sometimes, Mrs. Novack, a surprising amount can be accomplished just by getting people to talk things out. Perhaps some compromise is possible. Joint custody, say, or some visiting arrangement that would at least allow Sarah to see her son. She could also sit down with a Yugoslavian lawyer while she's there. She's going to need someone to represent her in negotiations and in court if it comes to that. I'm asking State to suggest some names—"

Sarah had stopped listening. Her mind was in turmoil. Belgrade would mean having to face Jovan again. Him and his mother, with all their hostility, their twisted rage and envy. But it would also mean seeing Joey again! And *that* would be wonderful. To hold him, to be with him . . . Maybe even bring him home with her if the lawyers could work it out. Was it possible? Did she even dare to hope?

Sarah spoke with Borden two and three times a day, as he confirmed facts, gathered information, reported on his progress. One day he called to say that he had discovered new charges that might be brought against Jovan if he refused to cooperate. Apparently he had obtained his NIH grant under false pretenses and may have perjured himself. As a condition for obtaining the grant, he had sworn in writing that he intended to become an American citizen and to teach in the United States upon completion of his doctoral degree. "Lying under oath on a federal document might well be grounds for criminal indictment and extradition," said Borden.

A day later, he reported that the U.S. Embassy in Belgrade had sent the names of three Yugoslav lawyers; one of them, a man named Dimitri Dimitrivic, had studied law at Harvard, and came highly recommended. "I suggest we work with him," said Borden.

The day after that, Borden was on the phone again, this time with instructions for Sarah to apply for a family passport —one that would include a recent photograph of both herself and Joey. Did she have such a photograph? No? Then she should go to a camera shop and have them prepare a composite: a single photo made up of two separate photos, so that it looked as if she and Joey had posed together.

"Is that really necessary?" Sarah asked.

"If everything goes well in Belgrade and you manage to get Joey back from your husband, it will make it easier for you to get him out of the country. He won't be able to travel with you unless his name and picture appear on a valid passport."

"But what if I already have a passport for myself. Will they give me another one?"

"Tell them you lost it."

_____

"You're c-c-coming, Mama? You're really c-c-coming?"

"Yes, Joey. I'm coming to visit you and Papa."

"Just to visit?"

"I'm afraid so, Joey. I'm sorry. But we'll make it a nice long visit, okay?"

"Yes, Mama," he said, but she could hear his disappointment. "Will you b-b-bring me Lionel and F-Fritz when you c-c-come, Mama? Mr. Monkey m-m-misses them."

"I'm sure he does, Joey. And you can tell him that his friends will be coming to stay, not just visit."

Lionel and Fritz were Joey's bedtime playmates and sometime "pillowfriends"—a cuddly pair of hand puppets made out of felt. One of them was a round-faced orange lion with

184

a yellow mane and the other was a gray pussycat. This past summer, when Joey had been at home with her, the two of them would often have long talks, using the puppets to tell each other things they would otherwise have found it hard to express.

"Sarah?" It was Jovan now. "When you come, bring him warm clothes. He has not enough and it gets cold here soon."

She said she would.

"What time does your plane come? We will meet you at the airport."

"No . . . I mean, I'm not sure yet."

"When you are sure, then you will let me know."

"Yes. Yes, of course."

She hung up. What would she do? Borden had told her to sit down with the lawyer first, before seeing Jovan. She couldn't let him meet her at the airport. She'd have to find some way of putting him off.

Stevenson, Davis, Russell & McLean
Attorneys at Law
Washington Building
Washington, D.C. 20005
November 10, 1976

Mr. Dimitri Dimitrivic
Attorney
Brace Jugovic 42
Belgrade, Yugoslavia

Dear Mr. Dimitrivic:

This confirms our recent telephone conversation in which you kindly agreed to serve as Belgrade counsel for Mrs. Sarah Novack Stefanovic (hereafter "Sarah"), in relation to the matter involving her husband, Dr.

185

Jovan Stefanovic (hereafter "Jovan"), and their five-year-old son, Joseph Stefanovic (hereafter "Joey"). . . .

Sarah and her grandmother, Mrs. Helen Heilicki, plan to visit Belgrade in about two weeks. Sarah hopes that, at the least, she will be able to see her son in Belgrade. She hopes there may be some chance that Jovan will allow the child to return with her to the United States. She and her grandmother will contact you upon arrival.

Officials of both the Yugoslavian Embassy and the U.S. State Department here in Washington are familiar with this case, as are officials of the Yugoslavian Foreign Office, the Yugoslavian Interior Department, and the U.S. Embassy in Belgrade. Representatives of both governments have shown sympathetic concern for the situation of this family, the plight of the young son, and the distress of the mother. I am confident that you will find a desire on the part of officials of both governments to cooperate with you and to contribute toward a humane solution which is in the best interests of the child and which affords both parents reasonable access to the child.

As our mutual client, Sarah, and I and members of her immediate family have discussed the problem, we trust that you will play a leading part in the endeavor to communicate with Jovan and to arrive at an understanding with him whereby the child spends part time with one parent and part time with the other parent—benefiting alternately from each of the parents, the countries, the languages, and the heritages involved. . . .

During her visit to Belgrade, Sarah will be most interested in learning, as you get into the problem, your assessment of the prospects for a solution through negotiation and, should that endeavor fail, the prospects for a solution reasonably satisfactory to her through litigation in Yugoslavia. . . .

There are two principal attachments to the present letter. One is a three-page summary of the facts of the case prepared by Sarah's father, Mr. Edward Novack. The other is an extensive Memorandum dealing with possible methods of influencing Jovan, prepared by me. This Memorandum sets out additional facts as well as legal considerations which I hope you will find to be helpful.

Other attachments to the present letter include copy of the consent decree of the New Jersey court concerning custody of Joey; copy of a New Jersey bench warrant for Jovan's arrest; copy of a communication to Sarah's parents from the law firm which represented her in the New Jersey proceedings; and copy of Joey's birth certificate.

Also attached are copies of letters of a Senator and a Representative of the U.S. Congress in response to appeals sent them. . . .

Sarah and her family look forward to working with you, as do I. With kind regards, I am

Very truly yours,
William L. Borden

Memorandum
Re: Possible methods of influencing the father, Jovan, toward sharing custody of the child, Joey, with the mother, Sarah.

1. *Sarah's willingness to share the child with Jovan.*
Sarah does not seek to monopolize her son if she

can negotiate a sharing of custody with Jovan. She recognizes that, when parents have separated, their child should have periodic access to each.

Sarah understands that she and Jovan represent two different heritages, and she wants Joey to benefit from both. . . . All questions of sharing custody are open to negotiation and reason . . . so far as Sarah is concerned. She fears, however, that Jovan will reject negotiation and reason. . . .

2. The alternative to negotiation and reason for Jovan.

If Jovan refuses to be reasonable, and if he therefore compels Sarah to seek relief in a Yugoslavian court, he may suffer loss of all rights of access to his son.

It is believed that, if the rules of evidence in a Yugoslavian court permit, the following could be proven:

(a) Jovan obtained student loans guaranteed by the Higher Education Services Corporation of the State of New York. The amount which Jovan owes on these loans is $13,886.

(b) Jovan also owes about $3,800 in student loans made to him by New York University, where he studied for his Ph.D. degree in Chemistry.

(c) Additionally, Jovan obtained Federal student training grants which assisted him over a period of 46 months. . . . Altogether the Federal grants added up to an estimated $25,000. The source of these funds was the U.S. Department of Health, Education and Welfare, acting through its National Institutes of Health. . . .

(d) While married to Sarah, Jovan lived mainly on largesse from her family totaling more than $10,000, on a total of some $17,686 in loans which are unpaid, on the estimated $25,000 in grants financed by the U.S. Treasury, and on unemployment compensation from the State of New York.

(e) Jovan, while driving an automobile registered in Sarah's name, was given numerous tickets for illegal parking by the New York City police. He now owes an estimated $5000 in fines to the City of New York.

(f) The New Jersey social worker who counseled Jovan and Sarah at the time when they were attempting to salvage their marriage believes that Jovan shows evidence of psychopathic tendencies.

(g) The order of the New Jersey court granting custody of Joey to Sarah and visitation rights to Jovan is based upon the consent of both parties. He had sued for certain visitation rights, and he obtained the rights he demanded. In taking the child to Yugoslavia, Jovan violated a court order which was not issued over his protest but which corresponded with his prayer.

(h) The New Jersey court has issued a warrant for Jovan's arrest, since he disobeyed the court's order and is therefore in contempt of court. . . .

(i) Jovan has not shown a willingness or a capability toward supporting the child.

(j) Sarah has an advanced degree in education and would be teaching now except for distress at the loss of her son. She is financially responsible and able to support Joey, if necessary, without any help from Jovan. Her record and character are unblemished.

In addition to the foregoing statements of fact which are believed to be provable, it is thought likely that a Yugoslavian court would accord great weight to the decree of the New Jersey court—not only for broad reasons of comity but also because the New Jersey court decree is identical with Jovan's own request.

It is believed, in any event, that the conscience of the Yugoslavian court would be shocked by the cruelty of Jovan's action in removing a five-year-old boy from his mother. . . .

3. Jovan's other incentives to be reasonable.

If court proceedings take place in Yugoslavia, Jovan will himself require legal counsel; and this means expense for him. . . .

Presumably Jovan is interested in pursuing his professional career in chemistry. His two principal professors at New York University have advised the undersigned . . . that Jovan had often spoken to them about his thoughts of further studies either in the United States, the United Kingdom, or France. . . . Anyone considering Jovan for further studies or for a job in chemistry would check [his] references. . . . These . . . will likely produce vivid expressions of concern about Jovan's character, so long as Jovan mistreats his son by cutting off mother-son relationships. . . .

Jovan can solve all such problems, simply by sharing his son with the child's mother. In this way he can move to regain the respect of others, obtain a position in his chosen field . . ., clear his debts and his record, and realize the rewards of long years of study.

It is hoped that Yugoslavian counsel for Sarah can help convey to Jovan an awareness of the incentive he has to be reasonable toward her and their son and thereby to change his own life for the better.

4. Possible civil and criminal sanctions against Jovan.

Because the decree of the New Jersey court gave Jovan precisely what he had gone into court to demand, with Sarah's consent, the decree of the court amounts to a contract between the two parties.

It is suggested that Belgrade counsel for Sarah consider whether, under Yugoslavian law, Jovan is liable to Sarah for damages on a breach-of-contract or other legal theory. The damages might include reimbursement of Sarah for her legal and travel costs, compensation to her for the suffering she has undergone, and exemplary or punitive damages to deter other persons from behaving as Jovan has behaved.

The Higher Education Services Corporation of the State of New York advised the undersigned that, if Jovan's student loans are determined to be in default . . . it will turn the matter over to U.S. counsel, who in turn may be expected to turn the matter over to a Yugoslavian attorney for purposes of bringing civil suit against Jovan in Yugoslavia for collection of the debt.

The text of the agreement between the U.S. National Institutes of Health and New York University, and the text of an agreement known to exist between New York University and Jovan, pertaining to the estimated $25,000 in grants bestowed upon him from U.S. Treasury funds, have not yet been obtained by the undersigned. [However,] it is expected that the papers will show that Jovan made certain formal representations to New York

University concerning his allegiance to the United States and concerning a commitment to teach for a period of time in the United States after completing requirements for his doctoral degree.

The undersigned has reason to suspect that Jovan's formal representations to New York University involve false pretenses to obtain money and/or perjury. If review of the papers tends to confirm such a suspicion, and if other measures to assist Sarah have failed, it is anticipated that the matter of these representations would be brought to the attention of the U.S. Department of Justice. If a criminal indictment of false pretenses and/or perjury were to ensue, it is anticipated that the U.S. Department of Justice would request the U.S. Secretary of State to institute extradition proceedings against Jovan under the extradition treaty between Yugoslavia and the United States. Article II of that treaty specifically lists both false pretenses and perjury as a basis for extradition. . . .

In the discretion of Belgrade counsel for Sarah, allusion to possible civil and criminal sanctions may be made in talks with Jovan as part of the endeavor to persuade him to accept negotiation and reason in relation to sharing custody of Joey.

6. Other measures.

No mother in the situation of Sarah can rest until she is reunited with her son. It is believed that, if forced, Sarah could appeal to numerous and diverse sources of potential sympathy for and support of her cause. Should she undertake such an effort, she has prospect of stirring the response of many people, in high places and low, in Yugoslavia and the United States.

The result would be growing pressure upon Jovan. In the end, it is believed, his only hope of continuing to separate child from mother would consist in his devoting essentially his entire energies to this atrocious purpose. Even his entire energies would seem likely to fail in keeping child and mother apart.

It is therefore hoped that Belgrade counsel for Sarah may help convey to Jovan some sense of the untenability of his position and of the likelihood that, resist as he may, child and mother are going to be reunited. . . .

7. Conclusion

It is believed that, in final analysis, Jovan has two and only two choices. He may dedicate his life to separating a small child from the child's mother; or else he may share custody of the child with the child's mother and be free to pursue a useful, respected, and remunerative career.

The assistance of Belgrade counsel for Sarah in helping Jovan to make the only sane election between these two alternatives will invoke the gratitude of the mother and of the child—and in time, the undersigned is certain, of the father himself.

November 10, 1976   William L. Borden

"Do you have everything, kitten? Passports? Traveler's checks?"

"Yes, Dad. We're fine. Everything's all set."

She took his hand and held it. He had improved a great deal

during the last two weeks. He was sitting in a chair now instead of propped up in bed, and the doctor thought he would probably be going home in another four or five days. But being so inactive was hard on him. Now, on this afternoon of her departure for Belgrade, Sarah knew he wished he were going with her.

"She's a sharp one, this girl," Gran said, smiling at Sarah affectionately. "She'll be all right."

"With your help, Gran," Sarah said. Once again Gran had offered to come along and keep her company and Sarah was grateful.

"Now, don't be silly, Sarah," Gran said. "We all know perfectly well that you'd do fine on your own; I'm just going along for the holiday. Instead of Florida this year I get to visit Yugoslavia. Who knows when I'll get another chance like this? Besides," she said, winking slyly, "I might just find one of those continental charmers for myself."

Sarah grimaced. "God forbid! One in the family was quite enough."

The jokes and banter, Sarah realized, were a reflection of the nervousness they were all feeling.

Unable to bear it any longer, she got to her feet. "It's late, Dad. We should be getting ready to go. Any last-minute instructions?"

"No. I think you'll do just fine, hon. Like Gran says." Reaching out a hand, he pulled her to him and kissed her cheek. "Good luck. Say hello to Joey for me."

"I hope you'll be saying hello to him yourself when we get back," she said.

He squeezed her hand and smiled faintly. "I hope so, too."

ten

"The name Beograde means 'white town.' Did you know that?" Gran asked without lifting her eyes from the guidebook. "And listen to this: 'The first fortified town was built there by the Celts in the fourth century B.C.' Imagine that: a city that's almost as old as I am!"

For Gran, the trip to Belgrade had been like a holiday right from the minute their plane took off from Kennedy. Having never been to Europe before, she had been enjoying herself immensely, chatting happily with the stewardesses and the other passengers, gobbling macadamia nuts by the fistful, even treating herself to an extra glass of wine with dinner. And now that they were only an hour away from landing, she was getting giddy with excitement as she avidly shared her guidebook revelations with Sarah.

Far from being annoyed, Sarah was grateful for the distraction. Without it, there would have been no escaping the anxiety she was feeling about what lay ahead.

" '. . . occupied by the Romans in the first century B.C.,' " Gran went on. " '. . . destroyed by the Huns . . . captured by the Turks . . . repeatedly burned and sacked . . .' My God, what a history! Can you believe it! '. . . Serbian rule since 1867 . . . bombed by the Nazis in 1941 . . . risen phoenixlike from the ashes to become the modern European city we see today. . . .' "

The city they saw when they were finally on the ground and speeding by bus toward their hotel was a city whose streets and buildings were blurred by a cold November drizzle. The trees lining the broad avenues were bare of leaves. In the gray light the rows of modern office blocks and highrise apartments looked more desolate than Sarah remembered from the first time she had been here. But of course it had been summer then. The sun was out, the trees were green, and the flowers were in bloom on the boulevards.

Nine years ago that was. She and Jovan had just been married and he had brought her to Belgrade to visit his mother and to see his homeland. It was their honeymoon trip, and Sarah had helped pay for it by cashing in the Paris-to-New York airline ticket her father had surreptitiously slipped into her hand on her wedding day. What better way to spend that money than to offer it to Jovan as her gesture of faith in him, as her way of letting him know—and letting herself know, too —that he was her future now and there would be no turning back. Indeed, in her own heart she had been secretly relieved to be rid of that ticket, for otherwise she might have been tempted to use it—to go running home and never find out what kind of life she might have had with this passionate dreamer whose wife she had just become.

No, she hadn't regretted her decision. Not for a minute. Not then. Because Belgrade had been so beautiful that summer and she had been very much in love.

Now, nine years later, in cold November, hardly anything looked the same.

———————

The Metropol, the hotel that she and Gran checked into, was described in the guidebook as the "smartest" in Belgrade. It was also said to have one of the best restaurants of any hotel in the city. Both recommendations had been enough for Gran. Although Sarah would have been perfectly willing to stay somewhere less fancy—and less expensive—Gran had insisted on nothing but the best.

"Listen," she had said, laying a hand on Sarah's arm, her many-jeweled rings glittering on her fingers. "Listen, when you're as old as I am, you don't want to take chances. You want good food and clean bathrooms. If it costs a little more, you pay the difference."

In actuality, it meant that Sarah's father would be paying the difference, since he had made it clear from the start that he and he alone would be picking up the tab for the trip: "And I don't want to hear any arguments about it."

Gran had berated him for being a stuffy old tyrant, "a regular Attila." But she had taken him at his word and now here they were, checking into the "smartest" hotel in Belgrade: an impersonal white stone block that looked more like an office building than a hotel. The lobby was all polished marble, sleekly elegant and cold as ice. But the clerks were friendly enough, and as she and Gran followed the bellboy to the elevator—Gran veering along on unsteady legs and too-small shoes—Sarah decided that maybe a little luxury was a good idea. It might just make it easier for her to get through these next few days.

"Awful weather out there," said a tall man who joined them in the elevator just as the doors were closing.

"Terrible," Gran agreed. "And to think I gave up Florida for this!"

The man smiled. "Enjoy it. It'll get worse tomorrow. Belgrade always does."

Gran chuckled appreciatively. Sarah glanced at the man

197

out of the corner of her eye. He wore a dripping raincoat and blue-tinted aviator glasses and he was remarkably well tanned considering the time of year. Something about the way he was dressed made him look English, but his accent and his casual manner were obviously American.

"Just arrived, I see." He looked expectantly at Sarah but she only nodded quickly and turned to watch the floor numbers lighting up over the door. Unlike Gran, *she* was not here on a pleasure trip. She had no interest whatever in striking up a conversation with any homesick American businessmen.

The elevator stopped at the fifth floor.

"Well, here's where I get off," the man said cheerfully. "See you again."

"What a nice man," Gran said after the doors had closed behind him. "And how nice to meet another American so soon. A good-looking one, too, with all that blond hair and that tan of his. I bet he's from California. Everybody's blond and tan out there. It's a law. They won't let you in otherwise."

But Sarah was not listening. She was thinking of Joey. He was somewhere very close now. Just a few miles from where she stood.

Their room was on the seventh floor: double beds, a desk and an easy chair, a window overlooking the Tasmajdan park and, beyond, the city center.

As soon as she and Gran were settled, Sarah picked up the telephone and called Baka's number. Jovan answered.

"Sarah, where are you? You sound so close."

"I am. I'm in Belgrade. At the Metropol."

"You are here? How does this happen? We are not expecting you until tomorrow. We were going to meet you at the airport."

"I— We had to change our plans at the last minute." It sounded so lame. She had to think of something else. And quickly. "The airlines. There was a mix-up with the airlines."

Silence. Did he believe her? She had never been a good liar. She rushed on. "I'm sorry, there was no time to call. But I'm here now. That's what's important. Can I come over later? I'd like to see Joey."

"Why later? Why not now?"

"I— It's four in the morning for us. We're still on New York time. I have to get some sleep or I'll fall over." What she could not tell him was that she also had to follow Bill Borden's instructions: she had to see the lawyer first. "I'll come this evening. About five."

There was a long pause. Sarah could hear muffled voices. He must be consulting with Baka. Finally he came back on the line: "Yes. Good. Come at five. You know how to come?"

"I have the address. I'll take a taxi."

Dimitri Dimitrivic was a small, elegant man in a crisp white shirt and a blue silk tie; his hair was combed flat and straight back. His English was only slightly accented, but he spoke so softly that even here in the quiet of his small, carpeted office, Sarah and Gran found themselves leaning forward in their chairs to catch his words. Was it just a quirk of his? Sarah wondered. Or was he afraid of being overheard? And if so, by whom?

"Your Mr. William Borden has done a magnificent piece of work here," he told them, his voice hardly more than a whisper. In his hand he held the memorandum that Borden had sent. "This that he wrote, it is something very beautiful, very moving. However, I am afraid, ah—"

"Yes?" Sarah asked. She did not like the note of reservation she was hearing.

"Mrs. Stefanovic, permit me please to be candid with you. If you were a Yugoslav woman, you would have no difficulty in getting back your son. Your claim appears to be a strong one. But—" he held up the letter—"these arguments that your Mr. Borden puts forward, they will have no effect here. What the judges will see when they look at you is an American woman who wants to take a Yugoslav child, a male child, out of Yugoslavia. And that—" he spread his hands in a gesture of hopelessness, leaving the rest unsaid.

"But my son is not a Yugoslav citizen," Sarah said. "He was born in America. He spent all of his life in American until two months ago."

"Yes, yes, I understand. But the boy is here now, living with his father. And that makes him—"

"Yugoslav," Sarah said, finishing his sentence.

He nodded. "Precisely," he whispered.

"But that's outrageous," said Gran, her voice sounding even more stentorian than usual compared to the lawyer's whispers. "An American court granted Sarah custody. She has the documents. She can prove it."

Dimitrivic shook his head wearily. "Your husband, Mrs. Stefanovic, he has documents as well. A certificate, for instance, showing that your son was registered at birth as a Yugoslav citizen."

"That's true," said Sarah. She remembered only too well the scene in the hospital when Joey was born. "But that was only a formality, a ritual. It didn't mean anything." She stopped, hearing the emptiness of her own argument.

"Mrs. Stefanovic, you must understand, there are many people in this country who mistrust America. They are hostile to everything America stands for. Not everyone, but many. Certainly the people who count, who make the decisions. Citing the ruling of an American court, this will not help you here."

"Are you telling me there is nothing I can do to get my son back?"

"I am saying that as far as the courts and government agencies are concerned you can expect very little in the way of—" Again his voice fell away to nothing.

"Assistance?"

"Probably none at all. I am sorry. But as your attorney it is my duty to speak realistically. I have seen too many such cases. Just a few months ago was one. A young woman came here from Scandinavia, from Sweden I believe, on a mission very much like your own. She too was trying to get her child back from her estranged husband. Unfortunately she was not very—what shall I say?—circumspect in her approach. She alerted the foreign ministry of her intentions. When she arrived at the airport with her lawyers, the authorities would not permit them even to enter the country. Officially, you see, she had no—"

"Recourse?"

Again the nod.

Sarah slumped in her chair. "You're telling me there is no hope then?"

Dimitrivic smiled and shook his head. "I am saying no such thing. You are here, inside the country. Already you have an advantage over the other woman." He got to his feet and came around his desk. "Mrs. Stefanovic"— his eyes were kind; so was his voice— "go to your husband. Have your visit with your son. See how things are with them. After that, we will have a better idea of how to—"

"Proceed."

"Yes, exactly so."

The light was already fading and most of the cars had their headlights on as Sarah's taxi sped down the Boulevard Revolucije. The day's rain had stopped but in the deepening

201

twilight the air seemed colder than ever and the taxi's heater did not seem to be working. Sarah pulled her coat collar tight around her throat.

She had come alone. Gran was still feeling the effects of jet lag and had gone back to bed, which was fine with Sarah. This reunion was going to be difficult enough without having Gran along to complicate matters.

On the seat beside her lay the package Sarah had promised to bring: Joey's two hand puppets and a new winter coat. She had more clothes for him back at the hotel, as well as toys and some children's books; but at Gran's suggestion she was saving those for later. "You might need them to buy your way back for another visit," Gran had warned, and she was probably right.

Not until the taxi turned off the boulevard and up a broad tree-lined street did Sarah begin to recognize where she was: Embassy Row. On either side, set well back behind high walls and hedges, were the great mansions that had once been the homes of Serbian aristocrats and were now the headquarters of foreign governments. And not far away, Sarah knew, was the official residence of President Tito. Uniformed sentries with machine guns slung over their shoulders were posted at the gates of the various embassies and at regular intervals along the street. Farther up, toward Tito's palace, the number of sentries increased.

"It is not the usual Belgrade neighborhood," Jovan had told her dryly the first time he brought her here. And indeed that aspect of it had not changed.

The taxi driver took a turn and they were in the narrow cul-de-sac that backed on the woods behind the presidential palace. Alongside a low wooden fence the driver brought the taxi to a halt. Sarah's heart began pounding. Just beyond the fence was Baka's home; the place where Joey had been living for the past ten weeks; the place where she was now about to see him again for the first time since Jovan had stolen him away.

The house looked the way Sarah remembered it from her last visit: a rustic stone cottage set amid lawns, shrubs, and flower beds. An eighteenth-century relic, the cottage had been wrangled for Baka by a relative who had connections in the government; it came to her free, as part of her war-widow's pension. Although the amenities were primitive—an outhouse in the back and a pump down the road, from which water had to be carried by hand—the setting was gorgeous, especially in the summertime, when it was like living in the middle of a private park.

But for Sarah, none of that mattered now. The only thing on her mind was one small boy—and the uncertain reception that awaited her inside.

She opened her purse. Her hands were shaking. When she went to pay the driver she missed his palm and the money spilled onto the seat beside him.

"Oh, I'm so sorry. I—"

"All right, missus. Is okay. Go. Go."

She picked up the package off the seat and got out. The taxi did a U-turn and drove away, leaving her standing alone in front of the gate. She took a deep breath and pushed it open. The gate squeaked on its hinges. At the sound, the door of the cottage flew open.

And there stood Joey, wide-eyed, with Baka looming in the doorway behind him. Joey: in old jeans and sneakers and a dirty sweater—taller and slimmer than she remembered, but her boy! Her Joey! With his tawny hair and his little snub nose.

"Joey," she said. "Oh, Joey."

Stooping down, she opened her arms to him.

But stopped.

Because something odd was happening. Instead of running to her, he was just standing there, watching her.

"Joey! Lovey! What's wrong?"

What she saw next chilled her to her very core: Joey glancing back at Baka and asking her, in her own language, "May I?" Asking Baka if he could go to his own mother!

With a smile of triumph that was like a knife in Sarah's heart, the old woman nodded. *"Idi naprijed. Idi svojoj mami,"* she said. "Go ahead. Go to your mother."

And stolidly Joey came to her: not running up the path, not flying into her arms, but moving robotlike, almost dutifully, as Sarah, shocked and bewildered, thought, My God, what have they done to you, my beautiful boy?

But then he was in her arms and she was pressing him to her as she was weeping and saying his name: "Joey, oh Joey. I'm here. I've come to you, just like I said I would."

And then at last she felt him respond, his arms tightening around her neck as he hugged her and whispered the single word that sang like the most exquisite music in her ear: "Mama, Mama."

Baka was beside them now, tugging impatiently at Joey's arm. "Come inside, come inside. Do not keep him out here in the cold. Already he is coughing. Do you want to make it worse?"

Only then, rising to her feet, did Sarah see Jovan. He was leaning against the doorframe, arms folded across his chest, head tilted arrogantly to one side.

"Well, well," he said, "look who's here."

The first thing Sarah noticed when she got inside were the drapes that adorned the sitting-room windows. They were the ones she had made for the apartment in Yonkers just after she and Jovan had moved in.

The next thing she discovered was that she would have no chance whatever to be alone with Joey. The cottage was tiny, consisting of a low-ceilinged sitting room, a kitchen on the other side of the fireplace, and a sleeping loft upstairs, under the eaves. Unless she took Joey up there, the two of them would have no privacy. The most she was able to manage was to hold Joey on her lap while she sat huddled in a chair before the warmth of the coal fire that smouldered in the grate. While Baka bustled around in the kitchen making coffee, Jovan sat perched on the edge of a chair, prodding her with questions about what she had been up to since her arrival in Belgrade.

"Up to?" she echoed. "I told you on the phone: we just got in this morning. When we got to the hotel, we went right to bed."

Avoiding Jovan's eyes, she busied herself with fussing over Joey. Setting him down in front of her, she held him at arm's length. "Let me look at you. Oh, you look so tall. I kept thinking of you as my little baby but I forgot how big you are. You're not a baby anymore. You're a big boy now, aren't you?" Lightly, lightly. "And look at your haircut. You just had a new haircut, didn't you?" It looked horrendous. As if someone had put a bowl over his head. All of his wonderful curls were gone, just as she'd feared.

"Baka cut it for me," he said flatly in Serbo-Croatian.

"Oh?" she said in surprise. "And you're learning the language, too. I'm impressed."

He beamed proudly. "I'm a Partisan now," he said. "Just like Grampa Stefan was."

"So I see."

She was forcing herself to be as cheerful as possible, but her heart was coming apart. So soon they had turned him into one of them! So soon. And if they had him longer? What would he be like then?

But it wasn't just the language that troubled her, nor the shock when she realized that she had forgotten how big he was. He *was* bigger than she'd remembered but he was also thinner than he had been two months ago. A lot thinner. He did not look well, and it was not just the haircut that made him look that way. He was pale and he seemed to have no energy at all, no light in his eyes. And his hacking cough came from deep inside his chest. Baka had been right to pull him in out of the cold. Yet the cottage itself was cold and drafty just a few feet from the fire.

"That doesn't sound good," she said after another coughing spell. "How long has he had this cold?" she asked Jovan.

He let out a snort of derision. "You mean you care?"

For a moment Sarah was too stunned to do anything but gape at him. "Jovan, how can you say that? *Of course* I care."

And then it struck her: had Jovan put the same thought into Joey's head? Was that what Joey thought too: that she didn't care? Was that why he had hesitated at the door? She hugged Joey to her. "I love my Joey. How could I not care?"

"Well, I'm surprised to hear it," Jovan taunted. "If you did care you would have come to see him long ago, not waited all this time. Over two months it's been."

"Jovan, my father has been sick. I told you that on the phone. I—"

But Baka cut her off. "Here, here is coffee. Drink. Warm yourself."

Sarah took the cup, then watched dumbfounded as Baka handed a cup to Joey, too. She was even more surprised when Joey sipped it without making a face. Apparently they had gotten him used to the stuff.

"What did you bring?" Jovan asked her.

"Bring?"

He nodded toward the package.

206

"Oh, I almost forgot." She was annoyed, feeling flustered and off balance. It was the way she usually felt around Baka —as if she could do nothing right. "I brought a few things for Joey. Here, Joey, you open it."

He did not wait for her to ask twice. Eyes wide, he tore eagerly into the paper bag. On top, he found the coat. It was of warm goose down, with a hood and nice deep pockets. Joey held it up without enthusiasm.

But then he looked again into the bag and saw what was at the bottom: his cuddly puppet friends, Lionel and Fritz.

"Oh," Joey said softly, holding them to his chest. "You remembered, Mama. You d-d-did remember."

The radiant look on his face filled her heart. At last she had done the right thing for him. And perhaps, if she was lucky, it had redeemed her a little in his eyes. Perhaps it had made up somewhat for all the lost weeks.

"Say thank you," Baka coached in Serbian.

"*Hvala vam, Mami.*"

Sarah shot the old woman a hateful glance. Baka turned away, a thin smile on her lips.

"You don't have to thank me, Joey," Sarah told him. "I brought you your friends because I love you and care about you more than anything else in the world. I have some other things for you, too. I'll bring them next time."

"You should have sent him earlier this coat, or sent us money to buy one. Then he would not have this cough of his."

"I? You're blaming me for the way he looks? When you told me he needed something I always sent it, didn't I?"

"It has not been enough," Baka hissed at her in broken English, before switching back to Serbian. "We cannot buy such things ourselves. We are not rich in our country like you Americans."

The remark was meant to be snide, but it was also obviously

a painful understatement of their situation. Aside from the drapes on the windows—*her* drapes—the place looked shabby and run down. Sarah did not have to ask whether Jovan had found a job. She knew from their phone calls that he had not. How they were managing to live she had no idea; it was not the time to ask. But it was clear that they were living very poorly indeed.

"How about a walk, Joey?" she asked him. "Shall we take a walk together? You can wear your new coat and you can tell me all about what you've been doing."

She thought she saw Joey's eyes brighten for a moment. But then, as if checking himself, he turned to his Baka. "May I?" he asked.

"Only a short time. It is cold outside."

Sarah was elated. At last she would have a few moments alone with him. But then Jovan dashed her hopes. "I'll come too," he said, moving to get his coat. "I can use some exercise."

With Joey between them, the hood of his coat buttoned tight around his head, the three of them walked hand in hand past the walled gardens, past the sentries standing guard outside the baroque stone palaces of Embassy Row.

"Just like old times, eh, Joey? You and me and Mama walking together?"

Joey looked up at Sarah uncertainly, then at his father.

"It is, Sarah, isn't it?" pressed Jovan, grinning. "Just like old times?"

"Yes," she said. "Just like old times."

She squeezed Joey's hand to reassure him and at last he smiled back at her.

And all the while Jovan hung onto Joey's hand. Not letting go. Not even for a minute.

———————

She left the cottage that night feeling trapped and depressed and angry.

"I've got to get my son out of there," she told the lawyer the next day. "As soon as possible. The way he's living, it's awful."

"Was it as bad as that?"

"Worse. The place was cold and damp. Joey looks terrible and he coughs all the time. Please tell me what I can do, Mr. Dimitrivic."

Gran leaned forward in her chair. "The last time we saw you, you mentioned the case of a Swedish woman. You said that *officially* she had no recourse. What did you mean by that?"

Dimitrivic gave a little shrug. He spoke very quietly. "There are perhaps unofficial ways."

"Such as?"

Dimitrivic picked up a pencil, turned it over in his hands. His voice fell to a whisper. "The young woman might have gone back to her husband. Long enough at least to reinstate the marriage and establish her residency in Yugoslavia. Then, after a certain length of time, she could have taken her husband to court and sued for divorce and custody, as one resident suing another."

"What length of time?" Sarah asked tentatively.

"Long enough to convince the court that she had no intention of taking her child out of the country. A year, perhaps. Two years."

Sarah flinched. Living with Jovan that long would be unbearable.

"And then of course," he continued, "it would take more time for the case to go through the courts. As in your country, the judicial system in Yugoslavia tends to be very—"

Sarah shook her head. "I just don't see how I—I mean, how that woman could do that, go back to living with her husband again for that long. Pretending to be happy. Living a lie. I don't see how she could ever do that."

Dimitrivic nodded sympathetically. "I understand. It would certainly be difficult. Very difficult. However, if she wanted her child back badly enough—"

But Sarah had heard enough. She rose from her chair. "Thank you for your help, Mr. Dimitrivic. I will think about what you have said."

"Please do." He got up to escort her and Gran to the door. "And may I ask what your plans are in the meantime?"

"I don't know," Sarah said. "I'll need some time to think."

But she had already decided what she was going to do next.

The two marines posted inside the lobby of the United States embassy looked very young and very serious. There wasn't a wrinkle in their dark blue jackets or in their light blue slacks. There was not a scuff on their gleaming black shoes. Somehow it was reassuring to see them there, as it had been to see the Stars and Stripes flying from the flagpole out front.

Sarah and Gran introduced themselves to the receptionist, at the front desk. The man they had come to see was the chief of the consular section, Fletcher Wethering, to whom Sarah had been referred by the State Department.

The receptionist punched the buttons on her telephone console. A few minutes later, Sarah and Gran were led to a small office on the second floor, where they were greeted by a young man who was so lean, his face so pinched and narrow, that he looked as if he had been pressed by the same iron that had creased the trousers of the marines in the lobby. He was very businesslike. He did not smile as he offered them chairs facing his desk.

There were no papers on the desk, no stray pencils, only a blank legal pad and a single, slim manila folder.

Another desk, another file, Sarah thought wearily.

Once more she heard herself going through the introductory pleasantries. Once more she heard in return the same protestations of helplessness.

"I wish there was something we could do," Wethering said blandly, his pale blue eyes focused somewhere over Sarah's head. "But I'm afraid since the boy is the child of a Yugoslav citizen his father is protected by Yugoslav law." He folded his hands on the desk top. His fingernails gleamed.

"Our lawyer told us the same thing," Sarah said. "But my son is also the child of an *American* citizen. Why isn't he protected by *American* law?"

"In America, he would be. But possession is still nine-tenths of the law, and your son is currently in his father's possession."

"Mr. Wethering, I'd like to know just whose side you're on. You sound like you're working for Yugoslavia instead of America."

Her anger left him unfazed. "We are here to protect American interests and to abide by the local laws and customs," he replied coolly.

Gran interrupted. "And do the local laws require that you lie to American citizens?" she asked.

The man's eyes flickered ever so slightly. Even Sarah was startled by Gran's question.

"I am afraid I don't understand," Wethering said, eyeing Gran cautiously, as if waiting for a trap to spring shut.

"My granddaughter was told by officials of the State Department that someone from this embassy had checked on her son," Gran declared. "She was assured that the boy was in good health and being well treated. Well, he's not in good health, Mr. Wethering, and he's not being treated well at all. Sarah saw him yesterday with her own two eyes and it was as clear as the nose on your face. The child is sick and he's weak and he looks like he hasn't had a decent meal ever since his father brought him to this miserable place."

When Wethering spoke again there was a steely edge on his voice. "Mrs. Heilicki," he said, "I am profoundly sorry to hear that the boy is not well, but I can tell you for a certainty that there was never any intention on our part to deceive anyone regarding his welfare. The reports we give to parents in situations such as this are based on the best information we are able to obtain under the circumstances. Besides, if I remember correctly, that report was given to us at least two weeks ago."

He began leafing through the folder on his desk, turning the pages with the tips of his fingers as if he were afraid of dirtying his hands. "Yes, here it is. This is dated October eighteenth. That's *three* weeks ago." His eyes slid up to meet Gran's. "Children do get sick, Mrs. Heilicki."

Gran straightened in her chair. "Young man," she said regally, her chin held high, "in case you haven't noticed, my granddaughter is a mother and I am a mother and between the two of us we know more about children in our little fingers than you will ever know in your whole body."

Wethering blinked. He looked at Gran sideways. For the first time he seemed at a loss for words. "Be . . . that . . . as it may," he began, recovering. "I assure you that we make every effort to do all we can with the resources we have at hand." He turned to Sarah. "As I am sure you can appreciate, Mrs. Stefanovic, we cannot keep a daily watch on every American in Yugoslavia."

"I'm not interested in every American in Yugoslavia," she shot back, emboldened by Gran's contentiousness. "I'm only interested in one small boy. And if you're asking me to be sweet and reasonable about that, I'm sorry but I can't. My son is the most important person in the world to me. And what I want to know is what my government is going to do to help me get him back."

The lids slid down over Wethering's eyes. "What we can offer you, Mrs. Stefanovic, is legal advice."

"Yes, I know about legal advice. You've already done that. And so far Mr. Dimitrivic hasn't been any more helpful than you have."

Wethering shifted in his seat. This conversation was obviously beginning to make him uncomfortable. "If legal recourse proves ineffective," he continued, straining to sound patient, "we can try to intercede on your behalf with the Yugoslav government. But beyond that—"

"Beyond that, Mr. Wethering?"

He smiled an icy, thin-lipped smile. "Mrs. Stefanovic, we're not about to go to war over this."

Every afternoon now, Sarah went to the cottage to see Joey. Always she brought along a gift: a sweater; a pair of corduroy pants; a soccer ball. The storybooks she took him were all in English. With a little luck, they and the other gifts might just help her to counter some of the influence that Jovan and his mother had already had on him, might help her to win back a little of what she had lost.

Now and then, to be on the safe side, she also brought things for Jovan and Baka. Bribes. It was as crude as that.

If Jovan or Baka suspected her motives, however, they gave no indication of it. On the contrary, they seemed quite content to let her provide whatever she wished toward their upkeep. And why not? They were hardly able to provide for themselves, let alone having to worry about feeding and clothing a third member of their pathetic little household.

"It is very bad for them," Jovan's sister Myra told Sarah one Sunday afternoon, while the two of them were cleaning up the dinner dishes in Myra's apartment. "When Jovan appeared here all of a sudden, we did not know what had happened. He had his son with him but no wife, no job, nothing." She gulped down the leftover wine from somebody's glass, then plunged the empty glass into the soapy dishwater. "It was so sad," she said. "He was like a little lost puppy."

Myra was round-faced and chunky like her mother, with the same broad cheekbones and almond-shaped eyes that Jovan had. She worked as a secretary at a printing company and lived with her husband Branko in this small apartment in the city's western suburbs. Three days ago she had telephoned Sarah at the Metropol to invite her and Gran for this Sunday afternoon get-together. Baka, Jovan, Joey—everyone would be there.

"It will be a real family reunion," Myra told her excitedly. "Please come, Sarah. It is so long since I have seen you and we used to have such good talks together. I remember them still. We were like sisters."

It was true. On Sarah's first trip to Belgrade the two of them had spent hours chattering away in French while sitting in the sun outside Baka's cottage. They had gone on shopping trips together, and one afternoon Myra had even taught her how to crochet.

It was with memories of that summer in mind that Sarah had consented to this Sunday afternoon visit. Maybe—just maybe—Myra might turn out to be the ally she needed: someone Jovan trusted; someone who could do what no one else seemed to be willing or able to do—persuade him to give Joey back.

Welcoming Sarah and Gran at the door, Myra had been as friendly and warm as ever. And the generous meal she served —lamb with rice and cabbage and fresh-baked bread—had

214

won Gran's approval immediately. But it was not until now, at the kitchen sink, that Myra and Sarah had a few minutes alone together to talk. In the next room, the two grandmothers had dozed off in their easy chairs, and Joey and the men had settled down to watch a soccer game on television.

"It was so insane," Myra was saying in French as she emptied another glass. "Jovan did not write to tell us he was coming or even to ask anyone what jobs there were for him here. One day he just dropped out of the sky, just like that, and expected that the university or one of the scientific institutes would have work for him. People thought he was a lunatic, perhaps even an American spy."

"A spy!" Sarah laughed despite herself.

"It was not a joke," Myra said. "No one trusted him. Branko knows some people at the university and none of them could understand why Jovan came back here. What is there for him here? Nothing! With his degrees he could be making lots of money in America." Myra sighed. "But what can we do? 'It is for my country,' Jovan tells us. 'I will not let America have my son.' You know how he talks."

"Yes, I know," Sarah replied, thinking, Do I ever!

Myra shook her head. "It is such a waste, him with that good head of his. He was supposed to be our mother's hope for her old age. But now look! It is she who is supporting him. And the boy as well. What she has from her savings and her pension is hardly enough for one to live on, never mind three. And still she gives him everything he wants. Money for concert tickets, money to see soccer. I ask myself, how long can they go on this way? It frightens me. And Jovan gets more unhappy all the time. Mother tells me that often he just sits and does nothing."

"I'm unhappy too," Sarah said quietly. "And so is Joey. Does Jovan ever think of that?"

She handed Sarah a dish to dry. "Oh, he does! I know he

does. He is not unkind. But he needs you back, Sarah. When you left him, it was a terrible blow to him."

"He gave me no choice." Sarah did not like the way this conversation was going. Instead of sympathizing with her, Myra was expecting her to sympathize with Jovan! "You don't know what it was like living with him," she said.

"I know what it was like. You forget, I grew up with him." Myra, the rice pot in her hand, was scrubbing fiercely. "I know how impossible he sometimes can be. But that does not give you the right to leave him. You took a vow. He is your husband. You are his wife."

Sarah felt her cheeks burning. Her teeth were clamped tightly together as she fought to control her rising anger. Very carefully she set the dish towel down on the countertop. "You do *not* know," she said evenly, trying to keep her voice down. "You have no right to judge."

Myra, surprised by her tone, quickly backtracked. "Yes, yes. I am sorry. You are right. What happens between a husband and a wife no one else can know. But when I see my brother so unhappy, and the little boy too, I cannot bear to even look at them sometimes." She wiped her hands on her apron and turned to face Sarah, a plea in her voice and in her eyes. "They need you. Both of them. They need your help. We try, Branko and I, but we cannot do it by ourselves."

"Do what? What are you talking about?"

"Helping them. With money. If you were here, you could get a job. You could teach English. We need good teachers here. Or perhaps your father could—"

Sarah cut her off. "No," she snapped. Suddenly everything was clear. Suddenly she knew why this friendly family get-together had been arranged. "No," she said again. "I won't listen to this. You're trying to use me just the way he is. I'm nothing but a money machine for all of you, a key to some-

216

body else's bank account. Well, you can forget it. Because I'm through being used."

"No. It is not like that. You're wrong."

"Am I? 'Poor Jovan,' you say. 'He needs help, he doesn't know what he's doing.' You're right, he does need help. I've known that for a long time. And I used to think I could be the one to help him. But I've found out differently. Nobody can help him because he doesn't *want* to be helped. Not in the way he needs to be. All he wants is for somebody else to take care of him so he doesn't have to take care of himself. He's almost forty years old and he doesn't want to grow up."

Tears glistened in Myra's eyes. For a moment she had no words. Then slowly, sadly, she nodded her head. "Yes," she said. "Yes, what you say is true." She wiped her eyes with a corner of her apron and stood staring down at the linoleum. "But it hurts me so to see him the way he is now. So mixed up. So confused."

Gently Sarah laid a hand on Myra's arm. "It hurts me, too," she said truthfully. "But I can't afford to worry about Jovan any longer. I've got to help myself now. And Joey, too. If I can."

"But how?" Myra looked at her. "What can you do? Jovan will never let you take Joey back to America. And how can you leave without him? So what choice do you have? Tell me that. What choice?"

"I don't know," Sarah said. "I wish I did."

———

Getting on the bus back to the city that evening, Jovan quickly slid into the seat next to Joey, leaving Sarah to sit across the aisle with Gran and Baka. Not even here was he going to let her have Joey to herself. Was he that jealous of her influence on him? That frightened?

217

"Will you stay with us tonight, Mama?" Joey asked as the bus neared the city.

Sarah glanced at Jovan. Had he put the idea into Joey's head?

"I'd like to be with you, but there's not enough room for me at Baka's house."

"Nonsense," said Baka. "There is room upstairs for you and Jovan together. Joey and I can sleep on the daybed."

But Sarah declined. There was no way she was going to stay overnight in the same bed with Jovan. "It's not a good idea," she said. "I'll go back to the hotel with Gran."

"Can I c-c-come visit you th-there, Mama? At the h-h-hotel?"

"Joey, that's a wonderful idea!" She hesitated. "Jovan, would that be all right?"

"Of course," he said. "We will come whenever you say."

His emphasis on the plural did not escape her. She nodded, resigned, and felt a weight of despair descending over her. It was like one of those lead blankets the dentists use to protect their patients from X rays, cloaking her body, pressing down on her, threatening to smother the life out of her.

"It's a crime what they're doing," Gran told Mr. Dimitrivic when she and Sarah went to his office the next day. "It's nothing but extortion. They don't want Sarah here. They don't even want Joey. It's just money they're after, all of them. They're—"

"Mrs. Heilicki," the lawyer cut in. "I have no doubt that what you say may very well be the case, but I doubt that you could prove it in court. The fact remains that Mrs. Stefanovic's husband, whatever his motives, still retains possession of the boy. And I'm afraid that possession—"

"Yes, we've heard," said Sarah. "Possession is nine-tenths of the law. And that leaves me just where I started: nowhere."

"Ah, ah." He wagged an admonishing finger. "Not so fast. Possession may not be the only factor here."

"What is all this?" Gran put in impatiently. "You're talking in riddles."

"The point," he continued, "is that if you insist on contesting your husband's possession of your son, I'm afraid you will have very little hope of success, for the reasons I have already—"

"Yes."

"However, that does not mean you have to give up all hope of seeing the boy."

"Are you talking about visiting rights?"

The lawyer nodded. "Our judges are not completely immune to human sympathies."

"But that's not—" she began vehemently but then caught herself. She looked down at her hands, saw them blur before her eyes. "I was going to say that's not fair," she said quietly. "But obviously fairness doesn't count, does it?"

"I'm afraid not," he replied.

Gran leaned forward. "Mr. Dimitrivic may be right, dear. You know what I've always said: half a loaf is better than none."

Sarah wasn't sure what to think. If she did as Dimitrivic suggested—stayed in Belgrade, got a job, found a place to live —she'd be cut off from her own world, with no friends, no allies, knowing no one but Jovan's family, who now mistrusted her as much as she mistrusted them. It would be hard, maybe impossible. Still, if it meant she could be with Joey . . .

"I'll need some time," she said. "It's a lot to think about."

"I understand," said Dimitrivic. He got to his feet, held out his hand. "When you have reached a decision, let me know. Then we will work out whatever legal aspects—"

She took his hand. She felt tired, weighted down. Clearly this man was not going to offer any more help. But then, maybe there was no help that he or anyone else *could* offer.

Part Two

Where to Turn

CHECKPOINT
Saturday, April 23, 9:40 A.M.

Ted slowed for an exit ramp and swung the BMW onto a secondary road.

"Pit stop," he said before Sarah could ask.

They had been driving steadily for over two hours, speeding southeast into the glare of the morning sun, Ted at the wheel, Wilkes asleep in the backseat. Sarah sat in front beside her father.

With the Hardys gone, there was plenty of room in the little car. The extra space felt positively luxurious. Even so, the drone of the tires and the whistle of the wind were as soporific as ever—and Sarah was glad to be stopping. Assaulted by the glare off the windshield, her eyes half-closed, she had been only vaguely aware of the country through which they'd been traveling: a wide, flat valley where lush pastures and vineyards periodically gave way to factories, refineries, train yards, oil storage tanks, the acrid smell of smoke and chemical fumes. They were in such a place now. It was like driving along the worst stretches of the New Jersey Turnpike, except that here the billboards and road signs were in Serbo-Croatian.

"Where are we?" Wilkes asked groggily from the back.

"Sign back there said Brod something."

"Slavonski Brod?"

"Right."

"Damn."

Ted shot him a glance. "You got a problem?"

"Bloody right. We should have been a hell of a lot farther along by now. Do you mind telling me why you've been going so bloody slow?"

"Look, mister, if you don't like it, you drive. I've been doing a good ninety kilometers an hour. What's that in miles? Sixty-five, seventy?"

"Christ, no wonder. Look, forget the sightseeing next time. Let's just get there, shall we?"

"What about the speed limit?"

"There isn't any. Not on the big roads."

"Swell. Thanks for telling me."

Their stop was coming just in time, Sarah realized. They were all getting on each other's nerves.

Not far off the highway, Ted pulled up at a roadside café. Several cars and a tour bus were parked on the gravel out front. Ted got out, slamming his door. Wilkes did the same. He led the way to the café.

Inside, they found a long line of people waiting to get into the single restroom. A harried waiter was making an effort to handle the dozen or so tables by himself.

Ted nodded at the inevitable portrait of Tito over the bar. "Old boy's all over the place, isn't he?" he said.

"Stow that," Wilkes hissed under his breath. "In this country, cracks like that can get you thrown in jail."

"That bad, huh?"

"Yeah, that bad."

Sarah wished Wilkes had stayed asleep. His snappishness was becoming oppressive.

224

The waiter finally came over. Wilkes gave their order in German: eggs, bread, coffee all around. When the food came, the three of them ate in numb silence. Sarah stared at her eggs, which were a runny version of scrambled. Her mind was blank. Her body felt as if it were still in motion.

The stop and the food helped. Once they were back on the road, they were all in better spirits.

"Step on it," Wilkes urged when they were back on the highway.

"Right you are," said Ted. "No more Mr. Nice Guy." He hit the accelerator and the car shot forward.

He and Wilkes were almost jovial—joking, making comments. In the backseat Sarah dozed and listened with half an ear while Wilkes told her father about the country they were traveling through: how it was really not a country at all but a crazy-quilt confederation of varied and often hostile nations and ethnic groups—Croats, Slovenes, Serbs, Hungarians, Albanians. Croatia, where they were now, was predominantly Catholic in religion and European in history and outlook; Serbia, where they were headed, was Greek Orthodox and its culture was heavily Byzantine; in the south, in places like Bosnia and Macedonia, the religion and culture were mostly Moslem.

"It's all quite mad, really," said Wilkes, lighting yet another cigarette. "All those different people struggling to coexist under one flag, in an area not much bigger than your state of Oregon. And the only person who's been able to hold it together is that chap in the pictures we've been seeing everywhere. Once he's gone, they'll all be at each other's throats again."

They drove in silence for a few minutes.

"How do you come to know so much about this place?" Ted asked.

Wilkes shrugged. "In this business, one makes a point of

being well informed. Otherwise one does not stay—shall we say 'active.' Not for very long at any rate."

"Sounds dramatic."

Wilkes grinned. "Can be."

"Have you ever had to use your gun?"

"I don't carry one."

"Not ever?"

In the backseat Sarah smiled quietly to herself. Her father sounded like a small boy talking to his first policeman.

"Rarely," said Wilkes. "It's just asking for trouble."

"Uh-oh." Ted was suddenly tense. His eyes were fixed on the rearview mirror. "Speaking of trouble, we seem to have a cop on our tail."

"Oh, hell."

Sarah froze, afraid to turn around and look. Was this it? Was this where they'd get caught?

"What if he's got our description from the border guards?" asked Ted. "What if they're looking for us?"

"I don't know," said Wilkes. "But you better pull over."

Ted slowed, then brought the car to a halt on the shoulder.

Sarah threw a glance out the back window. A white squad car was rolling to a stop behind them. A policeman got out.

"Let's make a break for it," Ted said, panic in his voice. "Now, while he's out of his car."

"Forget it. One radio call from him and we'll have police all over us. Just keep calm."

The cop stepped up to Ted's window. Obviously he had noted the car's German designation because he began speaking immediately in German.

"He wants to see your papers," Wilkes translated. "He says you were doing one-twenty in an eighty-kilometer zone."

"What zone?" asked Ted. "I thought you said there weren't any speed limits."

Wilkes shrugged. "There must have been a sign back there, when we went through that last town."

"Great. Now what happens?"

"You pay a fine."

"What, right here?"

"I'm afraid so."

"How much?"

"A hundred dinars," Wilkes said, only now beginning to crack a smile.

"Four dollars?"

"It's a very serious offense."

eleven

"Sarah, is it true?" Jovan asked. "This is wonderful. You have made me very happy."

"Mama, do you m-m-mean it?" Joey's bright eyes were so full of delight that it almost hurt to look at him.

"Yes, I mean it." She bent to hug him. "We'll try it for a while and see how it works out."

It had taken her several days but finally she had made up her mind: she would do as Dimitrivic suggested; she would try to find some way to stay in Belgrade on her own so that she could be near Joey. It was the only alternative she could think of. And now, walking in the park with them on this crisp fall day, with the dusty sunlight filtering through the tree branches and the ducks splashing playfully in the nearby pond, it seemed as if it might just be possible and that she might even enjoy living here.

"When, Sarah? When will you be moving in?"

She walked on a little way. Careful now. Careful. "Moving in wasn't what I was thinking of exactly."

"Ah, of course. I see. Yes. The cottage is too small. You are

228

right. We will have to get a place of our own. That will be better."

"No."

"No?" He stopped to look at her.

"I mean I don't think that's a good idea either."

"What are you trying to tell me?"

She did not answer immediately, but stooped to tie one of Joey's shoelaces, which had come undone. "Joey, why don't you go off and watch the ducks for a while. See the ducks over there?"

"D-d-don't want to watch the d-d-ducks."

"Joey," Jovan growled, his tone threatening.

"We'll be right here. Your father and I have some things to talk about."

Joey looked from one to the other with his big eyes, then looked down at his feet and turned away. Sarah watched him go. His hands were pushed deep into his pants pockets and he kicked at a stone as he went. Poor Joey, she thought. Her heart ached for him.

"Be careful," she called. "Don't go too close to the edge."

They sat on a park bench. Across the way, looming over the treetops, she could see the crenellated walls and turrets of the Kalemegdan fortress, the ancient Turkish citadel that stood guard over the place where the Sava River emptied into the Danube. Overhead flocks of pigeons dipped and wheeled, now flashing in the sunlight, now seeming to disappear as their dark sides turned against the sky.

Sarah took a breath. "I don't think it's a good idea for us to live together again."

"But you just said—"

"That's not what I said. Will you just listen to me for once? I want to get a place of my own. I want to be here, to be able to see Joey, to be near him."

"But not to live with me," he said tonelessly.

"It wouldn't work out. We've tried. It's just not good."

"And what about Joey? It's not good for him this way."

"It would be worse the other way. We'd be at each other all the time. You know that. This way he'd still live with you but I could visit him. He could visit me sometimes."

Over at the duck pond, Joey was hunkered down, watching the birds splashing and paddling about.

Jovan said nothing for a long time. Finally he turned to her. "It's a trick, isn't it?"

"A trick? No, it's not a trick. What kind of trick would it be?"

He pinned her with those strange yellow-brown eyes of his. "You think I'd let you do that? I know what you'd do. The first time I'd let you out of my sight with him, you'd take him on a plane back to America."

The idea astonished her. It had never occurred to her. "No," she protested. "It's not true. It's just not."

"I don't believe you. You're lying."

"But I'm not."

"Prove it, then."

"Prove it? How? How can I?"

His eyes narrowed. A new look came into them, cold and calculating. "There is a way." He took her hand. "Live with me again. That's the only way."

She tried to pull her hand back but he held it tight. "Let go. You're hurting me."

"You want to prove to me I can trust you? Live with me again. And give me another child."

"What! You're crazy. Let me go."

He was twisting her hand now, a look of cruel delight in his eyes. She realized he was actually enjoying this, the pain he was inflicting. He pulled her against him. "If you love me again, if you come to my bed and be my wife again, then you can be with Joey."

He gripped her chin with his free hand, forcing her head back. His face was inches from hers. "Otherwise I don't let you near him. I don't care how long you stay here. You hear me?"

Had he pushed harder Sarah was sure he could have snapped her neck. But suddenly Joey was there pulling at Jovan's arm, trying to get him to release his grip. "Daddy!" he screamed. "Stop it, Daddy! Stop it!"

Without taking his eyes off of her, Jovan finally let her go. As soon as she was free she leaped up from the bench and ran, her eyes burning with tears of hate and rage. Behind her she could hear Joey's voice crying, "Mama, Mama! Come back, Mama."

But she knew now there was no turning back.

Sarah stabbed her fork into her chicken kiev. "I could have killed him," she said. "I mean it, Gran. If I'd had a knife in my hand this afternoon, I swear I would have killed him."

"Now, child, be sensible," Gran said, savoring a mouthful of falafel. "A knife will never do. Much too messy."

Having worn herself out with an afternoon of shopping and sightseeing, Gran was in too fine a mood to take Sarah's anger seriously. "You should use poison, it's much tidier."

Sarah grimaced. "You're not being much help."

"No, I suppose I'm not. There'd be a problem with getting him to take it. Wait a minute! What about pouring it in his ear while he's asleep, the way they did it in *Hamlet*?"

Sarah shook her head. "Forget it. That would mean spending the night with him."

"You're right. Too bad." Thoughtfully Gran smeared butter on a piece of black bread. "Here's an idea," she said. "You've invited him here for supper, haven't you? We'll slip something into his food. A little cyanide in his bean soup."

Sarah laughed out loud despite herself. "Cyanide is no good either. It acts too quickly. At least that's what they always say in the murder mysteries. He'd keel over right here at the table, before we could make our getaway. We need one of those poisons like they give to rats, the kind they eat and then go off somewhere else to die. Then we couldn't be blamed."

"Mmm, that's right." Gran assumed a pensive mood. Suddenly her eyes widened and she began clapping her hands together in childlike delight. "I have it, I have it," she cried.

"What, Gran?"

"Mushrooms! Amanitas. Guaranteed effective. And I'll bet the woods around here are full of them. When he comes to dinner, we all order mushroom salads. Then, when he's not looking, we sprinkle a few amanitas into his bowl. Bingo! He's dead by midnight."

"Perfect! Gran, you're a genius." Sarah leaned over and planted a kiss on one of Gran's heavily powdered cheeks. "Are you sure you weren't a witch in a previous life?"

"Why, Sarah, dear! What a thing to say about your sweet old granny."

They sat in silence while the waiter cleared away their dishes and brought them coffee. A somberness had descended on both of them.

"What am I going to do?" Sarah said when the waiter had gone.

Gran poured milk into her coffee. "I don't know. I just don't know. As long as he's got Joey, there doesn't seem to be anything you can do. That's what the lawyer was saying: 'Possession is two-thirds of the law.' "

"Nine-tenths."

232

"Never mind. He's got Joey and that seems to be the only thing the lawyers care about. If you had Joey the law would be on your side. But you don't, so I guess that's that."

"I guess so."

But as Sarah stirred her coffee, Gran's last words kept replaying themselves in her head: *that's that*. Meaning there was nothing else she could do. But was that true? Or was she only making the assumptions that Jovan wanted her to make? Suddenly she had an image of him holding onto Joey's hand as they walked near the cottage that first night. Holding on and not letting go. Holding on for dear life. And again, on the bus, not letting her sit next to Joey. Afraid to leave Joey alone with her, even for a minute.

Yes, Jovan was afraid! She had known it before but not until now had the real meaning of it sunk in. He was afraid of *her*, and not just of her possible influence on Joey but of what she might *do*, of what she *could do*. He had said it himself in the park this afternoon. He was afraid that she would do the same thing that he had done: get Joey onto a plane and take him away.

"Gran, I've got it," she said aloud. "Why didn't I think of it before?"

"Think of what, dear? What are you talking about?"

"Possession, Gran. I'm talking about possession. Nine-tenths of the law. I'm talking about taking possession of Joey myself."

"*What?*"

"Why not? He took Joey from me!"

"But that's not—"

"Not nice? No, kidnapping isn't nice. And that's just the trouble. All this time I've been trying so hard to be so nice that Jovan's been able to get away with whatever he pleases."

"Sarah, dear, will you calm down and let me finish what I was saying? I don't care a crumb about what's nice. I care about what's legal. What you're suggesting is as illegal as what Jovan did to you."

"I'm aware of that."

"Are you? Then just what do you intend to do when you get Joey away from Jovan, assuming you can. Where will you go? You heard what Mr. Dimitrivic said. The authorities will never let you take him out of the country."

"I'll do what people do when they want political asylum. I'll take him to the embassy. Then Mr. Fletcher Wethering will *have* to do something."

In the morning Sarah and Gran arrived at the American Embassy just as the marine guard was opening the gate to the compound. At the same time, a taxi pulled up to the curb and the tall, lean figure of Fletcher Wethering stepped out. Every hair was in place; he and his pinstripes looked freshly pressed, and he had his briefcase in hand.

"Mr. Wethering," Sarah said, "you're just the person we've come to see."

For an instant he looked nonplussed, but he quickly recovered. "Mrs. Stefanovic, isn't it?" he said condescendingly as he stepped through the gate.

"Yes, and we want to talk to you," Sarah persisted, following him in.

"Of course. If you'd like to call my secretary for an appointment . . ."

"We want to talk to you now."

"That may be, but I have other matters to attend to this morning. So if you'll excuse me . . ."

"All right," she called after him as he started up the front steps. "But when I bring my son here and *you* have to figure out how to get him out of the country, don't say I didn't try to warn you."

234

Wethering stopped in midstride. Turning to face her, he studied her for a moment, his heavy-lidded eyes betraying just the slightest hint of uncertainty. It was enough. "You'd better come inside."

Sarah and Gran exchanged satisfied glances and followed him up the steps.

He led them upstairs to his office, where he asked them to wait. He went out, closing the door behind him. A minute later he was back. "Come with me, please."

Without another word, he led them down a corridor and through a door that bore the Great Seal of the United States. Striding past a secretary, he ushered them through another door and into a spacious office. Sarah was aware of thick blue carpet underfoot, an American flag prominently displayed in one corner, and, coming toward her, a big balding man in shirt-sleeves. In one hand he held a pair of steel-rimmed spectacles. The other hand was outstretched in greeting.

"Sir, these are the ladies I was telling you about. Mrs. Stefanovic and her grandmother, Mrs. Helen Heilicki. Ladies, I'd like you to meet Ambassador Laurence Silberman."

"How do you do," the ambassador said. "I'm glad we've finally had a chance to get together. I've been following your case closely, Mrs. Stefanovic."

Inwardly Sarah groaned. God, she thought, another smoothie. Next would come the expressions of sympathy, followed by heartfelt regret that nothing could be done. As he offered seats to them both, Sarah wondered why she had even bothered to come.

But the ambassador surprised her. "Damned fuddy-duddies," he said when the vice-counsel had left the room.

She blinked, startled, and he grinned at her reaction. "Oh, don't mind me," he said, with a wave of his spectacles. "It's these State Department types. Fletch, the rest of them. They're all alike. More worried about protecting their careers than they are about doing their jobs. You've got to plant a bomb under some of these guys to get anything done. 'Course, I'm lucky," he continued genially. "Now that the elections are over and we're about to get a new administration, I'll be able to leave here in a few months. Being a political appointee, you see, does have its advantages."

He swung around behind his sprawling desk, dropped into his high-backed leather chair, and cocked one foot on the edge of an open drawer. On the wall behind him hung a spectacular panoramic painting of a western landscape. Shafts of sunlight fell on rugged mountains and brightened the valley below, where Indian teepees stood and herds of horses grazed.

"I admire your persistence, Mrs. Stefanovic," the ambassador said heartily. Putting on his glasses, he plucked a file from amid the clutter on his desk and leafed through the papers he found there. "Why, I've got letters here from Congressman Vanderbeck, Senator Case, cables from State, notes on transatlantic phone calls from your Washington attorney." He slid his spectacles to the top of his balding head and leaned back in his chair. "You've certainly covered all the bases."

"Sarah is a very bright girl, I want you to know," Gran said.

"That seems apparent."

Sarah shrugged. She was determined not to be distracted from her purpose by geniality—and certainly not by flattery. "Most of that was my parents' doing," she said, nodding toward his folder. "I couldn't have done it without them."

"That's very loyal of you to say so, but it wasn't your parents who had Fletcher Wethering in a panic a few minutes ago." The ambassador laughed. "Why, he was carrying on like the place was on fire."

Sarah regarded him evenly. "I meant every word I said to him. I came here to get my son back and that's what I intend to do."

236

"And I intend to help you in any way I can," said the ambassador, adopting a tone as serious as her own.

"Thank you. I'm glad to hear it."

"I mean it sincerely. I've got children and grandchildren of my own and I know how I would feel if one of them ended up being abducted. Hell, I'd go to that house and get the boy myself if I weren't in the position I'm in here. But," he said, pointing his glasses at her, "it is exactly *because* I want to help you that I must tell you in all honesty that bringing your son to the embassy would be absolutely the worst thing you could do."

So that was his game. She'd been right to be wary. He was not trying to help her at all, just trying to make sure she did not do anything embarrassing. "Just who would it be worse for, Mr. Ambassador? For you? For the American government?" She was astonished at her own impertinence, but she had been put off too often and she was determined not to let it happen again.

"Sarah, the man's only trying to help," said Gran. Oddly their roles seemed to have been reversed. Now Gran was being the restrained one, while Sarah was being outspoken.

"I doubt it," she said, a challenge in her voice.

The ambassador looked pained. "Mrs. Stefanovic, I don't blame you for being cynical after everything you've been through. But let me make one thing clear. As you may have gathered, I am not especially fond of the Yugoslav government and they are not especially fond of me, which is one reason I'll be glad to be leaving this post come January. So don't think I care one way or another if the Jugs get their feathers a little ruffled. What I am worried about is what happens to you if you do bring your boy here."

"That would be your problem," she said stubbornly.

He shook his head. "It's not that easy. Oh, getting him in

237

here would be no problem. But there's a good chance you'd never get him out again. You'd be arrested the minute you tried to leave."

Gran let out a shocked little cry. "Arrested!"

But Sarah's determination had given her a cool calm that was new to her. She brushed back a lock of hair from her forehead. "On what grounds?" she asked evenly.

"The way they'd see it, you'd be kidnapping one of their citizens. You'd not only be breaking the law, you'd be offending their national honor. They're very touchy about things like that. They'd never let you leave. You could end up living here in the compound for years."

"At least I'd be with Joey," she declared staunchly. But suddenly things did not seem as certain as they had a few minutes ago.

"True. But are you sure that's the kind of life you want for your son? To grow up a prisoner inside these walls?"

"He's a prisoner now," she shot back. But she felt her resolve draining away. She let her gaze fall. Finally she relented. "All right, then, what if I don't bring him here? What if I just wait for a chance to take him out of the country?"

The ambassador shook his head. "Bad idea. They'd nail you at the airport and then things would be even worse for you. You could find yourself in jail."

"But what can I do then?" she cried out in frustration, angry at the tears she felt welling up. "What can I do?"

Gran patted her arm. "There, there, Sarah, dear. There, there."

"Look," said the ambassador gently, "there's not a lot I can do for you officially. But let me think about this a little. A few possibilities come to mind and I'd like to check them out. What I'd like you to do is just sit tight for a couple of days and give me a chance to see what I can come up with. Will you do that?"

She studied her hands for a moment. What alternative did she have? "Yes, all right," she murmured reluctantly.

"Will you promise me that you won't do anything, ah, precipitous in the meantime?"

She nodded again. "I promise."

"Good. Now, I can't guarantee you a quick fix, but there may be a way we can work something out—unofficially of course. For now, don't talk about any of this over the telephone. The Jugs are always very interested in anyone who walks in here to see me. If your phone hasn't been tapped already they'll certainly put a bug on it when they see you leaving here."

A shiver went through her.

"You're not serious," said Gran, echoing Sarah's own astonishment.

"Oh, yes," said the ambassador. "I'm quite serious. And I'd also advise you to stay away from that lawyer you've been seeing."

"Mr. Dimitrivic?" Sarah was puzzled. "But I thought it was you people who recommended him."

"That's correct. But none of us were aware at the time of just what your case entailed. Oh, Dimi is a good man, all right. We often call on him to handle routine legal affairs for us. But over here there's no such thing as confidentiality between a lawyer and his client. If the authorities questioned him about your case, he'd have to tell them everything he knows, including your intention to take your son back to America."

"But that's ridiculous," said Gran. "If she doesn't have a lawyer, how is she going to go to court?"

"To be frank, Mrs. Heilicki, going to court with this case would be a mistake. The chances of an American mother winning custody of a Yugoslav child—especially a male child —are almost nonexistent."

"That's what Mr. Dimitrivic told us," said Sarah.

"He was quite right, too. And after the court's judgment went against you, any attempt you made to take the boy on your own would be all the more perilous. If you got caught you'd be in clear violation of a court ruling. Then the Jugs would really nail you."

"Then what on earth am I supposed to do?" Sarah asked plaintively. "Can you tell me that? What am I supposed to do?"

"Sit tight for a few more days." Ambassador Silberman got to his feet. "Come see me on Monday. I should have some answers for you by then."

"I don't know whether to feel hopeless or optimistic," Sarah said as she and Gran left the embassy. "I couldn't tell if he was just putting me off or if he really has something up his sleeve."

"Oh, he was crafty all right," Gran agreed, easing her weight unsteadily down the front steps. "He sounded very sincere, but he never promised anything, did he?"

"Not a thing," said Sarah.

They walked to the curb and stood there in the cold November sunlight, waiting for a taxi to take them back to the hotel. As Sarah surveyed the street, her eye was caught by a movement across the way. A man sitting on a park bench was folding his newspaper. Was he the informant? she wondered: the person who would report their embassy visit to the police? Or was it that old man with the dog, the one just coming along the sidewalk over there? Or maybe it was that woman pushing the baby carriage.

Suddenly, standing there in the sunlight, Sarah felt very vulnerable.

She was relieved when she and Gran finally arrived back at the hotel. Even so, she found herself looking with new eyes at the people there: the idlers in the lobby; the seemingly friendly desk clerk who had been handing her her key every day for the last three weeks; the unsmiling old woman at the switchboard. (Who better to listen in on phone calls than the switchboard operator?)

All of which probably explained why she felt so inordinately happy when she saw that the familiar figure moving toward the elevator with her and Gran was the American businessman they had met here three weeks ago when they were just checking in—the man with the California suntan and the tinted aviator glasses.

Spontaneously she called out a cheerful "hello," and when he turned toward her she was pleased to see a smile on his face, an American face at that!

"Well, hello," he said in his husky baritone. "What a surprise." He nodded a greeting to Gran: "Ma'am," he said. Then, to Sarah: "You must be having a good time to have stayed so long."

"It's not exactly a pleasure trip," she said.

"That's too bad. Belgrade can be an interesting town if you know where to look."

"You must know where to look," said Gran. "You seem to spend a lot of time here."

"Oh, I'm in and out. My business keeps me hopping."

They all got into the elevator together. For a moment there was an awkward silence, broken only by the whir of the elevator motor.

"What kind of business are you in?" Sarah asked at last.

"Oh, lots of things. Casinos mostly."

She looked at him in surprise. "*Gambling* casinos?"

Her astonishment seemed to amuse him. "I've got a couple of places down on the coast," he said. "One's in Dubrovnik, the other's in Split. You should come down there if you get a chance. It's a great area. Good restaurants, terrific beaches."

The elevator lurched to a halt and the door opened.

"Well, this is where I get off. Nice to see you both again." He looked at Sarah. "Maybe we can get together for a drink sometime."

"Yes," she said, smiling. "I'd like that."

He held the door open. "You free tomorrow night?"

"Not tomorrow. I'm busy, I'm afraid. Maybe Saturday."

"Fine. I'll look for you in the bar downstairs. About five?"

"Yes. That'll be fine. Mister—?"

He held out his hand. "Flynt. Jack Flynt. And you are—?"

Sarah introduced herself and Gran. When the elevator door closed again, Gran was grinning from ear to ear.

"What a nice man," she said. "Now why couldn't you have fallen for someone like that instead of causing everybody all this trouble?"

"Gran, for God's sake!"

"Sarah, dear, I was only joking."

Back in the room, Sarah telephoned her parents as usual to give them a progress report. Conscious for the first time that someone might be listening in, she was careful to speak in only vague terms about having seen "a certain man" who she hoped would be helpful with "our project."

"I can't say any more right now," she told her mother, "but we're going to see him again in a few days."

But Sarah's evasions only piqued Emma's curiosity; she wanted to know more. Trying to find some way to get the message across, Sarah told her instead about how much she was looking forward to visiting Belgrade's natural history museum and viewing the entymology collection.

"They've got all sorts of bugs over here that we don't have back home," she said.

"Bugs! Sarah, since when are you interested in bugs?"

"The man I just saw today was telling me all about them.

I want you and Dad to understand about the bugs they have over here."

For a moment there was a mystified silence on the other end. Then all at once the message seemed to get through. "Oh," her mother said. "You mean those bugs!"

"Yes, mother."

"Are you sure?"

"No, but I'm told it's very likely."

After that her mother was more circumspect. She told Sarah that she had been keeping in touch with "our friend, Jack" (the man at the State Department), as well as with "Mr. B." (Bill Borden) and "Mr. V." (Congressman Vanderbeck). Meanwhile, she said, Ted was continuing to pursue new leads.

The conversation left Sarah feeling depressed. It was bad enough knowing she had failed in everything she had tried to do: failed with the lawyer, with Jovan's sister, probably with the ambassador as well. But it made her feel even worse, even more isolated, to know that every move she made, every word she said, was most likely being monitored.

"I think you should face it," Gran told her that evening as the two of them sat over dinner in the hotel dining room. "You've done all you can."

Sarah shook her head. "There must be something else. There's got to be. I can't just give up."

"I know, dear, but we can't stay here forever looking for a wild goose in a haystack. I can't anyway. I've been to every store and museum in Belgrade. If I never see another painting by 'the famous Yugoslav artist What's-his-name,' it won't be too soon."

"You mean What's-his-nameovic," Sarah joked, hoping to lift their spirits.

"I want to go back, Sarah. I want to be in my own home again and sleep in my own bed. And frankly, if you want my advice, I think you should go back too."

243

The prospect depressed her even further. Go back? Could she? And leave Joey behind? Would she ever see him again if she did?

"Gran, stay just a couple more days, can't you? At least through the weekend, until I see what the ambassador comes up with."

Gran sighed. Beneath the broad expanse of her silk blouse, her bosom rose like a tide, then fell back again. "All right, dear. I guess it's like I've always said: Rome wasn't build in a day. But I won't stay any later than Tuesday. Wednesday at the latest. After that, if you want to stay, I'm afraid you'll be on your own."

It was Friday evening. Amid the polished marble walls and pillars of the hotel lobby, Sarah waited for Jovan to appear with Joey for the dinner she had promised him. When she finally saw Jovan coming through the main entrance it was clear that he had dressed up for the occasion: dark suit, white shirt, unruly hair combed back from his forehead. He looked better than she had seen him the whole time she had been in Belgrade. But then, that was nothing to be surprised about. He had always known how to put on the flash when he wanted to. The surprise was that he had come alone.

"Where's Joey?" she asked as he came forward to greet her.

"Well, hello to you too," he said sarcastically. He leaned forward to give her a kiss. She turned aside, but not before she'd smelled the alcohol on his breath. Had he started drinking now, on top of everything else?

"I was looking forward to seeing Joey," she said coolly.

"Joey, always Joey. Tonight I wanted to be alone with you. Is that so bad?"

"Bad?" Sarah was incredulous. "After what happened in

the park the other day? How can you even imagine that I'd want to be alone with you after that?"

"Sarah, Sarah." He shook his head in exaggerated dismay. "Is that any way to talk to your husband?" He lowered his voice to a husky whisper. "Forget what happened in the park. Forget everything. I love you, Sarah. I want to be with you again, the way we used to be."

The combination of alcohol on his breath and his sweet cologne was overpowering. She looked directly into his eyes and saw they were bloodshot. "I don't believe you're saying this. Don't you understand yet what's happened between us? Don't you *see*?"

He took her by the arm. "I love you. That's all that matters."

She felt her stomach knotting up. God, it was starting.

"I think you'd better leave now," she said, keeping her voice down and hoping he would do the same.

"Leave!" He feigned astonishment. "But you invited me to dinner in your nice fancy restaurant! It would not be polite for me to ignore a lady's invitation."

"I invited Joey. You invited yourself."

"Well, Joey couldn't come so I'm here instead." Menacingly he tightened his grip on her arm. "Come. I'd hate for us to lose our table."

Afraid of making a scene, of triggering an eruption, Sarah allowed him to lead her into the restaurant. Gran was already waiting at a table in the middle of the elaborate room, with its tapestries and its muted lighting.

"Madam," he said, bowing formally to Gran and showing his teeth. His strong hand still on Sarah's arm, he pulled a chair out from the table and forced Sarah into it.

"What's going on here?" Gran asked angrily.

"Why, we're having a little dinner party, aren't we?" mocked Jovan. He lifted a hand and snapped his fingers.

245

"Waiter!" he called in Serbian. "Wine for the ladies and a vodka for me. Make it a double."

"Jovan, please," Sarah begged. She was aware that the restaurant had become very quiet and that people around them were staring.

"Poor Sarah," Jovan taunted. "Am I embarrassing you in front of all the rich people?"

"You're drunk," said Gran. "Why don't you go home and leave Sarah alone."

But there was no stopping him now. "Yes, I am drunk," he snarled. "You are absolutely correct. But at least I do not abandon my child the way this woman did." He sneered at Sarah. "*You!* You worry about being embarrassed. You, who run out on your husband and your only child! You *should* be embarrassed. You should be *ashamed!*"

"That's enough," Gran said. "If you don't leave, I'm going to have you thrown out."

He turned on her savagely. "Shut up, you bitch. This is none of your affair."

"Stop it! Jovan." Sarah grabbed his arm. "Just stop it."

But he shook her off and got to his feet, knocking over a wine glass and a vase of flowers in the process. "Oh, no," he said. "I will not stop. You will listen to me. Because I am telling you now, if you do not come back to live with Joey and me you will not be seeing him again ever. You come here, you live in your fancy hotel, you walk in and out on us like some grand lady, you bring your fancy presents and make Joey think you are better than we are. Oh, yes, I know what you try to do. I am not stupid. But you listen now. It stops now. No more games. No more talk about separate apartments. You want to see Joey, you want to be his mother, you first be my wife again. If you do not, you will not see him at all. And if you try, I will take him away from here and hide him in the mountains where you will never find him. Never."

Then, turning unsteadily on his heel, he barged past the startled waiters and out the door that led to the street. On the way he almost collided with an elderly couple who were just coming in. He dodged around them, and then he was gone, leaving Sarah sitting there, shaking, in the middle of the crowded restaurant.

"Oh!" Gran sputtered. "How could he! And in front of all these people! He's crazy. Do you know that? He's as mad as a hatter. He should be locked up."

Sarah closed her eyes. She felt as if she had been pummeled with fists instead of mere words. Drained and beaten. "I'm sorry," she said.

"Sorry!" Gran's mouth fell open. "What in heaven's name are you sorry for? You sound as crazy as he is. Sarah, *you* didn't do anything. You're no more responsible for Jovan's lunacy than the man in the moon."

"Excuse me," said a familiar voice over Sarah's shoulder. "I couldn't help overhearing. Can I be of any help?"

Sarah looked up, knowing already who was standing there. "Hello, Mr. Flynt," she said wearily. "Thank you, but I don't think there's anything anybody can do."

He tilted his head toward the door through which Jovan had stormed out. "Your husband?"

She nodded and looked away. Everybody knew. She wished she could just crawl away and hide.

"Her *ex*-husband," said Gran, careful as ever to avoid subtleties.

Flynt simply shook his head. He did not say he was sorry and Sarah was grateful to him for that.

"As a matter of fact, there is something you can do," said Gran. "You can have a seat and order us both a drink."

"My pleasure," he said. "What would you like?"

"Slivovitz for me," Gran said. "Sarah?"

"Oh—I don't know. Anything."

"A little cognac?" Flynt prompted.

She shrugged indifferently. "Fine."

She was not really in the mood to talk to the man and saw no reason why she should involve him in her business. But neither did she see any reason to turn him away. She really did not care one way or the other.

Soon, however, as the cognac began warming her cheeks, she was telling him everything, pouring out all her anguish and frustration. Even so, when she told him about Jovan holding Joey hostage and about his final vow to prevent her from ever seeing Joey again unless she came back to him, she was not prepared for the intensity of Flynt's outrage.

"Son-of-a-bitch," he growled through clenched teeth.

"Yes," Sarah said with a rueful laugh. "That, too."

But he did not smile. His fist looked as hard as a stone on the white tablecloth. "Lady, you want that man put away, you just say the word. I'm telling you, you just let me know."

"Put away?"

"It'd be very easy, believe me. There'd be nothing to it."

Alarmed, Sarah threw a glance at her grandmother. Was this man for real? Was he saying what she thought he was saying?

"I'm sorry, I don't think I understand—"

"You want him dead, I can fix it. Bastard like that doesn't deserve to live."

For a moment all she could do was stare at him, and it wasn't what she saw there that appalled her but what she did not see: not a trace of humor, not a hint. The man was not stringing together fantasies about poisoned mushrooms. He was absolutely serious. Suddenly in her mind flashed a picture of Jovan sprawled on the street in a pool of blood. How would it happen? Would he be shot? Run down by a car? Sarah shuddered and forced the image out of her mind.

"Thank you," she stammered. "I mean—" Good grief, how

248

do you tell somebody you don't want them to kill your husband for you? "I mean, I appreciate your concern but I really, you know, don't think—" She stopped then, took a breath. "I don't want him dead, no. I just want my son back. All right?"

He nodded, his expression softening. "Sure. All right."

Sarah breathed easier. The whole weird conversation had made her very uncomfortable and she was glad to be done with it.

But Gran was not finished. She leaned forward intently. "Just what do you mean, Mr. Flynt? What's all right?" She had apparently heard something in his tone that Sarah had missed.

"Getting the boy back. Isn't that what we're talking about? Of course, it would be more complicated than the other thing, and that means it would be more expensive. But sure, it can be done."

"That's not what Sarah has been hearing."

"She's been talking to the wrong people. There are ways, believe me. All it takes is money." He looked closely at Sarah. "Have you got money?"

The question took her aback. "Mr. Flynt, I don't know what kind of money you're talking about or what kind of activities but I think this conversation has gone far enough. Now if you'll excuse us, we'd like to get on with our dinner."

Behind his blue-tinted glasses Flynt raised an amused eyebrow. "As you wish," he said with a nod.

He pushed back his chair and got to his feet. "If you change your mind, you know where to reach me."

"I don't think that will be necessary," she said coolly. "Good night, Mr. Flynt. Thank you for the drink."

"My pleasure." He gave her a small bow and a smile. It was the same smile he had shown her earlier. But now it made her shudder. A killer's smile.

"Well, Gran," Sarah said when he was gone. "What do you

think of the nice man now? Do you still think I would have done better falling for someone like him?"

Gran winced. "God forbid."

Later that evening Sarah sat down on the bed in the hotel room and telephoned her parents.

"I'm going to see one of our friends again on Monday," she told her father. It was midafternoon in New Jersey and her mother was out at the store, so instead of the usual three-way conversation she found herself speaking only to Ted: "Gran and I will be getting a flight out on Tuesday morning. I'll call to confirm before we leave."

Only then, and only incidentally, did she tell him in guarded terms about the American who had just offered to handle "the project" for her. "I couldn't believe the things he was saying," she said, laughing. "It was like something out of an old Bogart movie."

But her father was not laughing. "Do you think he could do it?" he asked.

"Daddy, you're not taking this seriously, are you?"

"Honey, at this point I'm not closing off any possibilities."

"But, Dad—"

"Listen, I know what you're saying, kitten, and I agree with you. I'd rather not have to deal with somebody like that either. But if nothing else works out, this may be the only choice we have left. Now I'm on to a new lead here, and it looks promising. But we'd be foolish not to keep all our options open."

"Even something like this?"

"Look, all I'm asking you to do is to find out where we can get in touch with him later if we have to. Honey, it would be a last resort. That's all I'm talking about: a last resort."

Sarah peered out the window at the lights of the city. *You want him dead, I can fix it,* the man had said. She shuddered. Was this real? Was any of it real?

"You still there?" her father asked.

"Yes," she said. "At least I think it's me."

"How's that? This connection's not so good."

"I said yes, okay. I'll talk to him again."

"Good. That's great. Hey, looking forward to seeing you, kitten. It'll be good to have you home."

"Thanks, Dad. It'll be good to get back."

And she meant it, too. From the bottom of her heart.

twelve

When she and Gran were shown into Ambassador Silberman's office on Monday morning, Sarah could not help but notice that the sunlight in the landscape behind the ambassador's massive desk was brighter than the sunlight outside, where the weather had again turned gray and cold. Maybe that was why the painting was there, she thought: for days like today.

"I did some checking over the weekend," the ambassador said after his secretary had provided them all with coffee. "I think there might be something we can arrange. On the quiet, of course."

He pushed his steel-rimmed spectacles to the top of his bald head where they sat like another pair of eyes. Not far from the embassy, he explained, there was a school for the children of diplomats, journalists, and other foreign nationals stationed in Belgrade. "My wife tells me there's going to be an opening for a junior high school teacher. From what I know of your background I'm sure you wouldn't have any trouble qualifying."

"Oh," Gran said. "That sounds like a nice job, doesn't it, Sarah?"

"Wait a minute," Sarah said, waving Gran to silence. "Mr. Ambassador, what are you suggesting?"

"Just this. Once you were settled in, with a job and a place to live, you could work at gaining your husband's confidence. Ease his fears to the point where he'd be willing to let you see your son alone. Then, when the time was right, we could arrange to distract him long enough for you to get the boy on a plane and out of the country."

"Sarah!" said Gran, all excited. "Doesn't that sound perfect! It could be the rainbow at the end of the tunnel."

"Thank you," Sarah murmured, not knowing what else to say. "I'm very grateful."

"If you're interested, I could make the necessary arrangements, put you in touch with the right people. Unofficially, of course."

In the courtyard outside the window, the wind was blowing the last dry leaves from the trees. Sarah remembered being in the park with Jovan, and him telling her what he would demand of her in return for his trust. She remembered his drunken rage in the restaurant. She shook her head. "It wouldn't work," she said.

"Are you sure?"

Sarah nodded blankly. "It's too late. I could never make him trust me enough."

"She's right," said Gran. "There's been too much water over the bridge."

The ambassador took his spectacles from his forehead and began chewing on one of the ear pieces. "Well, I hope you'll give some thought to my suggestion. It is possible we could work something out. There is one thing I need to know, however."

"What's that?"

"A technicality, but an important one. It's the question of how your son came into this country. Was he on an American passport, do you know?"

She shook her head. "He didn't have one. Jovan got him a Yugoslav passport two or three years ago, when he was talking about bringing us over here for a visit."

"And that didn't make you suspicious?"

"No, not at the time. I didn't see that it mattered, what kind of passport he had."

"Unfortunately it matters a great deal. Without an American passport bearing a visa stamp that proves the boy was brought into Yugoslavia as an American, you won't be able to take him out of the country. In the eyes of the Yugoslavs, you'd be making off with one of their citizens. I'm surprised your lawyers never told you that."

"Mr. Borden did. He didn't mention the visa specifically, but he did say I should get a family passport with both Joey's and my picture on it." She opened her handbag and took out the little blue booklet. "This is what I've been traveling with," she said, handing it to him.

The ambassador put his glasses back on and studied the passport. "This is dated last month," he said.

"That's right."

"And the picture was taken when?"

Her heart skipped a beat. Oh, God, she thought, he's spotted it. He knows it's a forgery. "During the summer," she lied.

"Before Joey was taken, then."

"Yes."

"Hmm," he said, noncommittally. He handed the passport back. "It's a nice picture of you," he said. "More attractive than the usual passport picture. Joey's a handsome boy."

"Thank you," Sarah murmured in relief, hastily tucking the booklet back into her purse.

"Well?" Gran asked. "Is that what Sarah needs?"

"It's possible," he said cautiously.

"You don't seem very certain," Gran said.

254

"I'm not."

"But why not?" asked Sarah. "I have the entrance visa from when I came in at the airport. Wouldn't that cover Joey and me both?"

"It might," he conceded. "Under the normal procedures, I believe, each of you would need to have a visa stamp, even on a family passport. But you might get lucky. It's just the kind of wrinkle that the customs men would overlook. Yes, it might just work."

"Well?" Gran asked as she and Sarah rode back to the hotel in a taxi. "What do you think? Are you going to take the man up on his offer?"

Sarah shook her head. "It doesn't change anything. The visa is not the only problem. You know what I'd have to go through with Jovan for him to leave Joey alone with me. I can't do it. I won't. I'm not going to let him have that kind of power over me again. Not ever."

"Maybe you wouldn't have to, dear. Maybe if you were just here, just living nearby, he would be satisfied."

"I can't see it," Sarah said bleakly.

"Well, I just don't think you should dismiss the ambassador's offer out of hand. Remember what your father said about keeping your options in the fire. You shouldn't be slamming any doors."

Sarah turned to the window, to the bare trees that lined the boulevard, the people huddled in their heavy coats against the wind. "I'm afraid my options have just about run out."

Back at the hotel, Sarah called the airline and confirmed reservations on the morning flight to Paris, with a connecting flight to New York. Next she telephoned Dimi Dimitrivic to thank him for his help, such as it was. Finally, fighting off her resistance, she did as her father had asked and dialed Jack

Flynt's number, to find out where he could be reached in the States.

"Hey," he said cheerfully as she wrote down the information. "I'm glad we finally had a chance to have that drink together."

"Yes," she said, trying to sound as neutral as possible.

"I hope we'll be able to do it again. Maybe alone next time. Just the two of us."

"Good-bye, Mr. Flynt," she said. She hung up quickly. She had no intention of ever seeing him again. Not if she could help it.

That done, she was left with only one more chore, the one she had been dreading more than any other: she had to tell Jovan and Joey she was leaving.

If it had been only Jovan she would have done it over the phone. Maybe not have said anything at all. Just disappeared, shut him out of her life forever. No good-byes, no regrets. But there was Joey. No way she could not tell Joey. Still, she put it off as long as she could. She packed a few things, then wasted more time thinking about what she would wear on the trip home. A skirt and sweater? No, better wear slacks. It gets chilly on planes.

"If you wait too long," Gran said, "you won't have a chance to say good-bye at all."

"You're right, Gran. As always." She got up from the bed and got her coat out of the closet.

"Would you like me to come along?"

"No, Gran. Thanks. It's better if I go myself. You take a nap. I'll be back as soon as I can."

She went downstairs to the street and was about to catch a bus when, as an afterthought, she stopped in a nearby shop and picked up some candy and fruit and a little windup toy clown to take to Joey. No telling when he would get such treats again, once she was gone.

Back outside, she caught a bus on the Boulevard Revolucije. The city slid by beyond the windows but she saw none of it. She sat as if in a daze, trying to quiet the turmoil in her stomach, trying to think what she would say to Joey, how she could possibly tell him that she was going away and did not know whether he would see her again.

The bus pulled up near the Mongolian Embassy. Mechanically, Sarah got off and walked like an automaton up the street that led to Baka's cul-de-sac. Except for the sentry pacing at the corner, the little road was empty. A raw wind rattled the leaves in the gutters and set the bare branches of the trees scratching at the gray sky. From the cottage chimney flew a plume of blue-gray coal smoke.

Sarah pulled her coat collar closer around her neck and pushed open the squeaky gate. She walked up the path and knocked on the door.

It was opened by Baka, who seemed surprised to see her. "Oh, it's you," she said in Serbian. She was wearing an apron and a scarf around her head. In one hand she carried a broom. The wicked witch of the East.

"I've come to see Joey."

"He's sleeping."

"Would you wake him, please. I need to talk to him. It's important."

Baka eyed her warily for a moment, then stepped aside. "Close door," she said, switching to English. "We do not have money to throw away on coal."

Gracious as ever, Sarah thought. But she did as she was told.

Once inside, she glanced around the room and was relieved to see that Jovan was apparently not home. Maybe she could avoid saying good-bye to him after all.

Baka went into the kitchen and called up the stairs to the bedroom. "Joey, come down. Your mother is here to see you."

There was a whoop and in another instant Joey came flying down the stairs in his stocking feet. "Mama!" he cried and threw himself into her arms.

He was wearing all of his clothes, but apparently he had just emerged from under the blankets because as Sarah hugged him to her, she could feel the warmth of his small body, the smell of sleep in his hair. She drank it in voraciously, wanting to impress the smell and feel of him on her mind, to memorize every detail and store it away for the long months ahead.

"Hello, sweetheart. I'm sorry I had to wake you up."

"I'm n-n-not," he stuttered gleefully. "I'm g-g-glad." He hugged her again.

"Look, Joey! Look what I brought you. Here's some chocolate. And some apples. And I found this little clown. If you wind him up he does a little dance. See?"

"Oh, Mama. He's n-n-nice. Thank you, Mama." He clapped his hands happily and kissed her. His exuberance filled her with pain and delight at the same time. In the last three weeks he had gotten used to seeing her again. There was no more holding back, none of the untrusting restraint with which he had first greeted her. She had become part of his life again—and that was going to make it even harder to say good-bye.

"You want coffee?" Baka asked grudgingly.

"If it isn't any trouble."

"Always is trouble when you come." But she went to the sink to fill the kettle.

Sarah took off her coat and draped it over the back of a chair. She was just sitting down by the fire, drinking in Joey's excited talk about a new friend he'd made, when the door burst open, sending a draft of cold air across the room. Jovan stood there, a bucket of coal in one hand and an armload of kindling in the other.

"Well, well," he said as he kicked the door shut behind him.

258

"The grand lady honors us with her presence." Brushing past her, he set the bucket down and dumped the kindling into the box beside the fireplace. "Well?" he said, straightening up. "Are you going to tell us what you are doing here? Did you finally come to your senses, eh?"

Joey began to back away, his face shadowed by fear, but Sarah put an arm around him and held him near her. Despite the pounding of her heart, she managed to keep her voice calm and steady. She did not want to add to Joey's fear nor provoke another argument. That wasn't the way she wanted Joey to remember her. "If you mean did I decide to move in here, the answer is still no," she told Jovan over Joey's shoulder.

"Then why did you come? Did you forget what I said? You want to be with Joey, you be here with me."

"I didn't forget, don't worry."

"Then what are you doing here?"

"To tell you—" She turned back to Joey and took his hands in hers. She spoke to him rather than to Jovan. "To tell you that Gran and I will be leaving tomorrow. We're going back home, Joey. Back to America."

Joey froze. He stared at her in disbelief, his tender, sweet face hardening into a mask of stone. She would have done anything to have avoided this moment. Anything but stay here with Jovan.

"Leaving?" Jovan gave a snort of derision. "You can't leave. I won't let you."

Sarah ignored him, focusing all her attention on Joey, desperate to ease his pain in any way she could. "It's not what I want to do," she told him, searching his eyes, beseeching him to believe her. "What I want most in the world is to be with you."

"I won't let you," Jovan declared again, louder than before, and Sarah heard a note of panic in his voice. "In this country the husband makes the rules, the wife obeys. Do you hear? You will do as I say."

Sarah paid no attention. It was only Joey who concerned her now. "Grandpa Ted is still very sick," she explained carefully, feeling curiously calm and sure of herself even as Jovan teetered closer on the edge of hysteria. "He needs me there to help him get well again." She would not tell him the truth. She would not turn him against his father. Now more than ever he would need Jovan to love, to lean upon. "You want Grandpa to get well, don't you, Joey?"

"I will lock you in," Jovan shouted. Shoulders hunched, he was pacing in front of her like a cornered animal, and her calmness seemed to agitate him even more. Good, she thought. Let him. She was no longer afraid of his threats. He could do what he wanted. She had made her decision.

"Gran knows I'm here," she told him evenly as she got to her feet. Taking her coat off the back of the chair, she slipped it over her shoulders. "If I'm not back soon, Gran will go to the embassy and they will send the police."

The word brought a shriek of dismay from Baka.

"*Policija!*" she cried, her eyes wide with the fear. "They are coming here? The *policija?*"

More distracted than ever, Jovan hurried to reassure her. "No, *Mami*. Do not worry. There are no police coming." He turned back to Sarah, raging no more but pleading now, his face twisted in anguish, his eyes brimming. "For God's sake, Sarah, please do not go. I am sorry. I did not mean what I said just now. I was upset. It was not what I meant. Listen to me. You can see Joey whenever you want, take your own apartment, anything. Just do not go back. We need you." He reached out an imploring hand. "*I* need you," he whispered.

She knew he meant every word of it. Knew also that he was

capable of saying just the opposite in the next breath and believing that, too. She ignored the hand. "It's too late," she said quietly. "Last week, two weeks ago, it might have made a difference. But not now."

"Sarah—"

"No," she cut him off. "I'm going now. That's final." She turned to Joey. The sight of him broke her heart: head down, not looking at her, hands limp at his sides. Pale and cold as marble. She lowered herself to one knee, to where he could see her without lifting his head. Still he avoided her eyes. She reached out to him. "Will you give me one last hug before I go?"

Once, slowly, he shook his head and looked away.

"Joey, listen to me. I know you're mad at me and you've got good reason to be. I want to take you home with me, but I just can't. Not now. But that's why I need a hug from you, so I can take *that* home with me. So I can have that little part of you with me always."

For another moment he stood rooted to where he was. Then, still without looking at her, he took a single step forward, into her arms. And stood there. Rigid. Offering no warmth, no response.

"I'll be back, I promise," she whispered, her own tears welling up. His hair smelled like musty leaves and coal smoke; his sweater was rough against her cheek. "I want you to be a good boy and do what your daddy and your baka tell you. Will you do that?"

A nod against her shoulder.

"I know it's hard to be good all the time, but try and do the best you—" She stopped. It was all wrong. It was not what she wanted to say to him. "Joey, listen to me." She took his chin in her hand and forced him to look at her. "Whatever happens while I'm gone, I want you always to remember that your mama loves you. Don't ever forget that, Joey. Promise you won't forget that."

He nodded once. He was fighting his own tears now. Fighting them hard. He nodded again. "I promise," he whispered.

And that was all. Aside from one last *"Do vidjenja, Mami,"* as she stepped out the door, that was all.

Afterward she realized that it was probably the most she could have hoped for. There were already too many good-byes in his short life. Another one was simply more than he could bear.

And her own insides were raw for days after she and Gran got home.

CHECKPOINT
Saturday, April 23, 11:50 A.M.

It was just before noon when they crossed the bridge over the Sava River and found themselves skirting the edge of central Belgrade. Wilkes was at the wheel, watching for a particular turnoff.

Sarah watched the familiar sights flash past: the wide boulevards, the pointed gables of the Hotel Moskva, the copper-green dome of the parliament building. Off in the distance she could just make out the gray turrets of the Kalemegdan fortress, where it stood on its bluff overlooking the Danube. After this trip was over Sarah hoped she would never see any of those landmarks again.

Wilkes got off the highway in the newer part of town, amid rows of modern apartment blocks. No trees, no steeples broke up the boxy skyline. A single square tower stood taller than the rest, however, and as Wilkes drove toward it Sarah read the sign over the entranceway: HOTEL SRBIJA.

"I'm afraid it's not as elegant as the Metropol," Wilkes told Ted as he pulled into the parking lot. "But if we went there Sarah might be recognized. I didn't want to take any chances."

263

"It's also right off the main road," Ted observed. "Which means we can get out of town quickly."

Wilkes laughed once. A quick report, like a gun going off. "Dead right, Ted. By God, we'll make a private eye out of you by the time we're through. A regular James Bond."

They got out and Wilkes led the way up the front steps and into the hotel.

The lobby was as plain and unadorned as the building itself: teak paneling, photo murals of local points of interest, a long counter behind which a delicate-looking young man was bent over a paperback book.

Following the instructions that she had been given earlier, Sarah hung back near the entrance while Wilkes and her father stepped up to the reception desk. "Look shy and nervous," Wilkes had told her, and she had no trouble acting the part.

"Good afternoon," Wilkes greeted the desk clerk.

The young man stirred barely enough to raise his head from the pages of his book. "Yes?" he replied in English.

"We have reservations for two rooms. A single for my friend here and a double for me. The name is Wilkes. Peter Wilkes."

"A double for you, sir?"

"A double, yes. I'll be, ah, having a guest." He tilted his head meaningfully in Sarah's direction.

The clerk slid her a languid glance. Sarah's cheeks burned. She looked at her feet: tan pumps on a brown carpet. When she looked up again the clerk was busy handing out forms to Wilkes and her father.

"Fill in, please," the clerk said. "I need also to see your passports."

The ruse had worked. Obviously the private arrangements of the hotel's guests didn't matter to the clerk at all. Which was just what Wilkes had been hoping for: to pass Sarah off

264

as his local girl friend or perhaps as a call girl—a visitor, at any rate, rather than a paying guest. That way she would not have to show her passport to the clerk, who was required to enter in a police registry the names and passport numbers of all hotel guests. The name Sarah Stefanovic on an American passport was bound to raise awkward questions, maybe even spark the interest of a curious official. Nor did Wilkes want to make it too easy for the police to track Sarah down later.

When the forms were filled out and the clerk was finished examining their passports, Wilkes and Sarah's father were taken in hand by an aging gentleman in a frayed uniform, who lifted their suitcases onto a cart and led them toward the elevator.

"Come along, love," Wilkes called to Sarah across the lobby.

Sarah flinched. Wilkes' kept woman, his whore—whatever she was supposed to be, it was not a role she liked playing, especially since she had the distinct feeling that Wilkes himself was secretly enjoying this particular masquerade. But she set her smile and allowed him to take her by the elbow and escort her to the elevator.

They got off on the fourth floor, where the bellhop led them down a neon-lit corridor. Halfway along, he stopped, opened a door, and stepped back to reveal a narrow little cell crammed with teak furnishings; between the bed, the bureau, the table and chairs, and a writing desk, there was hardly enough space to turn around in. Still, the room was clean and bright, and the single large window had a sweeping view of the city.

Ted lifted his bag off the cart and stepped inside. For now, this would be his room; when the coast was clear, he would switch with Wilkes and share the double with Sarah.

"See you for dinner?" Wilkes asked through the open door. "How does six o'clock sound?"

"Let's make it seven. I need a good long nap."

"Seven it is," Wilkes said with forced good cheer. And with his hand still on Sarah's arm, he followed the bellhop down the hall.

Their room was only slightly larger than the one they had just seen. It had two windows instead of one, and two beds. But otherwise, it was exactly the same: same teak furniture, same gold carpet, same panoramic view of downtown Belgrade.

"Well, here we are," Wilkes said, once he had tipped the bellhop and closed the door behind him.

"Yes," she said. "Here we are."

He drew a glass of water from the sink in the corner, then let himself drop wearily into a chair. He glanced around the room. "I trust you will be comfortable here. It's not very roomy but it's got everything you'll need."

"Yes."

"Odd, though, isn't it?"

"How do you mean?"

"Two single beds. It's not very thoughtful of the management, is it? I mean, considering that we're supposed to be here for an assignation."

"Oh."

He smiled thinly, took another sip of water. "Typical socialist inefficiency, I'd say."

"Yes. I guess so."

It was awkward being alone with him for the first time . . . in a hotel room . . . even if it was only for a few minutes. He seemed to be feeling it, too. Or was he just playing with her? She couldn't tell. But she sat down on the bed nearest the window. She felt very tired.

"What about you and Dad being registered here?" she asked, to fill the silence. "Won't the police be able to track you down if something goes wrong?"

Wilkes shook his head. "The name won't mean anything to them. As far as they're concerned, I'm just an ordinary Englishman on a business trip."

"What kind of business? Or shouldn't I ask?"

"On the contrary." He flicked open his gold lighter and touched the flame to a cigarette. "It's better that you and your father know in case you're questioned." He reached inside his tweed jacket, withdrew his passport, and handed it to her. It identified him as Peter Wilkes of Maidstone, Kent, and listed his profession as salesman.

"What are you supposed to be selling?"

"Machine tools. It happens to be something I know a little about."

He also showed her photos of a woman and two children sitting on a park bench, and a letter from a Maidstone address. The letter was signed, "Love, Chrissy."

Well, Sarah thought, that explains the wedding ring.

"Your wife?" she asked. Not that it mattered, of course.

"Not mine. Somebody's, though."

"Oh." His answer was not at all illuminating but she was hesitant to press him further. She handed back the photographs. "So none of this is real?" she asked.

"Oh, yes. The passport itself is quite authentic. So is the name. And there *is* an executive at a manufacturing firm who's prepared to vouch for me." His grin was that of a small boy sharing the secrets of a particularly clever prank. Sarah couldn't help but smile back.

"You people have taken care of everything, haven't you?"

"I certainly hope so. For your sake as well as mine." His crystalline blue eyes rested on hers for a long moment and their warmth surprised her. Then, as if suddenly remembering himself, he got to his feet. "We'd all better get some rest," he said. "I'll stop back here at seven to pick you two up for dinner."

Then he was gone.

Wearily she kicked off her shoes and lay back on the bed. She was vaguely aware of her father coming into the room and falling into the other bed. Not until she was half asleep did she realize that she still knew absolutely nothing about Peter Wilkes except his name. And that he liked being mysterious.

thirteen

The ad caught Ted's attention one morning in mid-November, while Sarah was still in Belgrade. He was sitting in bed, leafing idly through the *Wall Street Journal,* when his eye fell on a black-bordered box at the bottom of an inside page:

SPECIALIZED INTERNATIONAL SERVICES
Highly trained, skilled professionals available for hazardous-type assignments. Security conscious, confidentiality protected. Licensed, insured, and bonded.

Interested parties were invited to address inquiries to a post office box number in Lakeland, Florida.

Sitting in his favorite easy chair in the living room, dressed in what had become his standard daytime attire of pajamas and bathrobe, Ted carefully tore the ad out of the paper and clipped it to the front cover of a manila folder. The folder was labeled "Joey" and it bulged with the notes, memos, and correspondence that Ted had accumulated in the weeks since

269

Labor Day; the clipping would help him remember to get a letter off to the Florida address this afternoon, after he'd had his nap and done his exercises. These days he was up and around for increasingly longer periods of time, and his health was improving steadily. But he still had to parcel out his energies.

A few weeks earlier, Ted would not have even considered responding to an ad like the one in the *Journal*. He had not forgotten the righteous indignation with which he had dismissed Bob Koenig's hints about "alternative measures." But things looked different now. Sarah's reports from Belgrade had been growing more discouraging every day, and even Bill Borden was beginning to sound less optimistic about their chances of getting Joey back through legal channels.

"I'm afraid we've hit another dead end," Borden had reported the other day. "Senator Case says he'll nudge the people over at State one more time, but beyond that there isn't much he can do."

"Goddamn it," Ted had fumed. "I'll bet if my name were Rockefeller or Kennedy, we'd get some action quick enough."

"Probably," Borden conceded. "But it's Novack and that's what we have to work with."

Then, just yesterday, Ted had had a call from Sherwood Brice, his well-connected friend in the brokerage business. Brice had been in touch with a former classmate at Princeton who now worked for the Central Intelligence Agency.

"My friend says you should forget about going through official channels," Brice reported in his pinched prep school accent. "He says you won't get anywhere that way."

"So what does he suggest?"

"He says you should hire yourself a professional. Or someone who has connections in the mob. The mob might be able to arrange something through Sicily."

"You're talking about the Mafia? Jesus, Sherwood!"

270

"Now hold on, Ted. Don't get me wrong. I'm not condoning any of this. I'm simply passing along my friend's advice."

"Well, thanks. But I'm not about to get involved with a bunch of gangsters. Besides, what if they did get Joey out? What guarantee would we have that *they* wouldn't then turn around and hold him for ransom?"

"Of course. You're right. Look, just forget I even brought it up."

"I'll do that. But let me ask you something else. When your friend suggested hiring a professional, what did he mean by that?"

"A private investigator, I assume."

"Any idea how much that kind of thing would cost?"

"Your guess is as good as mine. I imagine you'd have to talk to the person. Want me to ask my friend if he knows anybody?"

Ted hesitated. The idea appealed to his sense of adventure. But that was exactly the kind of reaction that made him distrust his own motives.

"No. No, thanks," he finally replied. "I guess I'd rather wait and see what else turns up."

Still, once the idea of seeking "professional help" had been planted in Ted's mind, it kept recurring, teasing at the corners of his consciousness. And now here was this ad in the *Wall Street Journal*: "highly skilled, trained professionals." Well, it certainly wouldn't hurt to inquire.

Ted drafted a letter that very afternoon. With it he enclosed a copy of the summary he had prepared for Bill Borden, outlining the facts in the case.

What happened next only seemed to confirm that he was on the right track. Hardly had Emma left for the supermarket with the letter tucked in her handbag, than Sarah was on the phone from Belgrade telling him about the surprising encounter she had had with an American who operated gam-

271

bling casinos in Yugoslavia. The guy sounded as dangerous as any Mafia hood. Yet it was encouraging just to know that such people were actually available, and that maybe all Ted had to do now was find the right one.

"I'm sorry," said Bill Borden when Ted broached the subject to him over the telephone. "That's not the kind of thing we here at the firm like to get involved with."

"I know, Bill. I don't like it either. I wouldn't even be asking you such a thing if there was any other way. But nothing else is working. You've been telling me that yourself. The congressman, the State Department people—nobody's getting anywhere. Or am I wrong?"

For a long moment there was no sound on the other end of the line. Finally Borden let out a long breath. "No, you're not wrong."

"Well, then, what about it? There must be people who would be willing to take on something like this."

"Sure there are. Lots of people. The newspapers are full of stories about private investigators who specialize in snatching kids in custody cases. It's a real growth industry. But you're talking about getting a child out of a Communist country. Not every flake in a raincoat could handle a job like that."

"I understand that. But—"

"And even if we did locate the right kind of person, there could still be problems. Even the professionals get caught. And if that happened, you could lose any chance of getting your boy back."

"The way things are going we don't have any chance anyway."

Again Borden hesitated, but this time only briefly. "Okay. Look, Ted, I'll have to talk this over with Colonel Stevenson. Give me a few days. We'll see what we can come up with."

Ted was pleased and relieved. But for a long time afterward, he kept having the niggling suspicion that Borden had agreed too quickly, that his show of resistance had been just that—a show. Ted wondered if there wasn't some rule in the lawyer's handbook about always making sure the client was the one who took the first step over the cliff.

Two days later, Ted picked up Sarah and her grandmother at the airport and brought them back to Sommerton. Gran only stayed long enough to have dinner. Then, exhausted from the trip, she asked to be driven home to Cherry Hill.

"You know what I always say," she told them solemnly as she eased her bulk into the car: "Home is where the heart is."

Sarah closed the door for her, then leaned in the window and gave her a kiss. "Thank you for everything. I don't know what I would have done without you."

"Oh, go on. You would have done just fine. Although, I admit, you did need a little help with your—"

To Ted it sounded like she said "mushroom salad," but he wasn't sure.

As soon as Emma and her mother drove off, Sarah took herself up to bed.

"Are you all right, kitten?" Ted called after her. He was worried. She looked terrible. Her complexion was pasty, her brown eyes dull, her face devoid of expression.

She murmured something about jet lag, but Ted knew it was more than that. The weeks in Belgrade had been an emotional roller coaster for her. And having to leave Joey behind had been devastating.

And yet, over the next few days, it became clear to both Ted and Emma that something in their daughter had changed. This time her depression did not immobilize her. And as they watched her moving about the house, making calls, catching up on what had been going on at home, they sensed in her a self-assurance, a quiet determination that they had not seen before. And when Bill Borden finally called back a few days later, Sarah was right there at Ted's side, watching while he took notes, waiting expectantly, eager to find out what their next move would be.

"Well?" she asked, as soon as he hung up. "What did Mr. Borden say? Did he come up with anything?"

Ted allowed himself a cautious nod. "He's been in touch with an American in London, a former FBI man named Harry Lipton who runs something called"— Ted consulted his notes—"Atlantic Information Systems. The man specializes in 'in-depth studies' for the big multinationals—Exxon, ITT, that kind of thing."

" 'In-depth studies'?"

"Spying," said Ted. "He also has another specialty: smuggling people out of Eastern Europe."

Ted telephoned London early on Monday morning, before the rates went up. His call was received by a woman with a perky British accent. She answered by reciting the last four digits of the phone number, followed by a polite, "May I help you?" No names mentioned—not Lipton's, not the company's. Just those anonymous four digits. It was, Ted noted approvingly, all very discreet.

"Mr. Lipton, please. My name is Novack. I believe he's expecting to hear from me."

Harry Lipton was cordial but businesslike. Yes, he said, Borden had filled him in on the general situation. He wanted Ted to understand that the firm did not usually handle "domestic" cases; as a personal favor to Bill, however, he would be willing to see the Novacks and talk in more detail. "Could you be in London during the second week of January?"

"Can't we make it any sooner?" Ted was impatient. There had already been too many delays. He was anxious to get started, to be *doing* something.

But Lipton would not be hurried. Monday, the tenth, was the earliest he could see them.

Reluctantly Ted agreed. When he thought about it later, however, he decided that having to wait three or four weeks might be a good thing after all. It would allow him just that much more time to regain his strength and make the necessary arrangements; plane tickets, hotel reservations. He'd no doubt need a new passport, too. His old one was almost certainly out of date. He'd got it in April '67. Almost ten years ago. When he and Emma were going to Paris for Sarah's wedding.

Later that day, while Ted was stretched out on the floor doing some gentle back exercises, Emma called him to the phone to take a long-distance call: "He didn't give his name, but he's got a Southern accent."

Ted took the receiver. "Hello?"

"Mr. Novack? I'm Tom Carleton. I'm calling about the letter ya'll sent? In answer to our ad in the *Wall Street Journal?*"

Tom Carleton identified himself as a lawyer representing a group of retired police officers, detectives, and security guards—"all professionals, you understand"—who hired themselves out for special missions involving security, surveillance, and undercover work. They referred to themselves, Carleton said, chuckling, as the "over-the-hill gang."

"Now, the kind of job ya'll are interested in would cost a good bit of money," he went on. "I mean to say, it could be pretty dangerous business, crossin' international frontiers an' all. Might even be some shootin' 'fore it's over."

"Shooting?"

"It's an eventuality we'd have to be prepared for. An' a' course, that's the kind of thing that pushes up the costs. The higher the risk, the higher the cost, if ya'll see what I mean."

"Yes, I see. Ah, just what kind of costs are you talking about, Mr. Carleton?"

"Well, as a ball-park figure I'd say we're talkin' seventy-five to a hundred thousand dollars, somewhere in there. It's hard to tell exactly without sittin' down with ya'll and goin' over the details. If ya'll would like to come down here for a little talk . . ."

Ted begged off. Not only did the fee sound outrageous, but so did the man's easy talk about gunplay. The boys in the "over-the-hill-gang" were going to have to find someone else to supplement their pensions.

"Hello, Joey. Happy birthday, sweetheart." Sarah fought to keep her voice steady as she spoke into the receiver.

It was Monday, December 20, 1976. Joey was six years old today.

"Hello, Mama." His voice was flat, without emotion.

"How are you, sweetheart? Are you having a nice birthday?"

"Uh-huh."

"Did you open your presents yet?"

"Uh-huh."

"I hope the clothes fit okay. Did you like the racing cars and the track that Gramma and Grampa sent?"

"*Da.*"

"Would you like to tell them that yourself? They're right here and they'd like to talk to you."

"Okay."

276

"Don't hang up now."

"I w-w-won't."

Sarah's mother got on the line and said hello and happy birthday, then her father did the same. God, Sarah thought as she waited, it's so hard. What could she say? How could she reach him over the phone when she hadn't even been able to do it in person?

"I hope you have a really nice birthday," she said when her father handed back the phone. "I wish I could be there with you. I miss you a lot, Joey."

When he answered, his voice was so quiet she could barely make out the words. "I m-m-miss you t-t-too, Mama."

———

Two days before Christmas, Jack Flynt called from California. How he had tracked down the number Ted had no idea; he was obviously a man of some resources. He told Ted he was prepared to fly East and discuss possible approaches to solving "your daughter's problem."

"Such as?"

"I'd rather not go into details over the phone, but as your daughter may have told you, I happen to have an interest in several resorts in a certain country."

"Yes, so I gather," said Ted.

"Naturally, in the course of my business, I come into contact with all sorts of people, including some well-placed figures in the government over there."

"And?"

"Well, as it happens, one or two of my more influential patrons had some bad luck recently and got in over their heads. If you'd be willing to cover their debts, I'm sure they could be persuaded to let your daughter take her son out of the country."

"I see," said Ted. The whole business sounded shadier than he liked. Still, if Flynt could make it work . . . "Just how much money are you talking about, Mr. Flynt?"

"Eighty thousand."

If Ted had not just heard a similar figure from the man in Florida, he might have been more startled. "That's a lot of money, Mr. Flynt."

"Amazing, isn't it? Some people can lose a bundle and still not know when to quit."

They all tried to make Christmas a happy day, even though no one's heart was really in it. Ted had gone out and bought a big tree as usual, and set it up in the bay window. On Christmas Eve, Sarah's brother Richard flew in from Berkeley, where he was teaching math and finishing up his doctorate. It was the first time in two years that they had all been together for the holidays.

On Christmas morning they sat by the tree and exchanged gifts and joked as usual, about saving the wrappings for next year. But without Joey, the holiday felt empty. By his absence he was more of a presence than if he'd actually been there.

Sarah was glad when the day was over. Now if only she didn't have to wait two weeks before the trip to London.

CHECKPOINT
Saturday, April 23, 7:00 P.M.

Having spent the afternoon catching up on their sleep, Sarah and her father had only just managed to drag themselves out of their beds when Wilkes came to collect them for dinner. Ted took a quick shower, but when he came out of the bathroom he still looked as pale as the bedsheets.

Sarah was worried. "Maybe you should stay and rest some more. You don't look well."

He made a gesture of dismissal. "I'm all right. I need food as much as I need sleep." He shrugged on his sportcoat. "Come on, let's go."

But Sarah knew he wasn't all right; he just didn't want to miss anything.

The café Wilkes took them to was in a cellar a few steps below street level. Its menu and its atmosphere had a Turkish flavor, complete with filigreed hanging lamps, rugs on the walls, waiters in fezzes, and the pungent smell of cooked lamb and strong cigarettes. In one corner, a drummer and a flute player set up a plaintive, wailing rhythm. The place was crowded with Russian tourists.

"This is one of their favorite hangouts," Wilkes confided.

What with the wailing of the music and the shouting and laughter of the people around them, Wilkes had to raise his voice to make himself heard by the waiter when he gave their order.

The drinks (beer) and dinner (moussaka for Sarah and Wilkes, cabbage and lamb for Ted) had a soothing effect on them all. After a while even Wilkes began to relax and open up a little about himself.

He was, it turned out, only in his mid-thirties, which surprised Sarah since the lines in his face and the weariness in his gray-blue eyes suggested that he was at least ten years older. He'd been educated at St. Andrews in Scotland and had planned a career as a history teacher before a stint in the army led him into intelligence work. After being "demobbed," as he called it, he had taught history in a public school for a few years before drifting back to intelligence work. "The pay was better," he explained laconically.

"Oh?" said Sarah. "Adventure had nothing to do with it?" She was needling him, wanting to break through that cool facade of his.

Wilkes grinned and took another sip of beer. "It *is* rather more stimulating than correcting the essays of schoolboys," he conceded.

"And how did you come to be assigned to our case?" Ted asked. He had been listening to Wilkes with obvious fascination, hardly touching his plate of cabbage and lamb. Clearly the man intrigued him.

"Eastern Europe happens to be a specialty of mine. I've worked in the Balkans quite a lot. And then of course"—he lowered his voice—"I've done this kind of thing before: helping people get out of well, other places like this. But those were adults, not children, and the cases were political not, um, domestic. Still, the requirements are similar."

"Yes, I imagine they are."

"I'll be frank with you, though. This is not exactly my favorite kind of job. I prefer to work for corporations rather than individuals."

"Oh? Why is that?" Ted asked. "I'd imagine corporate work would be much more demanding."

"It is. But—" Wilkes took another sip of beer. "Corporations don't cry."

fourteen

Atlantic Information Services was not included among the names listed on the registry in the lobby of Pemberton House. Neither was the name of Harry Lipton.

"Are you sure this is the right place?" Sarah asked.

Her father checked the letter he'd been given by the driver who had brought them from Heathrow. Like the registry board, the typewritten note bore no identifying information: no company name, no fancy letterhead; only the address in the upper right-hand corner and Harry Lipton's signature at the bottom. The man obviously valued his anonymity.

"Turn left out of the hotel, then right up Davies Street," the letter instructed. "Walk three blocks to Pemberton House, take the elevator to the top floor, then walk up one flight."

"This is it," said Ted. "Come on. Let's go up."

The walk had taken them along what must have been one of the most luxurious shopping streets in London—a street lined with fancy antique shops, art galleries, furriers, and designer boutiques whose polished brass nameplates listed outlets in New York, St. Moritz, Zurich, and Beverly Hills.

The shop on the street level of Pemberton House sold antique maps and prints.

Getting off the elevator on five, Sarah followed her father up a flight of red-carpeted stairs to a small landing. They found themselves facing a single white door. The small brass plate over the buzzer was inscribed with only one word: "Lipton."

Ted said, "This must be the place." He pressed the button.

They were admitted by a prim, middle-aged woman in sensible shoes. She introduced herself as Liz, and while she took their coats, Sarah had a moment to glance around the reception area: soft carpets, a comfortable sofa, a wingback chair, old-fashioned lamps on old-fashioned end tables. The place looked the way she imagined a rather stodgy men's club would look, and Lipton's own office turned out to be very much the same: sofa, coffee table, easy chairs, nautical prints on the walls. A humidor and a rack of at least a dozen pipes sat on a side table near the desk. The desk itself was off in one corner facing a wall, as though its owner was reluctant to allow business to intrude too heavily on the comfortable setting. It had nothing on it but a few books and a large ashtray.

"Hello, I'm Harry Lipton," said the man who was waiting to greet them. "I hope you didn't have any trouble finding us up here."

He was a big haystack of a man with a broad American accent—probably Midwestern, Sarah thought. Broad-shouldered, thick-necked, he had a head of bushy gray hair, a bushy mustache, and bushy eyebrows that flew up at the ends like feathers on a hat, giving him an oddly startled look. There was nothing odd, however, about his manner or the way he was dressed: crisp white shirt, dark blue three-piece suit complete with gold watch chain looped across the front of his vest. He looked very precise, very businesslike—more like a bank manager, in fact, than a private investigator. And as he offered them seats and made welcoming small talk—all very formal, very correct—Sarah had the distinct impression that she had just walked onto a stage set and was meeting an actor playing his role. The empty desk, the anonymous correctness of everything in the room including Lipton himself, made her suspect that this office was merely a showplace and that the real business of the firm was conducted elsewhere. But then, maybe that's the way it should have been, considering the kind of business it was.

"Before we begin," Lipton said once they had all been seated, "I want you both to understand right from the start that the work we do can be very costly. For the big corporations that's not a problem. They can write off our fees as a business expense. You won't have that luxury."

Sarah glanced anxiously at her father, who nodded soberly. "I understand," he said. "Just how much money are you talking about?"

"At this point I wouldn't even want to guess," said Lipton, picking up a pipe from the rack near his desk. "First I'll need a lot more information from both of you than I have now."

"What is it you want to know?" asked Sarah.

"Everything." He lit a match, held it to the pipe bowl, puffed it to life. "I need to know whatever you can tell me about your husband and your son. What they're like, where they live, how your husband spends his days. I want to know where he goes when he goes out, how he lives, who your son plays with, where he goes to school."

"He doesn't go to school."

"Why not?"

"He's too young. He just turned six."

"What does he do all day?"

She shrugged. "If the weather's nice he goes out and plays. There's a little boy who lives down the street. Otherwise he stays in with his baka."

"His what?"

"His grandmother. My husband's mother. That's where they're living. At her house."

"What's the address?"

"I've got it right here."

She talked for she didn't know how long, while her father chewed on his cigars and Harry Lipton took notes on a yellow legal pad and puffed on his pipe and plied her with questions.

Meanwhile Lipton's secretary slipped quietly in and out, delivering phone messages, producing coffees and Cokes on request, and even coming up with cookies and pastries as the afternoon wore on.

It was late in the day and already getting dark outside when Lipton finally called a halt. "We'll pick up again in the morning," he said. Both he and her father had long since taken off their jackets and rolled up their shirt-sleeves. By then, Lipton's original air of formality had softened considerably.

Sarah was glad for the break. But she would have been even happier if the interview had been over for good. How many more times was she going to have to go through this? she wondered: answering endless questions, tearing open her insides for strangers?

But the next morning, she and her father were back, this time filling Lipton in on their unsuccessful attempts to work through the lawyers and State Department officials, the embassy people, Sarah's own frustrating attempts to work out some kind of visiting arrangement with Jovan.

"Tell me more about the business with the visas," Lipton said when Sarah was recalling the meetings she and Gran had had with the American ambassador. "There was some suggestion that you might get Joey out on your family passport, is that right?"

"Yes."

"How would that work?"

"Oh, it was all very iffy. Ambassador Silberman thought that the customs men might overlook the fact that there was only one entrance visa on the passport. But the way they scrutinized my passport when I left, I knew it wouldn't work."

"Why not? What happened?"

She remembered the moment vividly: she and Gran had joined the queue at the airport's passport-control station. At a high counter two uniformed guards were checking the passports of the people in line. They were taking their time about it and Sarah was relieved to see that they were not being too finicky about regulations. Despite warnings posted in several languages to the effect that it was a criminal offense to take food or liquor out of the country, the guards gave little more than a glance at a woman carrying a wicker basket from which protruded a large salami. The guards' lack of interest was encouraging and Sarah's hopes were high. Maybe the ambassador had been right: maybe the guards really were careless enough that she would be able to sneak Joey past them.

But when her turn came and she stepped up to the desk and handed over her passport, hope vanished. Flipping open the booklet, the guard behind the desk suddenly came alert.

"Where is the boy?" he snapped, pointing at the composite photo of her and Joey. "He is with you?"

"No. He—I had to leave him home. He was sick. He couldn't travel."

The man got up off his stool, and leaned over the high desk, apparently to make sure that there really was no child at Sarah's side. His cohort, too, looked as if he suspected something was amiss and came around to the front of the desk. Then together the two men studied the passport.

"*Pogledajte,*" one said to the other in Serbian, pointing to a

286

page in the little blue booklet. "Look, there is only one entry visa. She came in alone." Then in English, he asked Sarah: "The boy, he travels sometimes with you?"

"Sometimes, yes."

The guard eyed the passport once more. Then, apparently satisfied, he stamped the purple exit visa on the appropriate page.

"Only then did they let me through," she told Lipton now. "That's when I realized there was no way the ambassador's plan was going to work."

"I see." Lipton puffed on a meerschaum. He looked troubled.

Ted said, "it seems they wink at the petty stuff but they don't take any chances when they think people are being smuggled out."

"Especially children," said Sarah.

Not until well after lunch—a cold buffet of sandwiches and salad whipped up by Liz in a kitchenette located off the reception room—did Lipton finally indicate that the interview might be nearing an end. Putting down his pen and legal pad, he leaned back in his swivel chair and gazed thoughtfully at a corner of the ceiling.

"I'll be honest with you," he began, relighting his pipe. "This is a difficult kind of case. When I first spoke with Bill I assumed it would be something we could probably handle by negotiation. But from what you've told me about your husband and about the reaction of the Yugoslavs, it seems pretty clear that negotiations are out of the question."

"Yes," Sarah said.

"I'm also troubled by the way the Yugoslavs checked your passport so carefully when you were leaving. Frankly I'm surprised they were as scrupulous as all that."

"But you can do it?" Ted asked. "You can help us?"

"That remains to be seen. It would certainly be a challenge. But then"— he offered a boyish grin—"I've always been a sucker for a steep hill."

He stretched, laid the pipe in an ashtray, and got to his feet. "I'll need a little time to think about this and to consult with a few of my colleagues. I've got several scenarios in mind, but I won't really be sure which of them will work best—if in fact any of them will work at all—until we've had a chance to conduct a feasibility study."

"How long will that take?"

"It depends, but you should figure on a minimum of two to three months."

"*Months?*" Sarah was shocked. "Why so long?"

"Mrs. Stefanovic, abduction is a risky business."

Sarah flinched. There it was. Laid out in the open for the first time. The last resort.

She glanced at her father. His gaze was steady, impassive. She felt she should raise some objection. What Lipton was suggesting was patently offensive. If they went through with it, they'd be doing just what Jovan had done; in her mind it was just as shabby and underhanded. Yet as much as she wished there could be some other way, she knew that there was not—not after all she and her parents had been through during the last few months: all the failed efforts, all the leads that led nowhere; all the expressions of sympathy followed by regretful assertions of helplessness. That they had finally arrived at this point now seemed almost inevitable. She lowered her eyes. She said nothing.

"I want to make certain," Lipton continued, "that the risks are absolutely minimal before I agree to go ahead. And that takes time. Safety has to be our paramount concern."

"Whose safety?" Ted asked warily. "Yours? Your men's?" He was remembering the Florida lawyer's frighteningly casual talk about gunplay.

"The boy's first and foremost, but everyone else's as well. If an abduction looked too dangerous we wouldn't go through with it."

Ted sat back, satisfied. "I don't think we can argue with that, can we, Sare?"

"No," she said quietly. "We can't argue with that."

Lipton nodded his shaggy head, refilled his pipe, and began to explain what the "feasibility study" would entail. For starters, he'd need a thorough briefing from Bill Borden on the legal aspects. Then, a team of operatives would be sent to Belgrade to survey the neighborhood where Joey was living with his father. The area would be mapped and photographed, with special attention given to the timing and routes of police patrols, the proximity of neighboring houses, the location of alternative entrance and exit routes. There would be a lengthy surveillance of Joey, his father, his baka, and other "significant" members of the family, with the aim of determining the pattern of their activities as closely as possible: when they went out, where they went, what they did, whom they visited, where they shopped. Careful surveillance could usually establish patterns of movement in two to three weeks, but Lipton felt safer with four.

All this research would involve several members of Lipton's staff. Additional personnel would be recruited at the local level to carry out specific tasks. For instance, conducting discreet surveillance every day for several weeks required different cars, so as not to arouse suspicion.

"It all sounds very thorough," Ted commented dryly.

"Oh, it is," said Lipton, his pipe cocked between his fingers. "People think of this as an adventurous business but a lot of it is just tedious legwork and attention to details. Careful preparation—that's the secret of success for us. Adventure is only the result of poor planning."

Sarah smiled. The man's professionalism was reassuring.

289

Although she felt impatient with the amount of time Lipton's study would take, she had to admit that two or three months of "research" was still better than two or three *years* of living a lie in Belgrade while she awaited her chance to take Joey— and an uncertain chance at that.

Ted rolled the ash off the end of his cigar. "I begin to see why this kind of thing gets so expensive," he said.

"I warned you about that," said Lipton.

"Yes," Ted said bleakly. "Yes, you did. Well, all right, what's the bad news? How much do you figure all this is going to run us?"

Lipton's gaze did not waver. "To begin with, we'd need twenty thousand dollars to conduct the feasibility study."

Sarah was stunned. She glanced quickly at her father. He was sitting very still.

"Twenty . . . thousand," Ted said. "For . . . just the study." He turned the words over slowly, carefully, as if he were not quite sure he had heard correctly.

"That's right," said Lipton. "If it then develops that the project is not likely to succeed within acceptable levels of risk, there can be no refund of that money. The work will already have been done, you see."

"Yes," Ted said. "I see."

"On the other hand, if we decided we could go ahead, you should figure on it running another forty or forty-five thousand."

Ted cleared his throat, studied the cigar in his hand. "We'll —we'll have to give this some thought."

"Take as much time as you need."

"Talk it over with the wife and so on . . ."

"Of course," said Lipton. He got to his feet. "Meantime, I'll have Liz give you the name and address of our bank. We could get started as soon as we've been notified that the initial installment has been deposited in our account."

290

With an effort Ted pushed himself up off of the sofa. Absently he extended his hand, thanked Lipton for his help, and started for the door. Sarah herself was still too stunned to do any more than follow his lead.

Not until they were downstairs and out on the crowded sidewalk was she able to vent her outrage and bewilderment.

"I don't believe it," she burst out.

Her father was barging along now like a rampaging bull, dodging around the people on the sidewalk, nearly knocking over a man in a bowler hat. Sarah had to almost run to keep up with him.

"Dad, what do you think you're doing? That man's talking about all that money and you're telling him we'll give it some thought! Why are you playing games? Are you getting some kind of kick out of all this, like it's one of those detective novels you're so fond of?"

"It's no game," he said without slowing his stride. "I said what I meant."

"But he's talking about sixty thousand dollars. Maybe more."

"Damn it, don't you think I know that? Do you think I like it any more than you do?"

"Then why didn't you just tell him he was crazy? Where on earth are we going to come up with that kind of money?"

"I'm not sure yet. It'll . . . take a little doing."

Sarah stopped in her tracks. "You mean you *have* that much?"

Ted stopped as well. People swirled past. He studied his shoes. "There are some stocks and things," he said vaguely. "And I guess the bank will give us a good bit for the house."

She stood there in the middle of the sidewalk feeling absolutely dumbfounded. "You can get that kind of money and you'd be willing to use it for—?"

He turned to her, his face a mask of rage and pain. "This

is Joey we're talking about. Your only son. My only grandson. I told you once before that the money didn't matter and I meant it. Now forget it, will you. Just forget it."

For once she faced his anger without flinching. "No," she said, facing him straight on, her eyes misting. "I won't forget it."

"Well, you better. Because that's—"

But before he could finish she had thrown her arms around his neck and she was hugging him with all her might. "Thank you, Dad," she said. "Thank you."

Ted snapped off the light over his seat and leaned back, hoping that the hum of the 747's engines would lull him to sleep. He glanced over at Sarah. Her eyes were closed. Her luxuriant waves of walnut-dark hair poured lavishly over her shoulders just the way Emma's used to do before she'd taken to cutting it short. Ted smiled to himself. Sarah's relief and gratitude made it easier for him to bear the weight of what he knew he would have to do when they got back home— made it a *little* easier anyway. Agreeing to Lipton's terms would mean giving up everything he and Emma had been planning and saving for all these years: early retirement, winters in Florida, maybe that Caribbean cruise they'd talked about. It would mean cashing in his few stocks, closing out their savings. And, yes, face it: he'd have to mortgage the house, just when it was almost paid off. It made him angry and resentful. And, God, what was Emma going to say when he broke the news to her?

Not that Lipton's fee seemed unfair. From what Ted had been hearing it was not out of line. Besides, he felt absolute confidence in Harry Lipton. If anyone could do the job—and do it safely—it was Lipton. But hell, Ted thought, a man deserved a break! He'd been working hard ever since he was twelve years old. Almost fifty years! And what about Emma? What about all the struggle and sacrifice she'd had to put up with all this time: skimping, making ends meet, putting away a little here, a little there, so that their future could maybe be a little comfortable. And here they were, their dream so close to reality that they could almost reach out and touch it, only to learn that they were going to have to throw it all away because of some dumb jerk son-of-a-bitch of a psycho son-in-law.

When Ted outlined Lipton's terms to Emma the next afternoon, he made an effort to break the news about the expense as easily as he could. But there was no gentle way to do it; Emma was as shocked as he had been at the thought of what it was all going to cost them—and what it would mean to their future.

For a long time she sat there at the kitchen table, sunk in gloomy silence. At last she said: "Maybe it would be simpler just to send Jovan that money in exchange for Joey."

Ted shook his head. "I wouldn't give that bastard the satisfaction. Anyway, it's not just the money he wants. It's Sarah, too."

Emma nodded. She knew as well as he did what their choice was going to be.

"Should I tell Sarah or will you?" she asked.

Ted reached for her hand across the table. "Let's both do it."

First thing the next morning, Ted telephoned Sherwood Brice with instructions to sell off his stock portfolio.

"All of it?" Brice asked, incredulous.

"All of it," said Ted.

Next he drove downtown to the bank, cashed in his and

293

Emma's savings certificates, and made out a form transferring the funds to Lipton's bank in Luxembourg. A tax haven, no doubt. The man didn't mess around.

That done, Ted cabled Lipton to tell him half of the down-payment was on the way and that the rest would follow in a few days. Then he went home to bed. He slept for seventeen hours straight.

Within a week of giving Lipton the go-ahead, the Novacks were being bombarded with phone calls and cables from London: requests for information; requests for photos of Joey and Jovan and Jovan's family; requests for documents—separation papers, the court order, the contempt citation. Sarah herself was told to be prepared to travel to Belgrade in the event that the project proved feasible. To avoid raising any questions about her recent trip to Yugoslavia, which was recorded in her current passport, she was told to apply for a new passport for herself as well as a separate passport for Joey; but as a precaution she was to hang on to her family passport as well—the one with the composite photo of herself and Joey.

From Lipton also came instructions that powers-of-attorney be drawn up for the two agents who would be carrying out the actual abduction if and when the project was given the green light. As drafted by Bill Borden, the documents stated that the two men—whose names would be filled in later—were acting as Sarah's "emissaries and representatives," that she had reposed in them her "full trust and confidence," and that they had full power "to decide and act in relation to my son as though I myself were acting and deciding." Thus, should the agents be arrested in the course of the abduction, they would at least have some legal protection.

294

Sarah, meantime, was instructed not to lose touch with Jovan.

"Write, telephone, keep on just as if nothing else were happening," Lipton advised her by phone. "Lull him into a false sense of security—that's the important thing. Get him to let down his guard. If he thinks you're on the verge of giving in to him, maybe he won't be quite so cautious."

That evening she went to the drugstore and picked out two Valentines. The one for Joey showed a clown being lifted into the air by a cluster of heart-shaped balloons. The card for Jovan was white with red hearts and a verse that she hoped wasn't too soupy; she didn't want to lay it on so thick that he wouldn't believe her. On the back she wrote of missing him and of thinking that maybe she had made a mistake by returning home, that maybe they could try again and make a fresh start. Lying, she discovered, could be frighteningly easy.

Jovan's response, which arrived a few days later, seemed to confirm that she had done a good job.

"How happy it made me to read your letter," he wrote. "I had almost given up hope. But then to have you tell me that you would want to try again to live together, it makes me so happy, I cannot tell you how much. Yes, we will try again, of course, it is the only thing I want in the world . . ."

The letter was everything Lipton could have hoped for. Sarah wished she felt pleased with herself. But she felt only disgust.

―――――――

It was a Monday morning in April. Sarah and her parents were in the middle of breakfast when the telephone rang. Ted picked it up.

"Hello? Oh, hello, Harry. How you doing? . . . Yes, we're all here." He exchanged glances with his wife and daughter.

"Yes . . . yes." He began to smile. "Wonderful! Glad to hear it."

Sarah felt as if her heart were going to burst. "What is it, Dad?"

He held a hand over the receiver. "Lipton's men have reported back." Then, into the receiver: "That's great, Harry. Terrific news . . . Right. Okay, we'll let you know . . . Goodbye. And thanks again."

He hung up. By now he was beaming.

"Well?" Emma said. "What did he say?"

"The field report looks good. They're ready to go ahead. They'll start as soon as we can get over there."

Part Three

Do It Yourself

fifteen

Now everything began happening very quickly.

On Wednesday, April 20, 1977, Sarah and her father caught a flight to London. Sarah's mother stayed behind; if things went badly in Yugoslavia, they'd need her at home, to make sure they got help.

Arriving in London on Thursday morning, they went directly to Harry Lipton's office, where he explained the intricacies of Yugoslavia's visa regulations. After weeks of research and detailed evaluations of various scenarios, including a plan to smuggle Joey out in a crate labeled "machine tools," Lipton and his associates had hit on a scheme that offered both a chance of success and a low risk of actual physical danger. The scheme, Lipton told them now, depended on a peculiar hitch in Yugoslavia's visa conventions: the fact that while Americans required visas to enter and leave the Federal Socialist Republic, citizens of Britain and other Common Market countries did not.

"Which means?" asked Ted.

Lipton ran a hand through his bushy hair. "Which means," he said, "that a child from Britain, say, could be used to impersonate Joey long enough to cross into Yugoslavia on Joey's passport. The passport then gets stamped with the necessary visa. When our people are ready to bring Joey back across the border, they will be able to prove that he entered the country as an American citizen and is therefore free to leave as one."

Sarah leaned forward. "And since the British boy doesn't need a visa, he can leave afterward on his own passport, is that the idea?"

"Exactly."

"I don't like it," said Ted. "It all sounds so damned round-about. Why can't you just forge a visa for Joey? Or pay some Yugoslav to get you a legal one?"

Lipton shook his head. "Too risky. I know of too many jobs that have failed because of botched forgeries. And bribery can be even worse. First thing you know, the guy you're paying off gets greedy and wants more. Or maybe he gets nervous and tells his boss. Before you know it, everyone's in trouble. No, our best protection is to do everything as legally as possible."

Finding a child to impersonate Joey had been the last detail.

"We lined up a boy just this past weekend," Lipton told them. "Of course, we had to hire his parents, too, but that's just as well since his father is a professional chauffeur and can help with the driving. At any rate, the boy's likely to be a lot more cooperative if his folks are along. Ah, here's Liz with the coffee."

They took a break long enough to fill their cups and pass around the milk and sugar. Then Lipton proceeded to outline the plans: Sarah would meet the English family at Heathrow Airport in the morning and fly with them to Frankfurt. There they would be met by a man named Wilkes, who would drive them across Germany and Austria and over the mountains into Yugoslavia.

300

"Wait a minute," Ted interrupted. "You're only talking about Sarah going. I assumed I'd be going too."

Lipton raised his eyebrows. "I don't know how you got that impression."

"Well, I did. I've never thought otherwise."

Lipton shook his head. "I'm sorry, Ted. Sarah needs to go along in order to help with Joey. Your going would only complicate matters. Besides, the car would be too crowded with six people."

But Ted would not be put off. "Come on, Harry. There's got to be room for one more. Hell, the boy can sit on my lap."

Sarah reached out and touched his hand. His insistence did not surprise her; she knew perfectly well how left out he had felt while she was in Belgrade the last time and how frustrating the waiting and the inactivity would be for him if he were left out again. But she was afraid that if he pushed too hard Lipton might get fed up and refuse to let either one of them go.

"I'll be all right, Dad," she told him. "Really. You don't have to worry about me."

"Dammit, Sarah," he shot back, "that's not the point. I'm not worried about you. I know you can handle yourself. You've proved that time and again in these last few months. Anyway, you probably know that place better than anyone else by now. The point is"—and here he turned to Lipton— "I really think I can be of some use if I go along. Look, Harry, I can spell the others with the driving. I can help Sarah with Joey. My being there might even help their cover. Sarah and I would be a father and daughter traveling together, being tourists together."

Lipton studied Ted for a long moment. "It's that important to you?"

"It is. Yes."

Lipton expelled a long breath. "All right. I'll call Wilkes

tonight and let him know. But remember this, you're to follow Wilkes' orders absolutely. You may be footing the bill for this little escapade but he's the one who'll be running the show."

Ted nodded soberly. "He'll get no argument from me."

There remained only one more piece of business: Sarah's signing of the documents that gave her power of attorney to Peter Wilkes and to an agent they would meet in Belgrade, someone named Vladimir Popovic.

"Wilkes is a good man," Lipton assured them. "One of the best. And he hired Popovic. You can trust them both."

Lunch then. Toasts to the success of their mission. A restless afternoon and evening. A night of unsettled sleep.

Finally the morning came. Friday, April 22. The drive to the airport. Meeting the Hardys and their downy-haired son. Then, as planned, they were boarding the flight to Frankfurt. For Sarah, the excitement was unbearable. Her stomach was in turmoil. At last it was happening. At last she was on her way back to Joey.

Then had come the long, cramped drive southward; the nerve-racking stop at the border crossing; the frightening uncertainty as they waited beside the road in the cold nighttime darkness, not knowing if they might be detained or turned back, until finally the drunken guard with the visa stamp appeared and sent them on their way, passports in hand.

It had worked! They had gotten Joey's visa—that innocuous-looking little smudge of purple ink that was going to be so critical when it came time to take Joey back across the border. *If* that time ever came. For as Peter Wilkes reminded them now, the real dangers still lay ahead:

"Once we've got the boy, that's when we'll have to worry."

They were just finishing dinner in the crowded little Turkish café in downtown Belgrade. The rhythm of the flute and the drum music was picking up and the place was getting hotter and noisier.

Wilkes took a sip of the thick, sweet Turkish coffee the waiter had just set before him. For a long moment his eyes were hidden by the steam that clouded the lenses of his horn-rimmed glasses.

"If we're caught with Joey in our possession and the police are looking for his kidnappers, we could all end up in jail. You two would probably be released pretty quickly since you're Joey's family. But I, on the other hand—" He pursed his lips and took a long drag on his cigarette. "I could end up spending the next twenty years in prison as a foreign agent." He eyed them sternly. "That's why I don't want any slip-ups. I've got too much to lose."

Sarah shuddered. Maybe he gave this speech to all the people he worked with. But it worked. She was scared.

The music had risen to a fever pitch. Now, abruptly, it stopped. A hush fell over the room. And held for one long beat. Then the drum began again, very slowly this time. The flute joined in, a languid wailing. And from somewhere nearby came a new sound: the clinging of tiny bells. Sarah turned to look. From behind a beaded curtain came a plump young woman with raven hair. She was draped in a flowing purple scarf and a gauzy, floor-length skirt, which was trimmed all over with gold and bangles. A veil hid the lower half of her face, leaving only her dark eyes visible. There were bells on her bare ankles and tiny cymbals on her fingertips, and as she undulated around the room to the rhythm of the music there seemed to be no part of her body that was not in motion. Whistles and cheers filled the air as first one veil, then another, fell away.

Sarah glanced at her father and found him entranced.

He winked at her. "Quite a show, eh?"

Sarah had to agree; it was indeed quite a show.

The girl had just come wriggling over to where Ted sat and was tumbling her ample belly in front of his very red face when Wilkes was suddenly on his feet and signaling toward the door.

Sarah pulled her attention away from her father and the dancer. Following the direction of Wilkes' gestures, she saw an orange-haired man standing at the top of the steps surveying the crowd. He had on a worn sportcoat and baggy trousers and his white shirt was open halfway to the waist, revealing a mat of curly reddish hair. With his drooping mustache and the cigarette that hung from his lower lip like a tusk, he reminded Sarah of a rumpled walrus.

"Who's that?" she asked.

"Popovic," was all Wilkes said. Having caught the man's attention, he now settled back into his seat to watch the dancer as she went jiggling away through the crowd.

Then, just as suddenly as the girl had appeared, she was gone, vanished behind the beaded curtain. More whistles and cheers, mixed with wild applause.

"Vladimir Popovic knows everyone in Belgrade and is related to at least half of them," Wilkes explained as the man sauntered in their direction. "He's been a great help these last few weeks."

Sarah recognized the name. This was the other man for whom she had signed a power of attorney back in Lipton's office. But seeing him now, all swagger and self-importance, made Sarah wince. Had she really signed over Joey's welfare to this character? Still, if Wilkes trusted him . . .

The man stepped up to their table. As Wilkes introduced him, he extended his hand with stiff formality. Holding his chin high, he regarded Sarah coolly down the slope of his broad nose. "A pleasure," he murmured in thickly accented

English. His manner seemed to assume that the true pleasure in the meeting must certainly be hers. But as he turned to shake hands with her father, Sarah realized that the haughty tilt of his head was probably as much a matter of utility as it was of temperament. It kept his carrot-colored toupee from slipping.

Wilkes ordered a slivovitz for the man, then passed on some surprising news: while Sarah and her father had been catching up on their sleep, he and Popovic had spent the afternoon delivering fertilizer to a certain old gardener that Popovic knew.

"Fertilizer?" asked Ted. The expression on his face mirrored Sarah's own bewilderment. "You mean to tell me that while you're supposed to be doing something about Joey, you're running a garden-supply business on the side?"

Wilkes grinned. "Vlad, why don't you tell them about it."

With an air of condescension, Popovic explained: the old man tilled a plot in the public garden across the street from Baka's cottage. "I know him now for several weeks. It is very convenient arrangement."

"Vlad cultivated his friendship, you might say," Wilkes interjected, his eyes twinkling. His earlier gloominess had vanished. He was obviously in high spirits.

Popovic ignored the remark and continued solemnly. "He gives me gardening advice, tells me stories, I bring him tea, sometimes other things. Pesticides last week. Fertilizer today. We drink and talk. This way I am keeping the lookout on the house where your boy is living, missus."

Sarah felt her heart jump. "You saw him today? You saw Joey?"

Vlad nodded. "He was there. He was playing in the street with his small friend, a boy from the Mongolian Embassy."

"Your husband was there as well," said Wilkes. "And there were other gardeners about, and strollers in the park at the end of the road. Too many people. It was not a good time to make a move. Probably just as well, too, since none of us is in any shape to face another long drive so soon."

Ted lit up one of his long black cigars. "When will you try again?"

"Tomorrow morning. We'll get there early, before the gardeners and the Sunday strollers begin turning out."

He and Popovic would arrive in separate cars. They would wait for Jovan to leave the house, wait for Joey to come out and play. If all went well, Wilkes would pick up Joey. Popovic would be waiting nearby in the backup car, ready to run interference if they were followed.

Wilkes turned to Sarah. "Have you got the blanket?"

"In the suitcase."

"Good. We'll take it along."

At Lipton's suggestion, Sarah had brought along the Snoopy blanket from Joey's bed; it was something Joey would recognize as having come from home, a familiar token that would serve to ease his fears in the first traumatic moments after he had been grabbed off the street by strangers.

"I know it's going to be hard to wait," Wilkes was saying. "But timing is critical. If there are too many people around it will be just too risky."

His mood had changed again. Now, as he gave Sarah and her father their instructions, he was all business.

Tomorrow morning, he said, while he and Popovic were gone, Ted and Sarah were to stay in their own room in the hotel. They were to keep their bags packed at all times and be ready to go at a moment's notice.

"Leave your room only to eat. And when you do go downstairs, don't use the elevators. The fewer hotel people who see you, the better."

Ted nodded. "How long do you think it will take?"

"Hard to tell. It could be an hour, it could take all day. But

306

when it happens it'll happen fast. So you have to be ready to move."

Sarah felt her breath catch in her throat. It was finally happening: what she had been waiting and hoping for for months; what Wilkes and his men had been planning for weeks. Her body was tingling all over with excitement. At the back of her neck there was a prickling sensation, as if her hair were standing on end. And then she thought: God, what if they failed? What if they got Joey and then Baka called the police and they were all arrested? She might never see Joey again.

"Keep an eye on the street," Wilkes was saying. "If you see us pull up with the lights flashing it means we've got Joey. Get your bags and come downstairs immediately. Leave your key at the desk and get out to the car fast."

Popovic leaned over and whispered in Wilkes' ear. Wilkes nodded. "One other thing," he said, turning to Ted. "Keep those cigars of yours out of sight. They draw too much attention. Smoke them in your room if you like but not in public."

"That's funny," said Ted, stubbing out the cigar. "My wife tells me the same thing."

He let out a giddy kind of laugh. Sarah shot him a glance. She realized he must be as nervous and excited as she was.

For a long time that night Sarah lay awake listening to the rhythmic sound of her father's breathing in the next bed and watching the shifting patterns made on the ceiling by the lights of cars passing in the street below.

Not two miles away, Joey was probably snug in his blankets, an arm outflung, lips parted in the soft kiss of sleep. Was he warm enough? she wondered. Was he even actually in bed? He should be; it was well past his bedtime. Not that Jovan paid much attention to such things. He'd keep Joey up all night if it suited his own convenience. He didn't care. All that concerned him was himself: his needs, his rights, his dreams, his pain.

No more, Joey. It will be over soon. Tomorrow.

God, was it possible? Would she really see him tomorrow? A few more hours? Hold him again? Her boy, her beautiful Joey?

Did he sense her nearness as clearly as she sensed his? Or had they so twisted him these past months that he had stopped even dreaming of her, had stopped hoping? She tried to push the thought out of her mind. She didn't want to even imagine it. But she kept remembering the last time she had come to Belgrade, kept seeing him standing there in the doorway of Baka's house and not moving when she called to him, only watching her impassively. She saw the hand on his shoulder then. Baka's hand? No, it was Jovan's, for now she could see Jovan himself in the doorway, sneering at her. He drew Joey back into the shadows and closed the door, shutting her out. Except now the door had become a dark window and she could make out Joey's face through it, his small hand waving as the train slid along the platform and away into the night, his voice reaching her on the train's rhythmic breathing, *Do vidjenja . . . Do vidjenja . . . Do vidjenja. . . .*

sixteen

Early the next morning, Sarah and her father watched from the window of the hotel dining room as Wilkes and Popovic drove off in the BMW.

"Keep an eye on the street," Wilkes had told them. "Be ready to move fast." In the meantime, all they could do was wait.

They finished breakfast and watched the traffic coming and going in the street outside. They lingered over coffee, both of them reluctant to go back upstairs and shut themselves up in their claustrophobic little room. But when the dining room began to empty and the waiter came to refill their cups for the third time, they both knew it was time to leave, before the staff began to take too much notice of them.

"You go first," Ted told her. "I'll take care of the check."

They were not, after all, supposed to be a father and daughter traveling together, but Peter Wilkes' friend and Peter Wilkes' mistress, staying in separate rooms.

Taking the stairs, Sarah reached the fourth floor and was just starting down the corridor when a pink-cheeked young man in a bellboy uniform came around the corner.

"Good morning," he said in English.

"Good morning," she replied automatically, then realized too late what she had done. How did he know she was English-speaking? Was there something about her that gave her away? Her makeup? The way she was dressed? Unless he knew all along and had been watching her. But why?

"You are a guest in the hotel?" he asked.

"Yes." If he had been watching her surely he would know. Unless he was trying to trap her. "I'm staying just down the hall," she said carefully.

"Yes? Which room, please? I did not see you come in."

"Room four-twelve. I—We arrived yesterday." She was getting increasingly nervous.

"I must ask to see your passport."

Oh, God, she thought. Not that. Wilkes had been adamant. "Why?" she asked, as calmly as possible. "Is there anything wrong?"

"No, no. Nothing wrong. Do not misunderstand. But in this hotel sometimes we have people coming in who do not belong here. Certain *kinds* of people. Women. You understand."

"Women?" She was more astonished than indignant, but it was indignation that she turned on him. "Certain kinds of women? Is that what you take me for? One of *them?*"

"No, no. Of course not. I only meant—"

"I don't believe it! If it wasn't so ridiculous I'd be insulted. In fact, I am insulted. Yes, I think that's just about the most insulting thing I ever heard."

"Miss, please," he said, glancing nervously down the corridor. To her satisfaction, he was beginning to look as flustered as she herself had been a minute ago.

"I am half inclined to report this to the management," she went on, pressing her advantage.

"I am sorry, miss. I did not mean to imply anything offensive."

"If this is the way you treat your guests in this hotel, I am surprised you have any guests at all."

"Yes, miss. I am sorry. I do apologize."

"Well, I certainly hope so. Now please get out of my way and let me pass." From her handbag she withdrew the room key, with its bulky metal tag, her proof of her right to be in the corridor. Then she straightened her shoulders and marched past him.

She kept her poise long enough to get her key in the door and open it. But by the time she had shut it behind her, her knees were shaking so hard she had to sit down.

"You should be proud of yourself," her father said when he finally returned to the room and she told him what had happened.

"I did carry it off rather well," she said with a smile of satisfaction. "I wish Gran had been there. She would have loved it."

Still, the encounter with the bellhop had shaken her and after that she was reluctant to leave the room. Nor did Ted feel up to tackling the stairs again; though he had taken the four flights at a slow pace, the climb had left him winded and frighteningly pale. The next time, he declared, he would use the elevator and to hell with Wilkes.

Sarah and her father took turns at the chair by the window. She discovered that it was incredibly hard to sit and do nothing but watch the street and wait for a particular car to appear, not knowing how long it would take.

One hour stretched to two. Two stretched to three. As the sun rose higher, Sarah watched the shadow of the hotel go sliding down the face of the apartment building across the way. Stabs of fear kept cutting into her. She kept thinking of what would happen if Wilkes failed, if she had to go home without Joey. Home? God, what home? What kind of home could there ever be for her if she had to leave Joey behind? What kind of life? To never see him again, to never again be part of his life or he of hers—it would be unbearable. Wilkes had to succeed. He just had to.

There was a knock. Someone at the door.

Sarah and Ted exchanged startled glances.

"Who is it?" she called.

The answer came in Serbian. A woman's voice. The maid wanting to straighten up the room.

Sarah breathed a sigh of relief. She realized she had been holding her breath. She sent the woman away, then went back to the window. Her father lay back on the bed and picked up the detective novel he had been reading. He had kicked his shoes off but they were close by, ready to be slipped on the minute the car appeared.

———————

The shadows were gone from the face of the building across the street and the sun was shining straight down onto the pavement below, but still there was no sign of the BMW.

"What time is it now?" Sarah asked.

She and her father had traded places again and now it was her turn on the bed. She had already read every article in the *Newsweek* her father had picked up at Heathrow, and she was reduced to leafing through the hotel's collection of tourist brochures.

Ted checked his watch. "Twenty after twelve."

"What can they be doing all this time?"

He shrugged. "Wilkes said it might take all day."

"What if something happened? What if they got arrested?"

"Come on, Sarah," Ted heard himself say. "Don't start imagining the worst. Wilkes knows what he's doing. They probably just haven't had a chance to make their move."

But the truth was that Ted himself was beginning to think something must have gone wrong. The waiting, the unrelenting tension and uncertainty, were beginning to work on his nerves too.

Feeling restless, he had just gotten up from the chair by the window and was stretching his muscles when the blue BMW turned into the parking lot below.

"They're here," he said.

His words brought Sarah bolting to the window as the car slid into a parking place and came to a stop. The headlights were not flashing.

"Are you sure it's the right car?" she asked.

"Look for yourself."

Sure enough, emerging from the driver's side was the familiar fair-haired figure of Peter Wilkes. But no one else got out of the car with him. He was alone.

"Damn." Ted turned away from the window.

In bleak silence, Sarah watched Wilkes walk toward the hotel and disappear beneath the canopy that sheltered the entranceway below. A few minutes later, there was a knock at the door. Ted went to open it.

"No luck?" he asked as Wilkes stepped into the room.

"Afraid not." Wilkes flung his jacket onto the bed and sank into the easy chair.

Sarah exploded. "Luck! You mean you're relying on luck?" She heard the shrillness in her voice but she did not care. Their bland acceptance of failure was infuriating.

Wilkes closed his eyes as if to shut her out. "Figure of speech, Mrs. Stefanovic," he said wearily. "Just a figure of speech."

"Well, will you kindly tell me what you have been doing all this time then? Where is my boy? Where is Joey?"

Her father reddened. "Sarah, please."

From the chair where he sat, Wilkes raised a patient hand. "It's all right, Ted. It's been a long morning for all of us. I'm sure it's not been easy for your daughter, sitting here waiting all this time."

His response only made her more angry. "Don't patronize me!" she shouted. "You've been doing that to me ever since we met. I am not a child. I'm a grown woman and I have not seen my son in six months. This may be just another job to you but it means a whole lot more than that to me."

"I'm well aware of that," Wilkes said icily.

"Well, then, act like it, will you!"

Wilkes rose from his chair. "Pardon me," he said, his manner all steely control, "but I do not need to sit here and endure the verbal abuse of an hysterical woman."

"Hysterical! You call me hysterical? You haven't seen me hysterical yet! But if you're not afraid of it, just hang around. I'll show you what it's like."

Wilkes was already to the door but Ted stopped him. "Peter, for God's sakes, come back here. And both of you, cut it out, will you? Damn it, things are bad enough without us getting at each other's throats."

Sarah turned on him. "Then when is this man going to start doing what he's being paid to do? When is he going to get Joey out of there? That's what I want to know."

"Sarah! I said stop it. That's enough!"

She and Wilkes continued to glare at each other across the room. Finally she turned away, her face to the window. Out over the rooftops she watched a plane lifting off from the airport on the other side of town. Behind her the room was silent. She heard Wilkes snap his lighter, smelled the smoke

314

of his cigarette. Then in his low voice he began quietly to explain what had happened that morning:

He and Popovic had watched Baka's house from eight-thirty on. They watched as the first dog walkers appeared. Then came the gardeners, with their forks and spades. Then the Sunday strollers, some with prams and small children, heading for the wooded park at the end of the cul-de-sac. Just before noon, Baka and Jovan and the boy came out of the cottage together.

"They walked to the corner and got on a bus," Wilkes said. "We followed them, of course, but from the bus number we had a pretty good idea where they were off to."

"Where?" asked Ted.

"To Jovan's sister's flat. It's the only place they ever go together. They usually go on Sundays and stay all afternoon."

"Does that sound right, Sarah?" her father asked.

She nodded sullenly and swept a strand of hair from her eyes. She was still angry, but she had to admit that Wilkes and his men had done their research thoroughly. They knew the pattern of Jovan's and Baka's lives inside out. She herself remembered all too well the gloomy Sunday afternoon she had spent cooped up in Myra's oppressive little apartment, the hours dragging on, the thick, soporific smell of boiled meat and cabbage, and Myra pleading with her to stay, to be Jovan's wife again. . . .

"Anyway," Wilkes went on, "there didn't seem to be much point in us hanging about. We'll try again tomorrow. It will be Monday, people will be at work. We should have a better chance."

He turned to Sarah. For once there was no condescension in his voice. "Look here," he said, "I'm sorry. I know this is frustrating. The waiting is the hardest part of this job, even for professionals. But you've got to understand. These things take time. They can't be rushed. The conditions have to be just right: the boy alone; no one in the way; as few witnesses as possible. And in this particular situation that's pretty difficult. You know what it's like over there, with all the embassies so close by and Tito's palace just up the street. That neighborhood is guarded like a military base."

Sarah heard no more. She did not know whether it was the cigar and cigarette smoke or what, but she suddenly felt herself going cold all over. Her head reeling, she bolted for the bathroom and slammed the door behind her. Then she threw up.

Wilkes was at their room early the next morning, his suitcase in hand.

"Feeling better?" he asked Sarah.

She nodded, smiling faintly. "I guess it was just—the strain. A good night's sleep helped a lot."

"Good. I'm glad to hear it." And from the way he said it, Sarah knew he meant it. "Ready to go?" he asked.

"All set," said Ted, picking up their bags.

A few minutes later they were in the car and on the way to a new hotel.

The move was a safety precaution. Having heard from Ted about Sarah's encounter in the corridor with the bellhop and later with the cleaning lady, Wilkes had decided it was time to change hotels. Sarah had been noticed by too many people at the Srbija.

The new hotel was the Moskva. Located at a busy intersection near the city's center, the Moskva was an elegant, old turn-of-the century building that had somehow survived the Nazi bombing of World War II only to suffer the indignity of having its interior "modernized" to look like a Howard Johnson's, complete with bright-orange vinyl furniture in the lobby.

316

At the check-in counter, Wilkes used the same ploy as before to get Sarah up to the room without showing her passport. The charade worked as well as it had the first time—better, in fact, since Sarah was now used to playing the role of the shy mistress. Hanging back near the entrance, she saw Wilkes tilt his head in her direction, saw the desk clerk raise his eyes to look her over. She let her own gaze fall away demurely, shifted her weight uneasily from one foot to the other.

"Well done," Wilkes told her once they were all safely ensconced in their new accommodations. "You are becoming quite an accomplished actress."

Sarah offered an elaborate curtsy. "Why, suh, Ah'm deeply honored to heah y'all think so."

For the first time since they'd met, Wilkes laughed out loud. "Scarlett O'Hara, I presume?"

"At your service, Mr. Butler."

Leaving Sarah and her father to have breakfast by themselves in the hotel dining room, Wilkes drove off to meet Popovic and to once again take up their surveillance of Baka's cottage.

Sarah and her father waited in their room for the rest of the morning. From their window they watched the pale morning turn to rainy noontime.

Around one o'clock Ted went down for lunch. After an appropriate interval, Sarah followed. In the dining room she started for an empty table; then, pretending to see Ted for the first time, she changed course abruptly.

"Why, Mr. Novack, what a pleasant surprise. Do y'all mind if Ah join you?"

Grinning, Ted got to his feet. "Please do, Miss Scarlett. I would indeed be honored."

She ordered a light lunch, but her stomach was still too unsettled for her to do more than pick at her food.

Later, back in the room, she and her father waited and watched as the wet afternoon dragged by.

Four o'clock came and went and there was still no sign of Wilkes or Popovic. All the fears of the day before had surfaced again. Sarah's fingernails had been chewed down long ago and now the skin around them was also falling prey to her voracious gnawing. Blood pooled in the corners where she had torn at the cuticles. What was happening? Had Wilkes been arrested? Would the police soon come knocking at their door? Was Joey all right?

At the window, Sarah picked up the pack of cigarettes Wilkes had left behind that morning. She had been pilfering them all day and now there was only one left. She considered saving the last one for Wilkes, then decided not to and lit up. A moment later there was a soft knock at the door.

"Open up. It's me, Peter."

Her father let him in.

"We didn't see you drive up," Sarah said.

"Oh." He avoided looking at her. Stepping over to the bureau, he reached into the paper bag he was carrying and pulled out a brown bottle.

"Where did you park?" Ted asked.

Wilkes glanced at him distractedly, as if seeing him for the first time. "We, uh, had to change cars. The BMW lost its clutch just after I left you this morning. Piece of junk. Anyone else care for a brandy? No?"

He fetched a glass from the bathroom, filled it half full, and took a swig. Then he collapsed into the easy chair, his legs stretched out in front of him. "This local stuff's not bad," he said, lifting the glass to the light. "Sure you won't try a bit, Ted?"

Sarah threw an alarmed glance at her father. It was the first time she had seen Wilkes looking so strung out, so defeated.

"Are you going to tell us what happened this afternoon?" Ted asked. "Or are we going to have to play twenty questions?"

Wilkes sucked in a long breath, let it out. "Nothing happened. Absolutely nothing. Oh, Jovan came out alone at one point and got on a bus at the corner. But that's all. We waited for the boy to come out to play, but he never did. The weather must have kept him in. It got quite raw this afternoon." He took another swallow of brandy. "Dammit," he said, pounding his fist on the arm of the chair, "they just bloody well never *go* anywhere. They just *sit* there. It's frustrating as hell."

But that wasn't all. Wilkes had more bad news. That morning, while he and Popovic were at the rental agency getting a new car, Popovic had let drop the fact that his driver's license had recently been revoked.

Wilkes let his head fall back and closed his eyes. "Reckless driving. Do you believe it? So much for our backup driver. Of course, *he* treated the whole matter as a colossal joke, the bastard. I was tempted to sack him on the spot!"

"Why didn't you?" asked Ted.

Wilkes shook his head. "We may still need him."

Popovic, it turned out, had a cousin who was a guard at a Hungarian border post; if they needed an alternate escape route, they'd need Popovic to get them through.

Ted took a breath. "All right," he said. "So he's lost his license. So we can't count on him as a driver. Let's face the facts and get on with it. What do you propose we do now?"

Wilkes got to his feet, went to the window, looked down at the street. Then he turned to face them. There was a sadness in his eyes that Sarah had not seen before. "Look," he said, "I

319

hate to say this, but I think we should put off trying to get Joey. Just for the time being, you understand."

Ted sat bolt upright on the bed. "You've got to be kidding."

"But—" Sarah was appalled. She could not believe what she was hearing. After all this effort, all this waiting, to quit now! It was unthinkable. "What about your grand lecture yesterday about these things taking time?"

"It would only be for a few months," Wilkes hurried on. "In the fall, when they send Joey to school—when he's away from the house and on his own—we'd have a much better chance. They won't be able to keep an eye on him every—"

"No!" Sarah shouted, cutting him off. "We're not quitting."

"Look," Wilkes tried again. He was almost pleading now. "There's no telling when we'll have a chance to get him if we just keeping hanging around. Besides, the police, the neighbors, someone's bound to get suspicious if they see us sitting there day after day."

But Sarah was having none of it. "Mr. Wilkes, I came here to get my son and I'm not going home without him. Maybe your big corporations don't cry but I'm willing to bet they scream bloody murder when the people they hire to do a job don't do it. Well, let me tell you something. If you're too timid to do the job, I'll do it myself and you can just go to hell! We've got the visa now. We don't need you."

Wilkes regarded her with those infuriatingly cool eyes of his, but she saw his jaws tighten, his hands go white-knuckled on the brandy glass. She looked over at her father. She'd been expecting him to try to quiet her. Instead, he said, "Sarah's right. We didn't come all this way to go home empty-handed. I'm not a rich man. I can't afford to keep flying back and forth to Europe every couple of months."

Wilkes shook his head. "But you won't have to. I can stay and get Joey myself. As Sarah's said, we've got Joey's visa

320

now, that's the important thing. Look, I feel as badly as you do about the way things have worked out, but—"

"You?" Sarah steel-eyed him. "I find it hard to believe you feel anything."

"Then you misjudge me."

"Do tell, Mr. Wilkes. Do tell."

"That's right," he said, his own anger rising. "Maybe you think you're the only one who's got any feelings about this. I can't blame you for that. You're Joey's mother. But I happen to have a boy of my own at home. He's just about Joey's age, and believe me, he's in my mind every time I go over there and sit outside that house and see your boy living the way he is, cut off from his mother, from his home, from everything familiar. I want to see him out of there as much as you do."

Sarah could not have been more surprised. "I—I had no idea you were even married," she stammered. "I mean, other than the marriage you made up for this trip."

"Divorced, actually."

"And your boy is—?"

"I have a girl as well. They live with their mother. But I see them every chance I get and . . ." He brushed the rest away with a wave of his hand, as if he had already revealed more about himself than he had intended. "Look, maybe I shouldn't have taken this job in the first place. It's too close to me. Maybe that's what's making me so damn cautious. But I couldn't live with myself if I walked away from it now and left Joey there in that hovel."

"I'm sorry," said Sarah. "I didn't know."

"Well, now you do." He stepped around her to the window, picked up the pack of cigarettes off the sill, saw it was empty, crumpled it distractedly. He turned to Sarah. He was very close to her now. "The point is, I want you to know that if we leave here now I will be back in the fall. I'll bring your boy back to you. I promise. I won't rest until I do." His eyes held hers and she knew he meant what he said.

"Thank you," she said, and meant that, too. "But I still think you're giving up too soon."

"So do I," said Ted. "We've only been here a couple of days. I'm prepared to stick it out a little longer."

Wilkes looked at them both uncertainly for a moment, then seemed to make his decision. "Right, then." He cleared his throat but his voice was still ragged. "We'll stay with it a few days more." He straightened up, made an effort to look and sound authoritative once again. "Now if you'll excuse me, I'll go freshen up a bit before dinner. What shall it be tonight? Croatian? Slovenian? Macedonian?"

They settled on Greek and agreed to meet in half an hour. Sarah showered, then left the bathroom to her father while she got dressed and sat down at the dressing table to fix her hair. She was just starting on her makeup when there was a sharp knocking at the door and Wilkes' voice urging her to let him in.

"We're not ready yet," she called.

"Never mind that. Just open up."

The urgency in his voice was alarming. Quickly she unlocked the door.

"What is it? What's wrong?"

He was in stocking feet and shirt-sleeves and his hair was still dripping from the shower. But instead of worry there was a smile of triumph on his face.

"I think we just got our break! Popovic just telephoned. Jovan boarded a plane for Paris half an hour ago. He's not due back until Thursday."

seventeen

Although Popovic had been unable to discover the reason for Jovan's abrupt departure, there was no doubt that he was gone and that he had left Joey behind with Baka. The old woman was now the only person guarding the boy. If Wilkes was going to make a move, this was the best chance he was likely to get any time soon.

That evening, over dinner at a sleepy little Greek restaurant, Wilkes explained the plan for the next morning. He and Popovic would meet at the hotel; then, as before, they would drive in separate cars to the cul-de-sac and await their opportunity. If the weather was fair and Joey was sent out to play—

"Wait a minute," said Ted. "You're still involving Popovic in this? What about the risk if he's caught without his license?"

"He'll be a backup, nothing more. Joey will be in my car. I'll pick you two up here, then we'll head west toward Zagreb."

Popovic, meantime, would follow as far as Slavonski Brod, the town where he had lost his license. He'd see the magistrate and try to get it back, then head for a town near the Hungarian frontier. In the event that none of their other exit routes worked out, he'd meet them there and get them across.

Sarah took a sip of the ouzo that Wilkes had poured for her. She made a face. The stuff tasted like licorice. She couldn't stand licorice. She switched to wine.

"There's something I don't understand," she said. "Why don't we just get a flight out of Belgrade instead of driving all the way to Zagreb? Wouldn't we get out a lot quicker?"

"It might be quicker, yes," Wilkes conceded. "Then again, it might take twenty years."

"Too risky?"

Wilkes gave a curt nod. "As soon as Joey is reported missing, the police will start watching the airport. It's the first place they'll look. And when they show up I don't want to be found sitting there waiting for an airplane. What we have to do is get away from Belgrade as quickly as we can." He pushed his empty plate aside and lit a cigarette. "Now, what do you two say to some coffee and then a little drive around to have a look at the city?"

"Sounds better than sitting in a stuffy hotel room," Ted agreed.

Sarah demurred. "I've seen Belgrade, thanks."

"Oh, come on," said Ted. "It'll do us both good to get out for a while."

The car Wilkes had gotten in exchange for the faulty BMW was a squared-off little green VW Golf—the European version of the Rabbit. With Ted beside him in the passenger seat and Sarah sitting in the back, Wilkes drove down a nearly empty boulevard. Although it was only a little after ten o'clock, the streets of downtown Belgrade were all but deserted. Now and then they'd pass a cluster of cars parked near the bright lights of a casino or a dance hall, but for the most part the city on this Tuesday night in April was very quiet. Socialist workers apparently went to bed early.

Soon Wilkes was driving them along a parkway that followed the banks of the Danube. Upon the river's inky surface danced the lights of the buildings across the way; barges ghosted along in the darkness.

The parkway swung around the base of a cliff and Wilkes, like a proper tour guide, noted that they were now passing under the walls of the Kalemegdan fortress. They skirted the bluff and a few minutes later they were back in the center of the city, amid darkened office towers and shuttered store fronts.

"The place looks more like a small country town than a capital city," Ted said.

"It's rather more lively nowadays than it was just a few years ago," Wilkes said. "People here used to say that no one in Belgrade could ever go anywhere on weekends; Tito always had the car."

Ted laughed. "Hasn't changed much, as far as I can see."

Sarah listened indifferently to their patter. Alone in the backseat, she paid little attention when Wilkes pointed out the National Museum, the Parliament building, the former royal palace. She had seen all she ever cared to see of Belgrade. All she wanted now was to have Joey in her arms and be on her way home. Still, it was a relief to get out of the hotel for a while. . . .

"What's that building?" Ted asked. "The one with all the guards around it?"

The building he pointed to was an elaborate pillared edifice that stood behind a high iron fence. The street in front of it was well lit and sentries were posted every thirty or forty feet, submachine guns slung over their shoulders.

"That's the presidential palace. Where Tito lives."

Sarah was suddenly alert.

"So Baka's place must be right nearby," said Ted.

Sarah answered instead of Wilkes. "Just around the corner," she said mechanically. She knew perfectly well where they were. She also realized that Wilkes must have been heading in this direction all along, whether he himself knew it or not—drawn here as if by a magnet.

"Like to have a look?" Wilkes asked.

"Sure," said Ted. "Why not?"

"Let's not," said Sarah. She did not want to be here, did not want to see this place again. Yet, despite herself, she could not take her eyes off the road ahead as Wilkes turned down the street toward the cul-de-sac. In reluctant, awful fascination, she found herself searching for the familiar landmarks. Yes, there it was: the high stone wall that surrounded the Mongolian Embassy. And there was the park bench where she and Jovan had sat with Joey one afternoon this past November.

"Are you sure it's safe?" she whispered, gripping the back of Wilkes' seat.

"Not to worry. It's dark. Nobody will notice. Here, it's just down here."

He turned a corner past an armed sentry, then drove on a little to where another sentry stood. The street lamps were dimmer back here and in the strange, pale light the shadowy form of the guard looked ominous and threatening.

"My god!" breathed Ted. "You were right about there being guards all over the place."

"Now you can see what we're up against."

Another turn and they were in the familiar narrow cul-de-sac, which ended a short distance ahead in a dark wall of trees. Wilkes slowed and came to a stop at the edge of the road. He switched off the headlights. On the left, behind a low wire fence, was the garden plot of the old man whom Popovic had befriended. Across the road, on the right, was Baka's cottage.

326

"That's it," Wilkes told Ted. "That's the place."

The street lamp at the end of the street cast just enough illumination to highlight the picket fence and the low, gabled outline of the cottage.

"That's it," Wilkes told Ted. "That's the place."

The lamp at the end of the street cast just enough illumination to highlight the picket fence and the low, gabled outline of the cottage.

"I don't believe it," murmured Ted. "That place is no bigger than a two-car garage."

Through one of the small, mullioned windows, they could see a light. Inside someone was moving about: a large figure. A grown-up. Baka, then, not Joey. But Joey was there—Sarah knew it. He was *there*— not fifty feet from where she now sat in the darkened car. She glanced at her watch. Ten-thirty. He was probably asleep by now. Still—

"What if we went in to get him?" she asked. "Right now."

Ted picked up her excitement. "Yeah," he said. "Let's do it now. While it's dark."

Wilkes was silent for a moment. "Tempting, isn't it?" he murmured.

"Well, then, come on," said Ted. "Let's go."

He had his hand on the door handle but Wilkes reached over and restrained him. "Don't," he said. "We've got to wait."

"Wait?" Ted burst out. "But why? Goddammit, why?"

"The setup is perfect," Sarah agreed. "What's the problem?"

She was wound up tight. All the anger and the frustration and the forced restraint of the past weeks felt as if they were ready to let go in her, made her want to jump out of the car and run to the house and grab Joey and never mind what happened afterward, she'd have him and she wouldn't ever let him go again. "No one's around except that one guard back at the corner," she hurried on. "And he probably can't even see us down here in the dark."

Wilkes shook his head.

"Listen to me," said Ted urgently. "Baka's the only one in there with Joey. If we go in now and just—"

"We don't *know* she's in there alone," Wilkes said. "She may have had a visitor since we last checked. Maybe Myra's there with her. Anyway, even if she is in there alone, it could still be dangerous."

Ted was at the end of his tether. "You're talking about an old woman. What's so dangerous? All we'd have to do is push her aside, grab Joey, and make a run for it."

But Wilkes held fast. "It's no good. She knows you, Ted. The police would know who to look for the minute we left. We'd never get Joey out of the country. It's got to be someone she's never seen before."

"Then why don't you—?"

"We've also got no backup right now. An impulsive move could ruin everything. Weeks of preparation could end up being totally undone. Besides—" He took a deep breath. "Look, there's something I didn't tell either of you before. The other day, when Popovic and I were sitting here watching the place, Jovan left the house and got on a bus. When we were quite certain that he was gone we decided to try going in after Joey. We thought that if we could just get the old woman to open the door we might manage it."

"And what happened?" Sarah asked.

"Well, she opened the door all right, but only an inch or two. Just enough to look out at us and ask what we wanted. Popovic gave her a story about wanting to leave something for his friend the gardener—plant food or something. But she didn't fall for it. She told us to go away. When Popovic persisted she began shouting and raising a royal rumpus. For some reason she seemed absolutely terrified of us. Of us or just of strangers in general, I don't know which. At any rate, I knew that if we were going to move we'd have to do it quickly. I was about to force my way in. She had opened the door a bit more and I could see Joey in the room behind her. He was right there, watching everything that was going on. But that's when I saw that the old woman had a kitchen knife in her hand."

Sarah felt goose bumps rising on her arms.

"A knife again," Ted murmured. If he had not faced the same angry woman with a knife in her hand he might have been more surprised. "She probably would have used it, too," he said.

"I certainly did not want to find out," said Wilkes. "Someone might have gotten seriously hurt. And *then* there'd have been a hell of a lot of explaining to do. That's why we backed off."

Ted shook his head. "It doesn't make sense. Why would she automatically open the door with a knife in her hand? She doesn't know we're in town. What's she so afraid of?"

Wilkes shrugged. "An old woman alone . . . perhaps she thought we'd come to rob her."

"Or that you were the police," said Sarah.

Wilkes turned to look at her. "Why police?"

"She knows what Jovan did was illegal. She's probably been just waiting for someone to come and take her away."

Wilkes adjusted his glasses on his nose. "You could be right."

"In any case," said Ted, "I guess there's no question of going in after Joey, is there?"

"Not if she's that jumpy," said Wilkes

"So what do we do?" asked Sarah.

"What we've planned to do all along. We wait until Joey comes out by himself."

The weather the next morning was perfect. Above the trees lining the boulevard, the sky was bright and clear, and from a flower stand on the corner a warm breeze carried the sweet scent of blossoms in through the window of the hotel dining room, where Sarah and her father sat with Peter Wilkes over morning coffee. Sunlight glared on the white tablecloth and shimmered on the breakfast dishes.

"If Baka is ever going to send Joey out to play," said Ted, "today has got to be the day."

Wilkes glanced impatiently at his watch. "And if that bastard Popovic doesn't get here soon, it's not going to matter one bloody bit whether the boy comes out to play or not."

Popovic had agreed to meet Wilkes at the hotel at eight forty-five. He was already twenty minutes late.

"Damn it," said Ted. "I don't understand why the hell you keep working with that guy if he's always screwing things up."

Wilkes ground his cigarette into the ashtray and reached for another one. "I can tell you this: if he doesn't show up soon, he's not going to be working for us again."

Sarah watched the sunlight slide over the edge of her water glass; the light shattered, sending brilliant slivers skittering across the tablecloth. From somewhere in her mind came the memory of another perfect day: a small boy jumping off a diving board, a blaze of sunlight, a stab of fear. Sunny days didn't mean a thing.

She lifted her eyes. "Look, Mr. Wilkes," she said, her anger seething, "you may feel like sitting around here waiting for your friend to show up, or for this piece or that piece to fall into place until everything's nice and neat. But I'm not." She kept her voice down; there was no need to shout. She was absolutely determined. "If you're not going to make a move,

I am. I'm going to go over there myself and get Joey. Do you understand? I meant what I said yesterday. I'm tired of waiting. I've waited for lawyers. I've waited for ambassadors and embassy attachés and while I've waited, nobody's done a thing. Well, I'm tired of it. I've had it." She stood up. "I'm going over there right now and you're either going to come with me or you're going to give me the car keys and let me get Joey myself."

Wilkes held her gaze. He did not move. "You're right," he said. "There's no point in waiting any longer." He got to his feet. "But I'm going alone. You're staying here."

"Maybe I should go with you," Ted said, "to handle the backup."

"No. We can't take a chance of Baka seeing you." He picked up his cigarettes. "Stay put, both of you. Watch for the car. Be ready to move when I get back."

Sarah sat down again. "What if Popovic shows up?" she asked.

"Tell him I've gone ahead. Tell him to meet me there."

He gulped a last mouthful of coffee, pushed his glasses back on his nose, then headed for the door.

"Don't forget Joey's blanket," she called after him.

He smiled. "It's in the car."

"Good luck," said Ted.

"Thanks."

He turned and strode briskly out of the dining room. From their table at the window, Sarah and her father watched him cross the street, climb into the VW, and drive away.

As soon as he was gone, Sarah began having qualms.

"Maybe I was too impatient." She began chewing on a cuticle. "Maybe I shouldn't have pushed him to go like that, before everything was ready."

Ted reached across and took her hand in his. "You did fine. He needed a push."

"If something happens—"

"Don't worry, kitten. You did the right thing." He passed her the breakfast rolls. "Here, have another one of these."

"I shouldn't."

"Go ahead. It's better than eating yourself alive."

She took one. Ted did, too, though he would dearly have preferred a cigar.

A half hour passed. Forty-five minutes. Wilkes did not appear. Neither did Popovic.

"I can hardly wait to hear what his excuse is going to be," said Ted.

"Who?" asked Sarah. "Wilkes?"

"Popovic. But Wilkes, too."

By now all the rolls were gone. Still the two of them lingered at their table by the window, watching the traffic outside, now and then catching the scent of flowers from the vendor's stand at the corner. Fortunately the restaurant was not crowded and no one hurried them to leave. The waiting, though, was hard.

Sarah had been folding and refolding her napkin. Before it had been squared. Now she was doing triangles. But finally she had enough. She crumpled the napkin into a ball and dropped it on the table. "I shouldn't have let Wilkes talk me out of going along," she said. "At least if I'd gone I wouldn't be just sitting here. I'd know what was happening."

Ted shrugged. His right leg, crossed over the other, had been bobbing nervously for the last ten minutes. Behind his glasses his eyes betrayed more worry than his voice indicated. "Peter is probably just sitting and waiting, too."

Sarah stirred the water in her glass. The table was in shadow now. The glittering sunlight had moved on. "Dad? What if he can't get Joey back? What are we going to do?"

He pressed his lips together, looked away. "I've been wondering that myself. I don't know. Maybe your friend the gambler—" But he stopped. Something out the window had caught his eye.

Following his gaze, Sarah saw it: the green VW. Wilkes was backing it into a parking space in front of the hotel. Her heart sank. The headlights were not flashing. And Wilkes was alone.

"Oh, no," she moaned, and turned away, her eyes suddenly stinging with tears of anger and frustration. So, he had failed again. Miserably, pathetically failed. Everything had been so right; Jovan was gone, the weather was perfect. And still he had come back empty-handed. God, what a fool she had been to have trusted him. To have trusted anyone but herself!

Overwhelmed with disappointment, she buried her head in her hands, wishing she could just blot everything out: this table, this room, this nightmare that her life had become.

But now her father's hand was on her arm. "Sarah, look."

And lifting her head, she saw that Wilkes had gone around to the passenger side of the car and was opening the door. For a moment his body blocked her view.

But then she caught a glimpse of the small figure, the tawny hair, and all at once she was on her feet.

"It's him, Dad!" she cried in disbelief. "Oh, God, it's Joey!"

He reached for her hand. "Steady," he murmured. "Steady." But his own voice was choked.

Her hands covering her mouth, her vision blurred by a mist of tears, she saw Wilkes taking Joey by the hand and leading him toward the hotel entrance.

"Steady," her father said again, but she broke free.

And then she was running. As if in a dream she ran through the door and into the lobby and he was there, Joey was there, holding onto Peter Wilkes with one hand, clutching his Snoopy blanket with the other, looking terrified and bewil-

333

dered as he peered about the strange big room with all the people. And then he saw her and his look changed to wonder and he was starting toward her, uncertainly at first, wide-eyed, disbelieving, until with a rush he was in her arms and she was sweeping him off his feet and hugging him to her and murmuring over and over through her tears, "Joey. Oh, my Joey, my beautiful boy, my beautiful Joey."

Oh, how wonderful it felt to hold him, to feel him holding her, to luxuriate in the bony awkwardness of his small, thin body. His hair smelled of his child's sweat and grime and Baka's wretched soap, but none of that mattered now. He was here. He was hers again, with his arms around her neck, his soft cheek against hers, the sweet music of his tiny voice in her ear, singing: "Mama, I m-m-missed you s-s-so m-m-much."

"I'm here now, Joey. Mama's here and everything's going to be all right."

Her father came over and was hugging them both and his own eyes were wet. But now Wilkes' urgent whispers were breaking in on them. "Come on, come on. Forget that now. We've got to get moving. If we don't get out of town fast we won't get out at all."

Quickly Ted ran upstairs to get the bags. While he was gone, Wilkes led Sarah and Joey out to the car.

"Get in. I'll help your dad and be right out."

He was just turning away when a blue sedan pulled up next to the VW, its horn blaring. Police, thought Sarah in sudden panic. We've been caught. Joey!

But then she saw who was driving: the orange hair, the drooping mustache. It was Popovic. He was grinning and waving and blowing his horn as if he had arrived at a wedding just in time to cheer the bride and groom. Around them heads were turning. People were staring. My God, thought Sarah, he's going to ruin everything.

Wilkes moved fast. Hurrying over to Popovic's car, he ordered him away: "If we have to, we'll meet you later, as planned. Now get the hell out of here."

Popovic shifted hard. Tires squealing, he sped off down the boulevard.

Five minutes later, Wilkes was at the wheel of the VW, driving through the back streets of Belgrade. Ted sat beside him in the passenger seat, clinging to the door frame. Wilkes seemed to know the city inside out: every cobbled alleyway, every one-way street. As he spun the car around corners and down alleys, he did not hesitate, not even for a second.

In the backseat, Joey, trembling, huddled under Sarah's arm.

"It's all right," she murmured, trying to keep her own fear out of her voice. "It's all right."

Using her free arm, she dug into her carry bag and pulled out the new clothes she had brought for him. New clothes had been Harry Lipton's idea: a way of foiling police identification once an alert was issued. But now Sarah saw that the change was a good thing in more ways than one. Joey was wearing a torn shirt; his shoes he must have outgrown months ago. And his trousers were soaking wet.

"Joey! What happened, sweetheart?"

He lowered his head, ashamed. "I had a a-a-accident."

"That was my fault," Wilkes said over his shoulder. "I'm afraid it was all rather upsetting for him, being snatched away by a big ugly bloke he's never seen before."

"Oh, Joey," she murmured. "I'm so sorry."

Wilkes swung the car around a corner and onto a wide

boulevard. Suddenly the car lurched to a halt. Wilkes had driven them straight into a traffic jam.

He punched the dashboard in frustration. "Bloody hell."

Ted fumed. "Now what?"

"I don't know." Wilkes craned his neck. "I can see the bridge we want. It's just up ahead. But I can't tell from here what's holding things up. Couple of cops up there, though."

"Oh, no," breathed Sarah.

"Roadblock?" asked Ted.

But no. There had been a collision between a car and a truck at the bridge approach. With cars ahead and others closing in behind, there was nothing they could do but wait.

It took a little time, but eventually the mess got sorted out. The traffic crept forward, then picked up speed. Soon the VW was sailing across the bridge, then speeding along the autoput through the western suburbs of Belgrade.

"So far, so good." Wilkes lit a cigarette. He was starting to relax.

Ted turned around and smiled fondly at Joey. "It's so great to see you again," he said, giving Joey's leg a squeeze. "I really missed you, kiddo."

Joey, still shaken, responded with a guarded smile. He huddled closer to Sarah. "Where is the m-man t-t-taking us?"

"Home, lovey. We're going home."

eighteen

They followed the same route they had taken on the way into Belgrade: the main autoput that ran the length of the Sava River valley, with its factories and chemical plants, its farms and pastures and picturesque villages.

Wilkes drove fast but not so fast as to attract the attention of any overzealous policeman.

In the backseat, Joey dozed, his small body tucked under Sarah's arm, and it seemed to her that he fit there as perfectly as a bird fits into a nest, his shoulder resting in that familiar place against her ribs, his head pillowed in the soft hollow between her arm and her breast.

She couldn't take her eyes off of him, couldn't help wanting to touch him, as if to reassure herself that, yes, he was real; yes, he was actually here with her again, after all this time—not somebody else's son but her very own, her Joey, her boy. His musky hair was all matted and stringy, but his skin was oh-so-soft as her fingers traced the curve of his cheeks, the gentle slope of his nose, the roundness of his chin.

His eyelids fluttered open. He smiled up at her and slid her hand into his, clutching it to him, embracing it—but also restraining her incessant, loving fingers.

Ah, yes, forgive me, she thought. It's all too much, isn't it? Too much, too soon.

He dozed again.

For a while they drove in silence. Then Ted turned to Wilkes. "What happened back there? When you took Joey, I mean. Did you have any trouble?"

"None at all." Wilkes glanced over his shoulder to make sure Joey was asleep. "The situation was just what we'd been waiting for. Joey was out in the road with a little playmate. Baka was nowhere in sight. The setup couldn't have been better. All I did was drive down to the end of the cul-de-sac, make a quick turnabout, and pull up next to the boys. I got out, scooped Joey up in my arms, and off we went. It all happened so quickly he was too surprised to even cry out. Of course, once I started driving away he did put up rather a fuss. But as soon as I told him I was taking him to his mother he quieted down."

Sarah stroked Joey's hair, thinking, Poor Joey, you must have been so terribly frightened.

"What about the other boy?" Ted asked. "What did he do?"

"The last I saw of him, he was running toward the house shouting for Baka."

"And the sentry? He didn't try to stop you?"

Wilkes laughed. "It was quite incredible, really. When we drove past the fellow, Joey was still yelling bloody murder and I was still trying to quiet him down. But all the sentry did was stand there watching. I expect he thought he was seeing nothing more than a frustrated parent trying to cope with an unruly child. Poor chap must be catching it from his superiors about now. 'Can't you even stop a child from being kidnapped from right under your nose, eh, Private Slivovitz? You, who are supposed to be protecting our beloved President?' "

338

"That's great," said Ted, laughing. "But what about the headlights?"

"Headlights?"

"They weren't flashing when you got to the hotel with Joey."

"Oh. Right. Fancy that. Must have slipped my mind in all the excitement. Awfully sorry about that."

As Sarah listened, all she could think of was the terror Joey must have felt. Her boy. Lying now with his head in her lap, his grimy hair spilling across his forehead.

"Mama, I have to g-g-go."

"Can we stop, Peter?" she asked.

"In a little while. Can you hold it, son?"

"*Da,*" he murmured.

Sarah, startled by his so-easy use of the word, glanced at him sharply. But then she realized why that simple little word had stung the way it did. It was a painful reminder of how far apart they had been all this time, of how different was the world that Joey had just come from. His features might be blessedly familiar; though he looked lean and underfed, he was still the same odd mixture of his father's looks and hers, with his almond eyes, his wide face, his small stub nose. Yet in the last eight months he had experienced things she had not been a part of, things she would never know anything about. What he had done during that time, where he had gone, what he had thought, what things had made him happy or sad—a whole part of his childhood had been stolen from her. Physically she may have gotten him back, but there was a large part of his life, of his growing, that would be forever lost to her.

They got off the highway and onto a back road, where Wilkes found a café in a small market town. Ted took Joey to the restroom. When they got back and their orders appeared,

Joey ate voraciously, shoveling down food not only from his own plate but from Sarah's and Ted's as well. Sarah had to restrain him for fear he would make himself sick.

"Lad's got an appetite," Wilkes commented dryly.

But it was painfully obvious to all of them that Joey's behavior was far from normal; he must not have had a decent meal in a very long time. No wonder he looked so gaunt and hollow-eyed.

When they got back to the car, Joey snuggled up once more under Sarah's arm.

"Remember the joke you told me?" she asked him. "About the cabbage and the faucet and the tomato that were having a race? Remember, Joey? Remember who would win?"

He looked at her blankly.

"The cabbage would be—ahead," she prompted gently. "The faucet—?"

A light came into his eyes. "The f-f-faucet would b-b-be running?"

"Right! And the tomato?"

"Would have to c-c-catch up!" he declared triumphantly. And then they were both giggling and laughing and Sarah was thinking, hopefully, that maybe everything hadn't been lost after all.

Wilkes was fiddling with the radio dials, stopping whenever he came to a station that had what sounded like news. Sarah did her best to translate, but as far as she could tell, there were no accounts of a child being kidnapped off the streets of Belgrade and no reports of any kind of police alerts.

Wilkes was not reassured. "There could be alerts out over the police channels."

"But wouldn't we have seen roadblocks?" Ted asked.

"We may have slipped through before they had a chance to

340

set any up. Anyway, by now, they'll certainly be watching the airports and the border crossings."

"What are we going to do?" Sarah asked quietly. Joey had fallen asleep again and she did not want to wake him.

"For now, we're going to keep driving. When we get to Zagreb we'll check the airport. If it looks clear, we'll try to get a flight out."

It was six in the evening before Wilkes pulled the VW into a parking spot in front of the Zagreb air terminal, where they had dropped the Hardys off for their flight to Rome. When was that? Sarah wondered. Only four days ago? It seemed like years.

"Oh, no," Ted groaned. "Look at that!"

Joey sat up and rubbed his eyes. "What's the matter, Mama?" he whispered. "Where are we?"

"Nothing's the matter, Joey. Do you feel better? You slept a long time." But something was the matter, otherwise why were all those police cars lined up at the curb outside the terminal?

"I hope they're not here for us," Ted said quietly.

"You three stay here," said Wilkes. "I'll go check it out."

He was back a short time later. Leaning in the window, he reported that the next flight to the West was to Munich. "But it's not due to leave for another three hours, and I don't want to sit around here waiting all that time. Not with all those chaps standing about." He nodded toward the police cars.

"Did you find out why they're here?" asked Ted.

"Guarding some visiting dignitaries, apparently. I don't think they're here for us. But I don't want to take any chances." He handed Ted the keys. "How about you driving for a while? I could use a rest."

Ted got out and went around to the driver's side. "Where to?" he asked as he turned the key in the ignition.

"Follow the signs to Ljubljana. We'll try Loibl Pass again. If it looks too risky, we'll turn around and rendezvous with

Popovic at the Hungarian frontier. Assuming he's managed to get his license back, he'll drive Sarah and Joey across. You and I will go another way."

"God," Sarah moaned in the backseat. "Do we have to go with that man?"

Wilkes let out an abrupt laugh. Over his shoulder he said, "Am I to understand that the lady does not relish the prospect of spending a few hours in a car with my trusted aide and adviser?"

"Not even a few minutes," she shot back.

He laughed again. "Well, there *is* another way, in fact. And we'll use it if Popovic comes a cropper. But it will take longer."

"What's the other way?" she asked.

"By boat to Italy. There's an Italian fisherman who's prepared to pick us up and take us across. But we'd have to hole up in a safe house for a while until things cooled down. It would mean many more days before you three got home."

Sarah was impressed. "You've really planned all this, haven't you?"

"It may not look that way at times," Wilkes said sardonically, "but yes, we have. It's what makes things work in this business."

"You know," said Ted, "Harry Lipton told us almost exactly the same thing back in London. And you know what he said?"

"I think I can guess," said Wilkes, grinning. "He said, 'Adventure is only the result of poor planning.' Am I right?"

"On the button," said Ted.

Outside of Ljubljana they stopped briefly for gas. At a nearby café, they got coffee and a snack and used the restrooms. Then they got back into the car.

"I'll take over now," said Wilkes, sliding behind the wheel.

They were on the final leg. Ahead of them rose the jagged peaks of the Karavanke Mountains, fading into purple shadows in the twilight. Somewhere up there was the border crossing, Loibl Pass. Once beyond it, they'd be home free.

"Are we alm-m-most there?" Joey asked sleepily.

"Not far now," Wilkes said. He was trying to sound casual but Sarah heard the strain in his voice. His usual cigarette was missing from between his fingers.

"What if—" Ted's voice broke. He cleared his throat, began again. "What if they detain us? What do we tell them?"

"Just what we planned to tell them all along," replied Wilkes. "We're tourists. You and Sarah brought Joey in with you. We've got the entrance visa to prove it."

"And you're just a friend along for the ride," added Ted.

"No," said Sarah. "He's my fiancé."

Wilkes glanced at her in the rearview mirror, his eyebrows raised in surprise. "I didn't know you cared."

"It makes the story more believable, don't you think?"

"Oh, absolutely." A smile wrinkled the corners of his eyes.

"All right then," said Ted. "That might work. But what happens if they've had an alert? What if they know Joey's been reported missing?"

"We stick to our story," Wilkes said. "You two came for a holiday and you brought Joey along so he could spend some time with his Yugoslav father and grandmother. Jovan and Baka started a fight with you and now they're claiming you've stolen the boy."

"That's a lie!" The high piping voice was Joey's. "That's n-n-not what ha-ha-happened."

"Hush, Joey," said Sarah.

"But it's n-n-not."

"I know, Joey. It's just for now. It's just make-believe."

"Joey's right," said Ted. "We should think about that. If

they check out our story, we're sunk. There's a lot of people who know Joey's been living here for the last eight months. We'll try it the way we said, but if the truth comes out I'm taking the blame. I'll tell them I took Joey on my own. Distraught grandfather and all that. Maybe they'll go easy on me."

"And Peter had nothing to do with it," added Sarah.

"Right," said Ted. "You're just a friend along for a ride." He grinned. "Or fiancé, if you two like it better that way."

Wilkes nodded solemnly. "Thank you. Both of you. I appreciate that."

It was after dark when they approached the checkpoint at the southern end of Loibl Pass. From a distance the floodlit plaza looked like a fishtank in a darkened aquarium, except instead of fish and miniature castles, what Sarah saw in the pool of light were guard booths and lines of cars and tiny figures moving about.

Over his shoulder Wilkes said: "We'll do it the way we did coming in."

She got the message. "Not a word now, Joey. I want you to pretend you're asleep. Will you do that? Here, stretch out and put your head on my lap."

"B-b-but, I want to s-s-see."

"It's just for a while, Joey. Please. It's very important. Good, now just stay like that. And keep your eyes closed. I'll tell you when it's okay to look up again."

There was more traffic at the checkpoint than there had been last time. Five or six cars were lined up at each guard house. And there were more guards on duty, too. Two at each gate. Guns on their hips. Other guards nearby.

Had any of them been on duty last Friday? Sarah wondered. Was one of them the man who had shined his light in her face? She couldn't tell. The brims on the guards' caps kept their faces in shadow.

Wilkes coasted into line behind the other cars. In nervous silence they waited their turn, motor running.

Sarah's heart was pounding. For a brief moment she thought, Let's go back! Let's get away! But then the interior of the car was lit by the headlights of a car taking its place in line behind them and she knew it was too late. They were hemmed in. There was no place to go but straight ahead.

Finally the car in front of them was waved through. The red-and-white striped gate went up and came down again, blocking their way. Wilkes edged the car forward and came to a stop.

The guard who stepped up to the car was not the same one who had checked them on the way in. Thank God for small favors, Sarah thought. And this one responded to Wilkes' "good evening" in English. He signaled Wilkes to shut off the engine.

"I'd rather not," said Wilkes. "If you don't mind."

The guard scowled. Obviously he was not used to being contradicted. "You will shut off please the car."

"I'd love to oblige you, old man," said Wilkes reasonably, "but I've been having a devil of a time with the starter. The bloody thing hasn't worked right since I picked it up. It's rented, you see. And I'm afraid that if I turn it off we won't get it going again."

The guard considered a moment, then shrugged. "Passports," he snapped.

Wilkes handed them over.

By the light of his flashlight the guard examined the booklets one by one. "You have had short visit," he said, eyeing the dates on the visas.

"Afraid so," said Wilkes. "Next time we hope to stay

longer. It's a beautiful country, especially this time of the year."

The guard grunted.

In the backseat Sarah squirmed. Suddenly the beam of the guard's light was slashing across her face. She winced. Joey flinched in her arms. His eyes flew open. She wanted to shield his face but knew she mustn't. "Shh, Joey. Be still," she whispered. "It's okay. Go back to sleep."

Then, blessedly, the light was gone and now the guard was turning away, taking the passports with him. In silence, Sarah, Wilkes, and her father watched him step into the guard house.

"I hope the man with the stamp isn't out to lunch," Ted whispered.

A muscle in Wilkes' cheek gave a twitch.

"I want to go h-h-home," Joey moaned.

"Shh," said Sarah.

Inside the guard house they could see the man showing the passports to his colleagues and nodding in the direction of the VW.

They know! thought Sarah. They're going to stop us! They're going to take Joey back!

The guard came out again. He did not have the passports in his hand. He spoke to Wilkes. "Registration," he said.

"Sorry," said Wilkes. "I don't understand. What—?"

"Registration. I must see please the registration for the vehicle."

"Ah. The registration. Yes. Of course." He reached across to the glove compartment, fumbled through the papers there, handed one of them over. The guard examined it under his flashlight, took it with him into the guard house.

"You think they know it's us?" said Ted.

Through clenched teeth Wilkes said, very quietly: "If they

346

try to detain us, I'm going to gun it and go through the gate. Be ready to duck. There may be shooting."

"Oh, God." The breath caught in Sarah's throat. This couldn't be happening. Not after we've come so far. Not now, when we're almost there. "Please," she begged, "Don't do it. Somebody might get hurt."

Wilkes glanced at her distractedly, but otherwise gave no sign that he had heard her.

"Please," she said again. "We'll go back if we have to. I'll take Joey back to Jovan, I don't care. Just please don't make them start shooting."

"She's right, Peter," said Ted. "It'd be too dangerous. Don't risk it."

Finally Wilkes gave in. "All right," he said. "But if we're arrested, don't forget the story we agreed on."

Sarah looked down at Joey. He was lying still but his eyes were wide open and he was clinging to her arm so hard that it hurt. She put a finger to her lips, then closed his eyes gently with her fingertips. Her beautiful boy! Whatever happened now, at least she'd had these few hours with him. These precious hours.

The guard was back. He was shining his flashlight on a little metal plate on the dashboard, just below the windshield, comparing the number he found there with the number on the registration form.

"I think he thinks we've stolen the car," said Ted.

The muscle in Wilkes' cheek twitched again. Carefully he eased the car into gear, his hand tight-fisted on the stick, his foot on the clutch. He was getting ready to gun it.

No! Sarah was about to shout.

But then the guard was at Wilkes' elbow again, handing back the passports and the registration, wishing them a good trip, waving them on their way. Almost before Sarah knew what was happening, the car lurched forward and they were through the gate and speeding up the open highway toward Austria.

Then suddenly the car was filled with their cheering.

"We made it!" cried Sarah, hugging Joey fiercely. "They let us through!"

"Whoo-eee!" Ted whooped. "Fantastic!" He grabbed Wilkes' free hand and began pumping it wildly. "Congratulations, Peter. Well done! Oh, boy! Fantastic!"

Sarah, laughing and crying at the same time, let go of Joey long enough to reach over the back of Wilkes' seat, throw her arms around his neck, and plant an exuberant kiss on his cheek.

"Hey!" He laughed with delight as he struggled to keep the car on the road. "Keep that up and I might just go back and do it all over again."

Ted reached into his jacket pocket and pulled out one of his long black cigars. "This one's for you, Peter. I've been saving it ever since Belgrade. Take a look. It's even got your name on it."

Wilkes flicked on the overhead light and glanced at the label. And grinned from ear to ear. The label read *El Caudillo*. The boss. The hero.

CHECKPOINT
Sunday, July 10, 1977

The gleaming blade sliced silently through the soft gray flesh: once, twice, three times. Swiftly, the plump mushroom was reduced to sherds. With the side of the knife Gran swept the pieces into the salad bowl. Then she started chopping the celery.

"I still think we should have offered Jovan a nice little mushroom salad, don't you, Sarah?"

Emma looked up from the stove. "I never knew Jovan was especially fond of mushrooms."

Gran caught Sarah's eye, winked slyly. "Oh, these he would have liked. They would have really put the gravy on his cake."

Sarah smiled. "Gran, you're incorrigible."

"Go on, you know I'm not a day over seventy."

Sarah shook her head. "What are we going to do with you?"

"You'll put up with me, just the way you always have."

Sarah laughed and gave her a peck on the cheek. "Right as always."

Reaching up, she took dinner plates down from the cupboard and carried them into the dining room. On the way she stopped to glance out the kitchen window. Although it was three months now since Joey had been back, she still found herself checking constantly to make sure she knew where he was.

At the moment he was on his hands and knees in the sandbox by the garage, racing his Hot Wheels with Michael and Jason. The two boys lived a few houses away and had come over to make friends with Joey within the first week after Sarah's parents had moved into this new house, this new neighborhood.

Three months! It was incredible to think it had really been that long ago. It seemed like just yesterday that Peter Wilkes had driven them over the border into Austria. She could still remember her elation, her relief, her joy.

Exhausted after the hours-long drive from Belgrade, they had stopped overnight at a hotel in Klagenfurt, where Wilkes had put through a call to London:

"Harry? Wilkes here. Mission accomplished."

That was all. No details, no excitement. Cool as a cucumber. Just another day's work.

After he'd hung up, her father had got on the phone and placed a call to Sommerton.

"Emma?" he said when the call finally went through. "Ted here. Mission accomplished." The smirk on his face was priceless.

While he was on the line, he left instructions for Emma to send Baka a telegram letting her know that Joey was safe with Sarah. As a precaution, Emma was to have Sarah's brother send the wire from California. It might just help to throw Jovan off the scent in case he came looking for Joey. They were not about to let Jovan near him ever again. Not if they could help it.

The next day, they drove over the mountain to Munich.

350

Wilkes had already called ahead to the airport. There was a flight back to the States that afternoon. Sarah and Joey and her father would be on it.

"Oh, Joey, Gramma Emma is going to be so happy to see you again," Sarah said as the four of them waited in the airport lounge for the flight to begin boarding. "And you'll see your old friends again and sleep in your own bed. Won't that be nice?"

"*Da*, Mama."

That word again. Should she correct him? No, not yet. Give him time. He needs time.

"What about you, Peter?" Ted asked from around his El Caudillo. "Where are you off to?"

Wilkes shrugged. "Home for a few days. Then back to work."

He said it so off-handedly that "work" might have been nothing more unusual than a job selling shoes or sitting behind a desk pushing papers.

"Anything interesting?" asked Ted.

Wilkes flicked open his lighter, touched the flame to a fresh cigarette. Behind the lenses of his glasses, a lick of fire flared in his eyes. "Might be," he said. "There's an American bank executive who's gone and got himself into trouble trying to smuggle art objects out of Afganistan. He's in Kabul at the moment, under house arrest. His company wants us to get him out."

Ted's eyes shone. "Sounds like a real adventure."

"Ah, ah." Wilkes wagged a finger. "Remember what Harry always says."

Ted grinned. "Oh, yes, I forgot." And laughing, he and Wilkes voiced the words together: "Adventure is only the result of poor planning."

The day after Sarah had Joey home, when she thought Jovan might be back from Paris, she picked up the phone and put a call through to Belgrade. She wanted to let him know what had happened. It seemed only fair. After all, he had called her when *he* took Joey. There was no need to torture him.

"Don't tell him where you are," her father cautioned as she waited for the call to go through.

When finally Jovan answered she was pleased with her coolness. The receiver did not shake in her hand as he poured out his rage. And as he turned to remorse, to pleading for forgiveness, to begging for another chance, she felt not the slightest twinge of sympathy. Which was just the way she wanted it.

Quieter then, more subdued, he told her how relieved he'd been to get the cable. Baka too. Until the cable arrived the police had assumed Joey was still somewhere in Belgrade, taken where or by whom they had no idea. Baka had been sick with worry. So had Jovan when Baka had reached him in Paris to tell him the news. He had hurried home immediately.

"What were you doing in Paris?" Sarah asked.

"Do not play games with me. I was seeing some people about a job and you know it."

"No, I didn't know it," she said, taken aback. "How would I have known it?"

"Because someone knew and they told you. Or they told that man who took Joey for you."

"You're wrong, Jovan."

"Then how did that man know I would be gone? How did he know to come for Joey on exactly the day that I went away?"

"He just knew you were going. He didn't know why."

"And how did he know I was going? Who told him, eh? Who told that man I was going away?" His voice was rising again. "And just who was that man anyway?"

"He was . . . a friend." She smiled to herself, remembering Peter's face, the light in his eyes, his caring. Yes, a friend. "But I don't know how he knew. He didn't tell me."

"You think I believe that? You think I am stupid? Eh? You and your friend think I am some fool that now you laugh at me together, you and your *friend*, because you think I will believe such stories? Who was it, Sarah? Tell me who told your friend that I would be away. It was Branko, wasn't it? It was my sister's husband. That bastard. I never trusted him."

"No, Jovan. It wasn't Branko."

"Then tell me who it was. Goddamn you, Sarah, tell me. Who was it? Who betrayed me?"

Two weeks later, an envelope from the State Department dropped through the mail slot in the Novacks' front door. Inside, Sarah found Jack Traymore's business card attached to photocopies of cables from the American Embassy in Belgrade. The cables reported that the Yugoslav newspapers—and presumably the government authorities as well—were shocked that the child of a Yugoslav citizen could be kidnapped off the streets of Belgrade in broad daylight—and from under the very noses of the soldiers guarding the residence of President Tito himself.

"It is not for us to judge who is right and who is wrong in this sad matter of parental custody," said a writer in Belgrade's *Politika Express*, "but that the national security could be breached in such a blatant manner was indeed alarming." Who was to blame? the writer asked. How was it possible that the kidnapper—whose identity was still unknown—had been able to get the child past the guards and then out of the country, despite rigorous security? The entire affair was scandalous! Shocking!

"My heart bleeds," said Ted sardonically, after he'd read the reports. Meanwhile, he had been taking his own security precautions. Through Bill Borden in Washington he had petitioned the Immigration and Naturalization Service to prevent Jovan from reentering the country. Borden thought the contempt citation and the arrest warrant would be sufficient grounds for INS action but so far he had had no definitive response from the agency.

The new house was another precaution: a new address in a new town, an unlisted phone number. This house was smaller and had less property than the one in Sommerton, but most of the profit from the Sommerton sale had to be used to pay the bulk of Harry Lipton's bill. (Even so, a substantial debt still remained.)

Sarah, too, would soon be moving to a new place, once she started teaching again. And Ted had promised that when Joey started kindergarten in the fall, he would be sent to a private school, so that his name did not show up on any public school records. If Jovan did manage to get back into the country he —or whomever he hired—was going to have a hard time tracking Joey down.

"I don't like it," Sarah's mother had said. "We're making hostages of ourselves."

But even she had to admit that the alternative was just too awful to contemplate: Jovan grabbing Joey again; all that effort for nothing. All that money. All that grief and heartache. None of them could bear to go through that again.

———

Joey and his playmates had grown bored with their sandbox games. As Sarah watched from the kitchen window, her hands full of dishes, the three boys ran helter-skelter for the swing set, where Joey and Michael began pushing and shoving to be the first one up the ladder of the slide.

"One at a time, boys," Sarah called through the window. "And be careful on the ladder. Hold on with both hands."

The words were hardly out of her mouth when the telephone rang.

"I'll get it," said her mother, wiping her hands on a dishtowel. "Sarah, are you going to finish setting the table? We're almost ready to eat."

Sarah took the dishes out to the dining room, then came back for the silverware.

"It's for you," her mother said, holding out the receiver. "It's long distance."

Sarah's stomach lurched. Jovan, she thought. But how did he know where—? "Hello?"

"Hello, Sarah? Peter Wilkes here. Remember me?"

She laughed, both with relief and delight. "Peter! Of course I remember. How could I ever forget? Where are you? You sound so close."

"I'm in Rome, actually. Another assignment. But I had a few minutes and I thought I'd ring you up and see how you're getting along."

"But how—?"

"Harry gave me you new number. Don't worry. It's safe with me. How are you? How's that boy of yours?"

"We're fine. We're all just fine."

"That's super. I'm glad to hear it."

Out of the corner of her eye Sarah saw that her mother and grandmother were listening. She pulled the phone cord around the corner and sat down at the dining-room table. "And how are you?" she asked, lowering her voice.

"Oh, I'm still in one piece. It got a little rough on that job I told you about, the one in Kabul. But everything worked out all right. Tell me about yourself and Joey. How are you managing?"

"Joey's just fine. Really. His stutter is almost gone. He was having trouble with his teeth for a while because of malnutrition but that's gotten better. The only thing now is that he still has trouble getting to sleep at night unless someone stays in the room with him. Other than that, he's coming along pretty well."

"And what about you?" he asked. "How are you getting on?"

She toyed with the phone cord. "Oh, I'm all right. You know, getting along. It looks like I'll be teaching in the fall. I'd like to help pay off some of these bills."

"Mine included?"

She laughed. "Yours especially."

"Surely your father isn't expecting—?"

"No, of course not. It would take me the rest of my life to pay everything off. But I'd like to help if I can."

"Yes, I see. Well, look here, the reason I'm calling is, I'm going to be in New York next week and I was wondering if you'd like to go out to dinner with me."

"I—" She hesitated. In her mind's eye she saw his warm eyes behind his glasses, his impish grin that first time he snuck her past the desk clerk at the Hotel Srbija. She felt the pressure of his hand on her arm, remembered the smell of his cigarettes and his tenderness with Joey. She also remembered something else: the fierce, hot light that shone in his eyes when he talked, so coolly, about his next assignment, his next gamble with his life.

"Hello," he prompted. "You still there?"

"I'm here. I'm just a little surprised."

"Pleasantly, I hope."

"Well, yes, as a matter of fact."

"Well, then?"

"I'll, uh, have to see if my parents will be free to stay with Joey. What if you call me again when you get in?"

"Come on, Sarah, you're stalling. We don't have to be coy with each other, do we?"

"I guess not. Not after all the hotels we checked into together."

This time it was his turn to laugh out loud. "So what about it? Will you let me take you to dinner?"

She took a deep breath. "Yes, all right. I'd like that. Yes."

Supper was ready by the time she hung up. She finished setting out the silverware, then went to the kitchen window to call Joey in.

He wasn't there.

Joey wasn't in the yard.

He wasn't anywhere in sight.

Panic. Sarah's mouth went dry. "Joey!" Her voice was a strangled whisper.

She ran to the back door.

And found him sitting on the steps, deep in conversation with his playmates. She closed her eyes. Thank God, she thought; thank God! And wondered if the time would ever come when she could bear to let Joey out of her sight again.

Outside on the steps, Joey and Mikey and Jason were discussing their new club.

The club was Joey's idea. It was a spy club. Joey was the boss and Mikey and Jason were his spies. Their job was to watch the street and keep an eye out for strangers or for suspicious-looking cars.

If they saw anything or anyone unusual they were to run and tell Joey about it right away.